DECAY

EDITED BY GHASSAN HAGE

DECAY

DUKE UNIVERSITY PRESS
Durham and London
2021

© 2021 DUKE UNIVERSITY PRESS. All rights reserved
Printed in the United States of America on acid-free paper ∞
Text design by Courtney Leigh Richardson
Cover design by Matt Tauch
Typeset in Minion Pro and Trade Gothic by Copperline Book Services

Library of Congress Cataloging-in-Publication Data
Names: Hage, Ghassan, [date] editor.
Title: Decay / Ghassan Hage.
Description: Durham : Duke University Press, 2021. | Includes bibliographical references and index.
Identifiers: LCCN 2021010242 (print)
LCCN 2021010243 (ebook)
ISBN 9781478013808 (hardcover)
ISBN 9781478014737 (paperback)
ISBN 9781478022039 (ebook)
Subjects: LCSH: Degeneration—Social aspects. | Degeneration—Political aspects. | Anthropological ethics. | Political culture. | Social change. |
BISAC: SOCIAL SCIENCE / Anthropology / Cultural & Social
Classification: LCC HM892.D433 2021 (print) | LCC HM892 (ebook) |
DDC 303.4—dc23
LC record available at https://lccn.loc.gov/2021010242
LC ebook record available at https://lccn.loc.gov/2021010243

Cover art: Photo by author

CONTENTS

Acknowledgments | vii

Introduction: States of Decay | Ghassan Hage | 1

1 Forever "Falling Apart": Semiotics and Rhetorics of Decay | Violeta Schubert | 17

2 Trash and Treasure: Pathologies of Permanence on the Margins of Our Plastic Age | Debra McDougall | 28

3 Infrastructure as Decay and the Decay of Infrastructure | Akhil Gupta | 37

4 The Waterfall at the End of the World: Earthquakes, Entropy, and Explanation | Monica Minnegal, Michael Main, and Peter D. Dwyer | 47

5 "Vile Corpse": Urban Decay as Human Beauty and Social Pollution | Michael Herzfeld | 58

6 Decay or Fresh Contact? The Morality of Mixture after War's End | Bart Klem | 73

7 Seeds of Decay | Fabio Mattioli | 86

8 Discourses of Decay in Settler Colonial Australia | Elise Klein | 99

9   Decay as Decline in Social Viability among Ex-Militiamen in Lebanon | Ghassan Hage | 110

10 Relational Decay: White Helpers in Australia's Indigenous Communities | Cameo Dalley | 128

11 Decay, Rot, Mold, and Resistance in the US Prison System | Tamara Kohn | 140

References | 153

Contributors | 171

Index | 175

ACKNOWLEDGMENTS

This volume is the product of a writing project initiated within the Department of Anthropology and Development Studies at the University of Melbourne. Some of the participants, namely, Michael Herzfeld and Akhil Gupta, are affiliated to other international institutions but have been yearly visiting professors to Melbourne. Bart Klem, Elise Klein, and Cameo Dalley, who were in the department when the project began, are now affiliated elsewhere. Still, the idea of a book written by members of the same department might appear parochial for a superficial gaze. We are all very grateful to Duke University Press for never gazing at the project superficially. We want to thank Ken Wissoker, specifically, for his enthusiasm and support, and the anonymous readers for their helpful and productive comments.

One key idea common to many chapters of the book is that the pace of decay is dependent on maintenance labor and external mechanisms that slow the inevitable processes of disintegration and decomposition. In a way, a departmental writing project is precisely one of those mechanisms in the era of neoliberal education where the intellectual culture of the university is rapidly decaying. It is no secret that, for many academics today, often one manages to live a rewarding life of intellectual pursuit despite rather than because of the university as an institution. As the project was underway, many of my colleagues were reflecting on the importance of the space created for and by the writing of this book. The notes of thanks accompanying many of the chapters clearly show the amount of collegial interaction that this space allowed. Carving out such spaces is a matter not only of skill but also of capacity. It can also be a matter of having support from within the university's administration. This is all the more so in a sociopolitical environment where successive neoliberal governments of all shapes see themselves in a state of enmity with the humanities and the social sciences. Here we want to thank Karen Farquharson, head of the School of Social and Political Sciences, for her unwavering moral support. Karen was also willing to support the writing project by financing a final retreat that could bring the writers together to finish the final draft. COVID-19 disallowed this from happening.

We have finished writing this book in what has been, by any standard, one of the most extraordinary years of our lives. In Australia, it began with the most lethal and extensive series of fires in Australia's history, which has forced many to come face-to-face with the effects of global warming and environmental degradation. This was followed by the global pandemic, which has altered and continues to alter our lives in fundamental ways. COVID-19 has forced us to further confront the ease with which whatever little control we have over the natural world can crumble. And as we write these acknowledgments, the Black Lives Matter movement has both shaken the United States and turned into a global movement that has awoken a broad and critcal consciousness to many traces of social decomposition and accelerated decay marking our lives. And as always with decay, amid the rot, new forms of life announce themselves at a macro and micro level. Three of us have given birth to, or seen the birth of, a child during the making of the book. The open-ended dialectic between the decomposition of old life-forms and the composition of new ones continues.

INTRODUCTION
STATES OF DECAY
Ghassan Hage

A statement such as "We live in an era of unprecedented social and moral decay" makes immediate sense today. But even though it "rings true," it is hard to substantiate empirically. This is hardly surprising. Decay, in the above sense, is not easily definable, let alone measurable. And it is not at all clear what "social" and "moral" reality one is referring to as "decaying." Still, if you make the above statement, you are less likely to be ridiculed than if you make a statement such as "We live in an era of unprecedented social and moral regeneration."

The mood of our time is depressive, and we are more likely to hear of social, moral, and urban, not to mention ecological, degradation, decline, and atrophy than the contrary. Especially when it comes to ecological decline, there is a sense that the very things that were the basis of modern expansion and development are now the drivers of contraction and dissolution: self-devouring growth, as Julie Livingston (2019) has put it. Interestingly, except for some marginal right-wing groups, not many speak of "national decay," as fascists did in the past. If you google "national decay," you quickly get to national statistics on tooth decay. Otherwise, serious and frivolous speculations concerning social and natural decay seem to be thriving. The imaginary of decay and the semantic field around it, conjuring experiences of ruination, decomposition, rot, disrepair, deterioration, decline, and disintegration, delineate what one can posit as a current "structure of feeling," in Raymond Williams's sense of the word. As Williams intimated in his classic piece on the subject, a "structure of feeling" works like an experientially grounded "hypothesis" (this is Williams's term) pointing to what things "are probably like" or are "experienced to be like" by a collective of people in their everyday lives (R. Williams 1977, 131–35). Violeta Schubert's description of the various ways the discourse of decay operates in Macedonia in chapter 1 offers an excellent illustration of this. As Claude Lévi-Strauss argued, this order of experience, and the meaningful world it gives rise to, is what anthropologists are interested in. Importantly, Lévi-Strauss (2013) did not oppose the order of "what it feels like to people" to a more "objective" order of "what things are actually like." He argued that both everyday experience and the more scientific objectivist gaze capture—or, better still, bring forth—actual dimensions of reality. Similarly, this book's chapters oscillate between these two orders of the real—between decay as observed by the analyst from the outside, and the sentiment of things decaying generated by people living through that process.

Decay: Normal and Pathological

But what is really meant when we say we are in a period of social, moral, or ecological decay? Or even, in a less general or abstract sense, when we note that our body or a building is decaying? This requires some reflection, given that most peoples of the world take it for granted that decay is the normal order of things. This is so even if some, like Charlotte Brontë's Shirley, might deplore this state of affairs: "Your god, sir, is the World.... All that surrounds him hastens to decay: all declines and degenerates under his sceptre. *Your god is a masked Death*" (Brontë 1993, 414). As Masashi Kishimoto's famous manga character Orochimaru tells us: "All things that have form eventually decay." The normality of this process of decay is accepted by most and incorporated into various cosmological conceptions of the world. When the Amazonian tribes first encountered the Spanish colonists, they were not sure whether they were spirits or bodies. They dumped the first Spanish people they caught in water to see whether they putrefied.[1] As far as they were concerned, decay was proof of bodily existence. For Christians around the world, Ash Wednesday (or Monday among Eastern Christians) marks a day of ensuring that believers remember that they exist in decaying bodies, that they are "of dust and to dust they will return." That we need to be reminded of this indicates that even our body's decay is not something that continuously preoccupies us.

Given that everything is decaying all the time, and with the exception of ethico-religious or philosophical reasons such as the above, making a point of spelling out that "things are decaying" seems banal. Yet, in what can ostensibly appear as a paradoxical fact, we do often tend to spell out that "things are decaying." Thus, the question arises: What kind of experience of decay makes "decay" come into our consciousness? Even a quick reflection immediately shows that this it is not the "routinized" and "normalized" processes that attract our attention when we declare things to be decaying.

Nietzsche, for one, differentiated between "normal" and "pathological" decay. For him, the latter was a specifically modern disease. It had to do with the generalized *ressentiment* and "slave morality" diffused by modern Christianity. The latter, he argued, created "mortals" who are now "physiologically deformed and deranged" and whose deformity is "an expression of the physiological contradiction—of being modern." As he put it: "When seriousness is deflected from the self-preservation and the enhancement of the strength of the body—that is, of life—when anemia is construed as an ideal, and contempt for the body as 'salvation of the soul'—what else is this if not a recipe for *décadence*?" (Nietzsche 1967, 292). One can note the etymological connections between decay and decadence here. As Heike Schotten explains, Nietzsche's "prognosis for modernity was terminal because the very definition of *décadence* entails death: it is a decay that has exceeded its healthy boundaries and convulsed the entire organism" (Schotten 2009, 52).

Schotten's interpretation of Nietzsche's passage touches on something important: as with the Huli people's experience of an earthquake detailed by Minnegal, Main, and Dwyer in chapter 4, decay has "healthy boundaries" that when exceeded "convulse the whole organism." It seems to me that this puts us, more generally, on the right track toward what brings decay into people's consciousness. Being a process, decay has a temporality, a pace or a tempo, and a spatiality, a mode of occupying and evolving in space. "Pathological" decay, the decay that marks us experientially such that we end up noticing it, is a decay that is happening at what we consider an unusual rhythm, often too quickly, but sometimes too slowly, and a decay that is progressing outside the confines of where we expect it to exist. We are therefore speaking of a decay that is either, as Mary Douglas famously put it, "out of place," or a decay that is "out of tempo," or both, as in the case of plastic that is decaying way too slowly in places where things ought to be decaying quickly, as examined by Debra McDougall in chapter 2. In both cases, decomposition and disintegration are no longer happening imperceptibly, where and how they should. "I can see things crumbling before my very eyes," say exasperated people witnessing their institutions decaying (we academic anthropologists inhabiting the university system need not go on a long ethnographic trip and live in an exotic culture to recognize the experience behind such tropes). Martin Demant Frederiksen has written a rich ethnographic piece detailing the oppositional politics triggered by public renovations that have decayed too soon in Tbilisi. As he put it: "The central issue was that any of the newly built structures began to decay shortly after having been built, turning immediately into ruins despite being envisaged as political visions of the future" (Frederiksen 2016, 50). Frederiksen's piece conjures the specter of so many housing, agricultural, or industrial development projects in the world that begin as a vision of a better future but then decay too soon. It also conjures images of the new consumer products that capitalism increasingly produces and that are purposefully designed to disintegrate too soon, so as to ensure that economic activity continues in the industries producing them—though here one needs to differentiate between and examine the complex relation among malfunction, mechanical disintegration, and decay, as they are not the same.

But of all the pathologies of decay, none has activated the macabre side of the modern imagination the way the idea of an "advanced but arrested decay" has. In its "normal" mode of existence, bodily decay indicates a direct relation to dying. It does so in that, the more "advanced" the living body's state of decay, the more it is a sign of its approaching death. However, this relationship is made more ambiguous by two facts. The first is the fact that decay continues after death: while an increasing decay brings us closer and closer to death, death itself does not bring an end to bodily decay. Second, and related to the above, is that even in old age our conception of ourselves is more that of an ageless soul than of an aging body—an imaginary played out in the opposition between embalming and crematory practices. It is the fissures created by these ambiguities that open the imagination to the figure of the not-yet-dead, or, more ominously, the zombie, the figure of the should-be-dead-but-isn't. Here we have the pathology of an extreme state of decay that stops being a process—a transitional state that actually becomes a permanent condition. The entire resources of the anthropologies of liminality and in-betweenness can be productively brought to bear to deal with such a figure and the questions it raises. As zombie film fans often ask: "Zombies must have a half-life. They exibit [sic] signs of decay as soon as they transform into the undead. Their rotting flesh would attract decomposers, like flys [sic] and beetles. Those insects should be able to quickly break down rotting zombies and reduce them to bone through the action of their maggots, but they don't. Why do the Walking Dead zombies stop decomposing?" (Major Stackings 2012). Although we might seem far from any sociological or anthropological concerns, we are not. A not-so-different question has haunted radical political theorists for whom capitalism is the ultimate manifestation of the should-be-dead-but-isn't zombie: on the one hand, it seems to be increasingly rotting and decomposing, ready to die in any moment, as it moves from one crisis to another; on the other, it seems to be able to last in such a decomposed state forever.

In Marxist thought, the idea that material conditions must be suitable for a revolution was crucial. Capitalism was bound to increasingly crumble and decay under the weight of its own contradictions. This is an imaginary that radical political theory has largely inherited and originally accepted. However, as capitalism continued to evolve without such a revolution taking place, the more pessimistic idea started to materialize that capitalist decay might be itself an alternative future rather than a road to revolution and a better future. Thus, in some of the voluntarist trends of Marxism that emerged in the 1960s around figures such as Herbert Marcuse (2007), which also fed into the left-wing terrorism of the Baader-Meinhof Group and the Brigate Rosse, capitalist decay was indeed the sign of a capitalism that was "overripe" for a revolution that had failed to come. No one managed to pick the ripe fruit at the right time, so now it's become overripe and is starting to rot, as Marcuse often argued. It is at this point that we see the emergence of a zombie capitalism that should be dead but that continues to live in a state of arrested decomposition. While this conception of capitalism lacks the optimistic teleology of the classical Marxist theorization, it is nonetheless not totally pessimistic. For the revolutionary "voluntarism" that has marked this period, one can still opt for a Hegelian optimism in the face of such decay and hope for something unexpectedly new arising from the decaying present. This something new, however, will not come simply because the structural conditions for its emergence exist. It will come because certain people are willing to push the decaying zombie down the cliff. It is not "history" but the action of these revolutionaries that ignites the Hegelian fantasy whereby "the gradual crumbling that left unaltered the face of the whole is cut short by a sunburst which, in one flash, illuminates the features of the new world" (Hegel 1977, 6–7).

In the above, Hegel's optimism is expressed in a sense of differential scale; the decay happening at one level is not showing at another level. This multiscalar perspective is crucial for gaining a better understanding of all forms of decay, for not thinking them uniformly as a downhill process of disintegration. We can watch a rotting leaf on the ground and speak of decay. But from the macro perspective of the rainforest where the rotting leaf is located, it is part of the process of the forest's regeneration. Likewise, from the micro perspective of the rot itself, decomposition is an effervescence of a multiplicity of forms of life. In that regard, Charles Baudelaire's (1869) famous "Une charogne" (A Carcass) is an avant-garde text. In it Baudelaire sees decay not merely as a process of decomposition but one where nature gives back "a hundredfold all she together join'd":

> The flies the putrid belly buzz'd about,
> Whence black battalions throng
> Of maggots, like thick liquid flowing out
> The living rags along.
>
> And as a wave they mounted and went down,
> Or darted sparkling wide;
> As if the body, by a wild breath blown,
> Lived as it multiplied. (Baudelaire 1869, 12)

Because scale joins space and tempo as an analytical dimension, decay is a fertile ground for thinking through the agency of microorganisms of the kind that multispeciesist and chemo-ethnographies are increasingly highlighting today (Shapiro and Kirksey 2017). But the fact that what is decaying and disintegrating is teeming with new life is something that can also be captured at the level of human experience. This is highlighted in Tamara Kohn's chapter.

Toward an Analytics of Decay

The above makes it clear that the knowledge that "everything decays" is hardly enough from a socioanalytical perspective. Things decay in very different ways, and knowing the principle behind particular kinds of decay is important. Some things decay quicker and more extensively than others, some processes of decay are welcome and some are resisted, and we need to know the many internal and external factors that shape such differences. Things can decay because they are too exposed, and they can decay because they are too closed. There are processes of endo-decay, where things decompose from the inside, and processes of exo-decay, where disintegration is caused by external environmental factors. This differentiation between endo-decay and exo-decay is hardly ever neat, and the two processes can often be entangled in the making and unmaking of social processes. In a way, all the chapters of this book are concerned with these differential processes and the ways they are experienced, though the chapters by Michael Herzfeld and Bart Klem are most explicitly so.

Given the pervasiveness of the differential experiences of organic, physiological, physical, organizational, moral, and social decay in everyday life, it has attracted relatively little explicit social scientific attention. One strand of thought, influenced particularly by Norbert Wiener's theorization of cybernetics (1948, 1950), has shown an interest in entropy. In anthropology, the work of Gregory Bateson (1972) clearly stands out, but so does the structuralism of Lévi-Strauss. In sociology, one also finds reflections on entropy influenced by Wiener, but also partly inspired by Bateson's and Lévi-Strauss's work. In France, Edgar Morin's work on "complexity" (2005), which has included reflections on entropy, has been developing from the 1970s and well into this century. In the United States, Kenneth D. Bailey has specifically developed a "social entropy theory" (1990) that aims, according to one reviewer, to "measure the natural decay of the structure" (François 2001, 537). Because of the influence of cybernetics and systems theory in all these works, entropy, as the very idea of "decay of the structure" indicates, speaks more of organizational entropy. Even biological entropy is thought of in this "systemic" way in that, from this perspective, biological entities are conceived as organizational systems. To be sure, decay does involve such formal entropic dissolution, though this is only one dimension of the process, and not necessarily the richest ethnographically. Georg Simmel, in his essay on ruins, has offered us a descriptively richer and more substantial (as in "associated with substances") sense of decay. He sees decay as a taking over by natural forces of architecturally inspired spaces (buildings), where a kind of balance between human design and nature prevail.

> Decay appears as nature's revenge for the spirit's having violated it by making a form in its own image. The whole history of mankind is a gradual rise of the spirit to mastery over the nature which it finds outside, but in a certain sense also within, itself. If in the other arts the spirit bends the forms and events of this nature to its command, in architecture it shapes nature's masses and inherent forces until, as if of their own accord, they yield and the artistic conception is made visible. But the necessities of matter submit to the freedom of the spirit, and its vitality is expressed without residue in nature's merely weighing and carrying forces, only so long as the building remains perfect. The mo-

ment its decay destroys the unity of the form, nature and spirit separate again and reveal their world-pervading original enmity—as if the artistic formation had only been an act of violence committed by the spirit to which the stone unwillingly submitted; as if it now gradually shook off this yoke and returned once more into the independent lawfulness of its own forces. (Simmel 1965, 260–61)

More recently, there has been an interest in modernity-driven processes of ruination, influenced or inspired by Simmel's work (see Hell and Schönle 2010). Akhil Gupta's chapter explores some ramifications of thinking this ruination in terms of decay. I also critically engage, in chapter 9, with an important anthropological work that deals with the relation between colonialism and ruination: Ann Laura Stoler's article on imperial debris (2008).

Despite the above, it can still be said that analytical, and particularly ethnographically oriented, works showing an interest in the differential modes of decay traversing the entities that make up the social world are rare. And while we started this section by saying that "the knowledge that 'everything decays' is hardly enough from a socioanalytical perspective," the fact is that most social science and social theorizing seem oblivious to that basic truth and its analytical consequences. Social scientists seem to need more than anyone else the Christian injunction to remember that we are "of dust and to dust (we) will return." In fact, the absence of a preoccupation with questions of decay is so systematic that one begins to suspect that mechanisms of repression, avoidance, and displacement might be at work there. Take, for instance, the various theories of reproduction and social change. While the absence of a focus on decay in theories of reproduction might perhaps speak for itself, one would think that the same cannot be the cases with theories of social change. Yet theories of social change touch on every possible form of social change other than decay.

One begins to suspect that the first part of Antonio Gramsci's famous formula, the "optimism of the will," continuously overshadows the second part, the "pessimism of the intellect," in this domain, and thus makes analysts blind to the obvious. Even the sociology and anthropology of aging,[2] which one would think is most confronted with the decaying human body, evades this confrontation. It is more centered on the overcoming of the limitations of aging (e.g., persistence of agency, relations of care) than on describing aging itself.[3] In the previous section, we noted how decay draws attention to the not-yet-dead: how decomposition highlights the living by continuously pointing to its future disintegration. However, one cannot fail to note here how the figure of the not-yet in social theory is the figure most associated with hope in the work of Ernst Bloch. For Bloch, the not-yet is the future that is already present, that is, the potentialities that the present is already pregnant with. As a figure of hope, the not-yet for Bloch meant the "not-yet-born." To be sure, no one is arguing that it is wrong to see such traces of a hopeful future in the present. It nonetheless takes a particular form of blindness to see the present as pregnant with the "not-yet-born" without also noting that it is equally pregnant with the "not-yet-dead," a more certain not-yet than any of the intimations of hope that the body can carry.

The blindness to this one-way-traffic-to-oblivion type of social change that decay represents is all the more manifest when we consider how the interest in the way things perpetuate themselves has been elevated to the highest meta-philosophico-theoretical order today. This is particularly so thanks to the way social theory has taken up Spinoza's concept of *conatus*, famously announcing that "each thing, as far as it lies in itself, strives to persevere in its being" (Spinoza 1988, part 3, prop. 6). From Louis Althusser and then Gilles Deleuze's ways of taking the concept on board, to the current debates between Judith Butler, Jane Bennett, and Caroline Williams on subjectivity and humanism that it is generating (see C. Williams 2016), *conatus* is seen solely in terms of the power to exist that it represents. Yet, for all the talk about perseverance, the concept cannot be understood without an implicit understanding that "each thing is bound to decay." Indeed, even more so, it cannot be understood without understanding that, tragically, the tendency for things to age, decay, and disintegrate will always, in the long run, win over their tendency to persevere in their own being. If not for an inexorable force toward disintegration, persevering in one's being would not be a "striving." Both the ideas of "persevering" and "striving" imply a force "trying to" achieve its aim in the face of another force operating in the opposite direction. In this sense, *conatus* is in fact an indication of how slowly a thing, "as far as it lies in itself," decays. It is the core variable affecting what we called above endo-decay. It tells us the extent to which a thing's inner constitution influences its mode of decay.

The Book's Chapters

It is against this backdrop that the uniqueness and inventiveness generated from centering on the problematic of decay—qualities that mark all the works that make up this book—come to the fore. Given the novelty of the space being investigated, the contributors were encouraged to think of their pieces as mixing formal ethnographically grounded style of academic work with a more free-flowing essay form that raises issues and invites the readers on new thinking paths. The chapters oscillate between an analytic and a lay experience of decay, though they differ in how they oscillate and where they tend to dwell. In much the same way, they explore a terrain located between decay as a condition or a property of the social and decay as a history or a materialization of this condition. Some are more interested in decay's significance as a material process of infrastructural decline, and others are more interested in it as a phenomenology and as a condition of social and personal demoralization, but most are interested in both. Because of the entanglement of this multiplicity of issues within them, the chapters can be arranged in many ways. I have aimed to maximize the feel of an overall narrative flow. As indicated earlier, I've chosen to begin with Violeta Schubert's chapter because it offers a good sense of the way a discourse of decay constitutes a "structure of feeling." The chapter examines the way varieties of modes of talking and thinking with and against decay circulate within Macedonian national space. For those Makedonci and Balkanci with whom Schubert is working, the sense that everything is corrupt and malfunctioning creates an experience of perpetual coming-apartness. This, in turn, is invested into the sociopolitical realm, and decay becomes a characteristic of all national politics at all times. Her chapter works in a general way in relation to all those in the book. But in its Macedonian specificity, it works particularly well in conjunction with Fabio Mattioli's more particular investigation of a specific type of decay that he shows to be flourishing in Macedonia.

After Schubert's chapter, I have tried to arrange the following pieces as a movement from chapters treating the way certain features of decay in society are attended to, or are experienced, in broad political and cultural terms, to chapters that center on individual experiences of social decay. Mediating between the two sets are chapters with a stronger sense of a politics of decay. I'll briefly detail what each of the remaining chapters entails and the issues they give rise to.

The ungovernability of waste, whether in the form of toxic chemicals in rivers and soil or greenhouse gases in the atmosphere, is one defining dimension of the global ecological crisis (see Hage 2017). This ungovernability can be caused by the increased volume of waste and the inability of the earth's environment to absorb it, transform it, and dissipate it, and it can be caused by the undissolvable nature of the waste itself. In chapter 2, Debra McDougall traces the penetration of plastic packaging to a rural island of the southwestern Pacific. If Spinoza's *conatus* refers to the ability of things to perpetuate their own being in the face of decay, it can be said that plastic, because of its inner constitution, has a particularly healthy *conatus*. What is of interest to McDougall, however, is not simply that plastic does not decay easily. Plastic packaging is designed to perform a function and then be disposed of. It is here that it emerges as a practical and a classificatory problem. For most people, what is valorized and what is devalorized coincides with what to keep or exchange as a gift, and what to dispose of, which also coincides with what should endure and what should decay quickly. Plastic packaging however is something devalorized, to be disposed of, but nonetheless does not decay. This is at a time when people under the assault of globalization see their cultural values, something they like to imagine as durable and even as eternal, begin to decay (see also the chapter by Bart Klem).

A short piece in the *New Yorker* revisits the 2007 book *The World without Us* and its author, Alan Weisman. One of the book's chapters is said to describe "how quickly nature would reclaim New York City if humans were removed. The decay would likely begin from below. Every day, the MTA pumps millions of gallons of water out of the subway system; if the pumps stopped, within half an hour tunnels would begin to flood. Soil under pavement would leach away. Streets would buckle." According to the author, "The unstated but absolutely resonant message throughout that book is how important maintenance personnel are to make sure that these things don't fall victim to entropy" (Khatchadourian 2020, 13–14). It is this work of maintenance that is of concern to Akhil Gupta in chapter 3.

If decay is the natural order and direction of things, what has always stopped it, or at least slowed it down from the outside, are structures, institutions, assemblages, and forms of labor whose function is maintenance. As such, just as there are external and internal factors that induce, facilitate, and accelerate decay (what we termed endo- and exo-decay), there are internal and external factors that slow it down. And if, as we have already seen, the *conatus* is the main factor that affects endo-decay, it is the work of maintenance that is the main exo-factor that slows it down from the outside. Gupta thinks through the issue of maintenance in relation to infrastructure. He examines two interlinked registers for thinking the relation between infrastructure and decay. One concerns how infrastructures decay over time because their materials rust and wear out; the other points to the ruination caused by the infrastructures of the Industrial Revolution, which in turn were literally fueled by decaying organic matter (fossil fuel). Maintenance keeps infrastructures functioning, staving off decay, but maintenance is seen as unglamorous and uninteresting compared to the heroic masculinized activity of invention and construction. Gupta finishes by asking: What would giving priority to the loving care of maintenance imply for the ruination engendered by the infrastructures of the Anthropocene?

The problematic of maintenance also raises the issue of human agency in the face of decay. In a way, the distinction between endo-decay and exo-decay differentiates between the decay that can be influenced by human agency (exo-decay) and the decay that, short of changing the very nature of things, cannot (endo-decay). But the boundary between the two is hardly a stable cross-cultural matter. In chapter 4, Minnegal, Main, and Dwyer explore the way this question of agency played out in a remote mountainous area of Papua New Guinea when people had to deal with the devastating consequences of a magnitude 7.5 earthquake in February 2018. As the physical world around them collapsed and decayed, many sought to understand what had happened within ontological frames grounded in science and Christianity. Both these speak of decay in physical or moral order, and an inexorable end without human cause. The ultimate effect of these new schemas negated the possibility that earthquake-affected local people might view themselves as agents of cause and control with respect to natural disasters, contrasting profoundly with traditional beliefs and practices.

A different dimension of the relation between decay and agency has to do with attributing responsibility for something decaying. Particularly in the face of a decay attributed to external elements, we often witness a whole political field where creative strategies of blame are produced and propagated. In chapter 5, Michael Herzfeld offers us an excellent example of such a process as it plays out in Rome. In a city famed for its durable and visually impressive monumentality, many locals view migrants' presence as both the cause and the essence of what they consider an evil degradation of the city's material and social fabric. Cosmological models as well as economic and demographic change thus together drive the disturbing current drift toward a racist and embittered populism.

In chapter 6, Bart Klem also treats a situation, in postwar Sri Lanka, where social change is experienced negatively as a process of social and moral decay. If in Rome's case the undesirable decay is the result of outsiders inside the gate, in Sri Lanka's case they are outsiders who are actually located outside the nation but whose influence is seen to have increased as a result of increased openness and interaction with the outside world. Drawing on Jonathan Spencer and Karl Mannheim, Klem argues that we must interrogate the political work that such narratives do. The dominant narrative interprets the sudden changes at war's end in terms of decay and purity: the opening floodgates to the world bring unwanted mixture and require purification. To confront the implied exclusivist, patriarchal, and potentially xenophobic positioning of this narrative, he suggests an alternative reading: rather than decay, exposure breeds fresh contact.

In chapter 7, Fabio Mattioli, treats creatively a kind of decay that disturbs a neat separation between exo- and endo-decay. Here the cause of decay is something external, a recurring experience of crushed hopes, that ends up lodging itself into the social body in the form of "a seed of decay." As indicated above, there are important connections between Mattioli's chapter and Schubert's chapter 1. Mattioli offers an analysis of a specific kind of decay that emerges in the discursive landscape that Schubert analyzes more generally. The chapter shows how, in the Republic of (North) Macedonia, decay germinates from fragments of broken social expectations, nested within the social imaginary of working- and middle-class citizens. In the postsocialist context of an endless transition, decay appears as a constant existential state that feeds on the delay of future progress and on the impossibility of equality and democracy—a burdensome structure of feeling that Macedonians try to address by embracing nihilist politics. If Macedonians gave up on hope, Mattioli argues, the material conditions that gave birth to their abnormal lives would not disappear. But the Macedonians might stop hurting.

Attributing blame for decay can take the form of scapegoating, but that it is not always what happens. There are many historical instances, particularly in colonialism, where social disintegration and decomposition was a willful strategy. Ann Stoler rightly preferred the active verb "ruin" to refer to the "ruins" produced by imperialism. This allows her to ascribe agency to colonialism and imperialism and to assign blame for such ruinous states. We noted above that while decay is a natural process, social spaces are clearly dependent on that whole battery of mechanisms, apparatuses, and labor aimed at slowing down decay that we have referred to as the labor of maintenance. With this in mind, decay's acceleration can be induced simply by withdrawing maintenance. As Simmel noted in the case of ruins, while decay is indeed the work of nature, sometimes nature does its work unhampered because humans let it do its work. Reflecting on what "characterizes a good many urban ruins, like those, still inhabited, often found in Italy off the main road," Simmel notes: "In these cases, what strikes us is not, to be sure, that human beings destroy the work of man—this indeed is achieved by nature—but that men *let it decay*" (1965, 263).

This seems to me important in thinking settler colonialism in places like Australia and Israel. Thinking the tempo and speed of decay as dependent on the labor of maintenance makes clear that the politics of public health is a technique of maintenance of the human body. Because such biopolitics is at its core a politics concerned with the differential decay of bodies, it is a politics concerned with choosing which population is given which resources to slow down its decay. In Australia, we have a settler colonialism that began like any other, with robbing the colonized of their lands, along with acts of extermination through killings and massacres, then through attempts at cultural eradication. Yet what characterizes the exterminatory nature of this colonialism today is that it precisely takes the form of "let it rot," "let it decay." Having destroyed Indigenous people's own maintenance mechanisms, the social and cultural forms that propelled them into the world, British colonialism and later Australian governments failed to replace those mechanisms. This withdrawal of maintenance works to "let Indigenous people decay." It is a form of extermination that resembles finding a spot on the farm to hide a truck that you have broken, that is no longer working, and leaving it there to rust and rot. Clearly, Indigenous people in Australia have more agency than such a truck and are still struggling to produce their own maintenance mechanisms to prevent their decay.

"Let them decay" is therefore a form of active colonial racism remains with us today. However, what interests Elise Klein in chapter 8 is something more insidious. Having initiated the forces of accelerated decay among Indigenous people, the Australian turns this decay into a characteristic of the Indigenous people themselves. That is, they discursively transform what is a colonially inflicted exo-decay into an endo-decay, blaming it on Indigenous people themselves. The chapter is about how this discourse of endo-decay has been deployed by the Australian state to legitimize punitive interventions and further attempts at assimilationist politics in First Nations communities. These programs actually perpetuate and even accelerate the very social decay that they purport to stop. It is clear in Klein's chapter that individual bodies just as much as collective ways of being are equally implicated in this politics of decay. This is true of all the remaining chapters.

In my own chapter, though looking at a very different social phenomenon, I also examine the way that the gradual disappearance of maintenance mechanisms leads a process of accelerated decay. The Christian Lebanese ex-militiamen I work with are left with very little social or economic support. What interested me in their situation is the role of social fantasy, as a less enduring variety of myth, in slowing down their decay as social and bodily subjects. In the early stages of my research, listening to the militiamen define themselves as "defeated," I simply took their experience of defeat as having a causal effect on their sense of social decline and even on their bodily decay. At a later stage in my interaction with them, I came to realize that a discourse of defeat that still constructed them as warriors actually worked to give meaning to their lives. I thus came to analyze "the defeated warrior" as a fantasy that works as a technology of maintenance against decay. But what happens when the assemblage that is slowing down the subject's social decay itself begins decaying?

Cameo Dalley's chapter 10 also deals with decaying bodies. Her chapter explores the lives of non-Aboriginal helpers who live and work in remote Aboriginal communities in Australia and the various ways they end up relating to the ambient decay. Tasked with providing programs and services addressing decay among Aboriginal people, these Whitefellas often embody through their own ill-health the dominant culture's disappointment at the inability to enact desired change. These experiences result in ambivalent relationships to those whom they are tasked as helping, typified by kinds of "relational decay." This relational decay is rooted in historical settler colonial relationships and symptomatized in socio-spatial distributions of people and the kin relations they form to one another. In an interesting twist on the topic, Dalley takes her own decaying body as a starting point, raising methodological issues concerning the body of the anthropologist working with people who are themselves suffering from severe decaying social conditions. She argues that understanding how relational decay frames experiences allows a refiguring of relationality on Australia's colonial frontier.

In chapter 11, Tamara Kohn is also concerned with people subjected to a type of "let them rot" governmentality. Her work, however, focuses on US maximum security prisons and the people "inside" on life or death sentences. While many do perish there, some rise to the challenge of defying institutionally maintained physical and mental decay through their own productive and creative practices. Her chapter describes how decay, mold, and rot are produced, interacted with, and resisted. It asks readers to recognize and question their own expectations about the bodies and places hidden from public view that foster decay as well as their own participation in reproducing those expectations. Through long correspondence with an individual who has survived thirty years in solitary confinement by "calling out" mold and evil wherever it presents itself, decay becomes reframed (beyond entropy) as a structural condition that invites an active political response that contains elements of hope. As the whole collection makes for some rather grim reading, I felt that it was good to finish with Kohn's chapter, which explores the possibilities of resistance and hope amid the rot.

Notes

1. "In the Greater Antilles, some years after the discovery of America, whilst the Spanish were dispatching inquisitional commissions to investigate whether the natives had a soul or not, these very natives were busy drowning the white people they had captured in order to find out, after lengthy observation whether or not the corpses were subject to putrefaction" (Lévi-Strauss 1976, 329).

2. Andy Dawson's piece (2002) on the aging body of miners is an exception to the rule.

3. In sociology see Higgs and Gilleard 2016; and Grenier, Phillipson, and Settersten 2020. And in anthropology, Buch 2015 provides a good summary of the existing scholarship.

1

FOREVER "FALLING APART"

Semiotics and Rhetorics of Decay

Violeta Schubert

In a media incident, a popular Macedonian television game show host posted on her Instagram profile that her account had been hacked and photos deleted (Infomax 2018). One indignant commentator to her post wrote: "The village is burning, and grandma combs [her hair]! For us, our country is falling apart, to you, two photos on your profile were deleted, and for three days, half of Macedonia is talking about that" (Infomax 2018). The use of the folk phrase "Selo gori, baba se češla" (The village is burning, and grandma combs [her hair]) is immediately comprehensible to Macedonians. It is not simply a matter of someone being so self-absorbed as to be oblivious to the enormity of what is happening (i.e., "the village is burning" or "the country falling apart"). Instead, it points to the collective experience of a decay, "falling apartness," that remains perpetually unattended.

In Macedonian, the intransitive verb *raspagja* (falling apart) resonates with the Middle English *decay* and the Old French *decaïr* in referring to falling down, a *gradual* decline in strength, soundness, wasting or wearing away, or decline from a bad to a worse condition.[1] Yet there are additional nuanced variations in Macedonian. Stating that something is in a state of "falling apartness" makes it difficult to pinpoint "from bad to worse," cause or instigator, purposive action or disengagement (inaction). The prefix *ras-* connotes some kind of scattering or dispersal rather than a fall or a linear progression from "good to bad." The same prefix appears in a range of words also often used in a similar context to *raspagjanje* (the gerund of *raspagja*). For example, *rasipani* (broken, rotten) is a standard descriptor for those who are "corrupt bastards" (*rasipani kopilina*). Likewise, the term *rastureni* (past-perfect tense, meaning "dispersed, scattered, crumbled") connotes a sentiment of regret, the emotional state of an undesirable condition of having "fallen apart," as in "dispersal of migrants across the world" (*rastureni niz svetot*) or living in small units, lacking coordination or structure. Further, *raspušteni* (a state of being relaxed, letting go) is typically used to refer to "loose" morality, such as women who indiscriminately "scatter" their sexual favors or youths who lack self-control or morality. The term is also frequently found in analyses of disintegration: of the Socialist Federal Republic of Yugoslavia (SFRJ; *raspagjanje na SFRJ*), the Ottoman Empire, communism, Macedonia (*raspagjanje na Makedonija*), and even families (*raspagjanje na semejstvoto*).

The utility of deploying the term *raspagjanje* here is that it captures the sense and experience of decay, where its source is everywhere and nowhere. Spaces of suspension, of arrested thought and action, invariably appear at some point or in some context of human experience and shape the ontologies of life, experience, and identity. Such experiences may be fleeting or perpetual, but they provide a glimpse into dystopian or alternative modes of framing the limits of human agency.

The National Imaginary and Perpetual Falling Apart

As part of an ongoing research project of exploring contemporary Macedonian society, villages have been a central concern for me since the mid-1990s, when I commenced fieldwork for my doctoral thesis.[2] Macedonians, as in other places, often draw on villages as a collective topos of self-identification, but the aversion to villages is undoubtedly stronger.[3] From the mid-1990s to the present, both villagers and commentators alike frequently mention *raspagjanje na selata* (decay or disintegration of villages). As a predictable outcome of modernity—with the call of the city, a better life, a better "me"— the deliberate neglect and mismanagement by both people and successive governments have merely sped up (rather than arrested or reversed) village decay. In the 1990s, many would say that villages are for the "old and dead," and even if economic circumstances allowed for a return to living there, the objective is to leave, to get rid of the undesirable association with them (Schubert 2020; Halpern 1965, 163). Today countless villages in Macedonia lie empty, their land unused and houses decaying. Others are populated only by the walking dead—a few older people without the means to move away, who live in crumbling houses and struggle to maintain the *bavči* (garden plot) for personal sustenance, while the *nivji* (fields) are left to ruin. The traditional migratory pattern of *pečalba*—that is, of individuals going to make their economic fortunes and then returning to settle back in villages (see Bielenin-Lenczkowska 2010; Halpern and Halpern 1975)—has in the past few decades significantly changed. Ex-villagers are reluctant to return, and the collapse of villages makes for an eerie rural landscape of "falling apartness" that no measure of political will or development intervention can reverse. Indeed, rural decay has become a laboratory for political experiments and imposing Western mimicry of standards and values as "reforms."[4] But rural decay defies intervention.

The experience of village decay is a mere microcosm, however, of the broader social and national context. The expression "Our country is falling apart on us" (*Državata ni se raspagja*) quoted in the opening of this chapter evokes various aspects of the complexities among the love of country, patriotism, and the particular cultural experience of perpetual decay, which has plagued those who refer to themselves as Makedonci, and frequently as Balkanci (people of the Balkans). To be from a region that continues to be a locus of geopolitical machinations and contestation inevitably shapes local discourses about unique identity—a mode of engaging with the world grounded in the experience of, and ability to navigate, perpetual decay. Notwithstanding Western imaginaries of "the Balkans" as a crossroads of European civilization (cf. Todorova 2009), the discourse of Macedonian exceptionalism has led to the hyperbole of "trouble," "question," "problem," "complexity," and even "sickness."[5] As a "borderland of borderlands" (Pond 2006), "the Balkans of the Balkans" (Gal and Irvine 1995, 982), a "*salade de macedoine*," or an "ethnic chessboard" (Cowan and Brown 2000, 9), Macedonia is perpetually caught in a state of being in-between, in limbo, or at "the crossroads" (see Friedman 2010). In fact, the rhetoric deployed by Western commentators and negotiators in the late nineteenth century via the "Macedonia question" (see Danforth 1995) continues to reverberate. The checkered history of the autonomous Macedonia movement and the multiplicity and fluidity of identities not only defy the stereotypical logics of claims to ethnonational integrity but also offer little explanation for the idea's persistence.[6] There is no particularly coherent historical, cultural, or political golden age to refer to in the discourse. Ethnic conflicts, as Stanley Tambiah argues, "constitute a dialectic" (1989, 347). The tensions between "universalizing and homogenizing" and "the claim to be different," to use Tambiah's phrases, remain unresolved.

They are akin to "discursive dead ends," a term Olga Demetriou uses to describe Greece's perennial problem of minorities existing in a state predicated on ethnonational homogeneity (2006, 295). This is especially notable in the case of the people who claim an ethnonational identity as Macedonians.

Nonetheless, there is a familiar pattern in the public rhetoric of decay in Macedonia: namely, evoking selective histories, sites, and agents as the source of good as much as of bad. For instance, the state uses strategies in its politico-romantic revisioning of the national imagination, such as selectively commemorating the ancient—and, for many, dubious—link with ancient Macedonia. Intensifying archaeological digs, projects to invigorate cities, such as "Skopje 2014," and the "ancient Macedonia" monument-making endeavor—all have received much scrutiny (see Janev 2017, 153–54) and have even been mentioned as causes of the government's fall (see Clapp 2016). In the constant identity struggle and shape-shifting, undesirable associations and histories, such as the era of communist Yugoslavia, are left to decay, to die on their own, rather than being addressed.

In this, the rhetorical deployment of decay reflects a dissociation between self and others that serves as a mode of diversion, moving attention away from the rhetorician's (rhetor's) own behavior, corrupt doings, and transferring blame (see Herzfeld 1982). As Elizabeth Fay aptly notes, the purpose of rhetoric is not to persuade but "to dissemble the rhetor's actual goal beneath a simplified account or defense or attack meant to divert the audience's attention" (1994, 122). The diversion or dissociative aspect of decay presupposes illusory agency and naming decay agents in the general rather than the specific.

Political actors, ethnonationalists, conservatives, and moralists seek to tap into people's understanding of decay strategically by focusing on what seems to be reparable. But few are co-opted wholeheartedly by the promise of eradicating decay. Cynically, perhaps, most people in Macedonia view the democratizing of opportunities afforded to both majority and minority ethnicities to be corruptible and corrupted by power. Thus, though one is likely to hear that the collapse of communist Yugoslavia was a definitive act of getting rid of something "bad," it is just as likely that the trope of the rotten dispositions or decadence and corruptibility of some actors is brought forth as the reason for lack of progress or resolution to individual or social precarity. That is, hopefulness about change in the social order soon brings about resignation that this particular premier is no less corrupt or corruptible, no less implicated in instigating and selectively addressing decay than the previous leader. Thus, though urban and rural subjectivities present differing articulations of how decay is dispersed, they share in the experience of suspension, unfinished thoughts, and angst about possibilities in the face of perpetual chaos, conflict, and decay. Abandonment—in other words, leaving some histories, experiences, or categories of people to decay—does not resolve internal rot (decadence) or the sense of dispersed and perpetual decay that comes to afflict the human condition. In this sense, independence from Yugoslavia in 1991 seemed like a moment to arrest entrenched decay but soon gave way to the return of familiar discourses and rhetoric of fated subjectivity as Makedonci (Macedonians).

"Falling Apartness" and the Rhetoric of Fated Subjectivity

In a society of decaying spectacles, decay is abhorred just as it is utilized to mark a distinction—where *knowing* decay *reproduces* it. Indeed, decay can be a powerful social anchor. In assertions of their distinctiveness as Makedonci or Balkanci, for instance, many locals that I spoke with during fieldwork would often describe "Westerners" as "naive" (*naevni*) or "delicate" (*nežni*), judged wanting in their capacity to navigate perpetual "falling apartness," decay, and the ensuing chaos. Likewise, villagers would often describe urbanites as "delicate" in a similarly derogatory manner. Paradoxically, though the capacity to live in and navigate perpetual decay is a mark of distinction, there is also, on occasion, a sense of despondency and troubling irreconcilability with the inability to arrest decay. That is, the sense of the shared experience of decay and the homing in on the craft of survival in the face of precarity bring forth contrary discourses and rhetorics of heroism (alluding to individual agency) as well as fated subjectivities and positionalities.

The way the rhetoric of fatalism is deployed—that is, withstanding rather than eradicating decay—means that attempts at changing the condition are merely fleeting. Folk rhetorics of fatalism abound. For instance, older informants say, "Taka je napišano" (that's how it is written). Acceptance of perpetual decay, their "fate," compels nonengagement and passive conformity to the will of the powerful. In colloquial Macedonian, an acceptance of fated positionality goes with notions of suspension and irreconcilability, best illustrated in the subtle differences in framing rhetorical questions in the intransitive form, "Što da se prae?" (What to do?), as opposed to the transitive, "Što da pravam?" (What [am I] to do?). That is, discourses of *raspagjane* and fated subjectivity reflect a particular way that individuals come to express the experience of the limits of human agency and the affordances they are given in being able to navigate entrenched social, economic, and political precarity.

To give an example, in a 2018 visit to Macedonia I caught up with "Dana," a woman who had been referred to as *stara čupa* ("old girl," i.e., an unmarried woman past the social age of marriage) in the 1990s. Dana, still single, continued to work as a waitress in the town of Bitola. She spoke of some "Scandinavian tourists" who had left the restaurant as I arrived. The Scandinavian couple had shared internet-sourced pictures of garbage collection in their country, condescendingly talking about how much cleaner their country is, demonstrating the lack of cleanliness in Bitola. She told me how frequently foreigners (tourists or UN and development people) think it's okay to criticize her country, asking rhetorically, "What should I say? . . . 'We do it this way; we do it that way' . . . They just show off!"

Like many others, Dana followed the well-worn tracks of the rhetoric of fatalism, saying, "That's how it is for us [here]" and "There is no chance, that is that [it is what it is]." But, contrarily, Dana was also resentful of outsiders who point out the rubbish, chaos, or decadence (i.e., the behavior of some individuals or the general state of corruption, criminality, or immorality). Dana exclaimed, "We know how it is." But she soon added despondently, "No one knows," "They haven't got a clue," and "If anyone knows what to do here, I'll give them ten stars." Dana concluded the story summarizing the condition of life with the same phrases that many locals used during my fieldwork in the 1990s. In the first two decades of the twenty-first century, such phrases have gained a new currency with the particular experiences of precarity: "All is a struggle for life" (*borba za život*).

There is no shortage of local phrases to describe life's precarity under the condition of perpetual falling apartness. Many would say, "Kaj nas se je katastrofa" (Here [for us] it is all a catastrophe), and in imagining no escape from such a condition, they feel that "nema spas" (there is no salvation). The deployment of words such as *katastrofa* (catastrophe) and *haus* (chaos) are familiar cultural tropes where social decay is experienced as "sve je rastureno" (all is fallen apart [collapsed, let go, scattered]). Locals such as Dana, in other words, understand the obvious rubbish on the streets (which for the Scandinavian tourists might be surmised as an outcome of inefficient municipal services, poor governance, or simply poverty) as part of the condition of perpetual falling apartness. Constant chaos breeds endless decay, and, conversely, perpetual decay produces constant chaos.

As Michael Herzfeld argues, "To some extent, all social groups exhibit a tension between self-display and intimate self-recognition" (1987, 47). In this sense, the "appeals to fate" Herzfeld notes in the case of Greece are "invocations of imperfection [that] always occur after the event, never as an excuse for prospective passivity" (120). Appeals to fate in the case of Macedonians are likewise often "after the event." To be sure, like Herzfeld I reject the notion that some people or the entirety of the population wholeheartedly embrace fatalism, "passive and total resignation to future events" (36). But repeated experience teaches one lessons about how to navigate perpetual decay and the manifestations of power it produces. Moreover, where agency is evoked, often they rely, as Keith Brown (2003, 1) notes, on "idioms of the taken-for-granted—the things one cannot help—for explanatory efficacy."

For locals, the "explanatory efficacy" of perpetual decay and the inability to shift one's circumstances often backfire in the normative cultural frame of "putting on a face" or "two-facedness" (*dvoličnost*). For instance, a man who struggled to find a job after completing his degree in 2014, found one working with foreigners in the capital city, Skopje. The foreigners, according to the man, would naively accept *at face value* boasts by local "partners" of the reforms that they had achieved. Like many others, the man pointed out to me the appearance of a good life, "all that shines from afar" (*sve sveti od daleku*). "Look at how everyone lives," he continued. "They drink, eat, go out, smile. . . . All youth dress beautifully. Beautifully adorned but they have no resources, don't have jobs. They all want to escape from here." The man soon added his spin on the moral of the tale: "Things that look shiny to outsiders are rotten, but you can't tell them the truth."

If *raspagjanje* is taken for granted as a condition of life, social performativity compels putting on a "face," presentation of *čisto lice* (clean face), hiding the "true" nature of things by deploying *dvoličnost* (two-facedness) to keep experiences of falling apart (such as problems with one's health, family, or finances) away from prying eyes and potential harm. It is a matter of not only pride but also self-preservation; if one fails to "put on a face" and thus shows weakness in such a context, one is liable to be exploited.

"Strašni Raboti" (Scary Doings) and What Lies beneath the Surface

That other people may exploit one's revealed weaknesses is nowhere more apparent than in the copious stories of ghosts and *vampiri* (see Siegel 1996) in a state of perpetual decay: that is, those who have not transitioned into death (the finality of a decaying process). The fear, too, that some disgruntled members of one's community may deploy curses and black magic (*magija*) to harm is embedded in the cultural repertoire of navigating decay. The recourse to *magija* and curses, in other words, is also deployed to excuse personal failure. As Vassos Argyrou notes for Cyprus, people who draw on magic for explanations of events and actions "are employing a *strategy* aimed at redefining problematic situations to their advantage" (1993, 259, emphasis in the original). Grounded in perceptions of irreversible decay, for instance, some curses evoke falling apart, such as "hope to God that your house [family] fall apart" (*daj Boźe da ti se rasturi kukjata*). In one village, a childless couple proclaimed to me that, because of such a curse being placed on them by a spiteful woman that they knew, their house (symbolic of the agnatic *familija*)[7] had "fallen apart." Further, such beliefs are invoked by war veterans reacting to the Bitola municipality's 2007 decision to remove twenty-six monuments to communist partisans from the city park: "The dead heroes of Macedonia, albeit as ghosts, will rise against all of you who will decide to give your support to this harmful plan. Through the destruction of the monuments of the antifascist war, you destroy the present and the future of our country" (Marinov 2010, 1). In the perpetual state of decay, there is neither morality nor respect for the past. And in some cases, no amount of guarding oneself by "putting on a face" is adequate protection.

From a different perspective, in a conversation with a self-proclaimed *običen čovek* (ordinary man) working long hours in a restaurant in the heart of the capital city Skopje, the law's inability to provide protection emerged. The man emphatically argued, "There are no laws [rules]" (*Nema zakoni*). Obviously, laws exist in the literal sense; indeed, making new laws is the preeminent performativity of identity as reformists. Privileged protection, however, is afforded to the powerful (see Hislope 2008). The man thus spoke of an incident in which a youth was killed in a car accident but the driver didn't go to court, as it was deemed an accident. "It just went away," he said, putting forward an explanation for such "sweeping away" as a product of corruption: "They are all rotten bastards. Corruption is so deep, doesn't change; don't believe in any of the talk of reforms. I see people drive in cars that would make people in the West jealous. They park wherever they like, the police give parking tickets to everyone else but not them." In the absence of rules, there are only *rasipani kopilina* (rotten bastards).

Typically, the sweeping statement that "they are all rotten" is deployed equally to refer to locals and the foreign actors who have infiltrated the society post-independence. There is much bending over backward to attract foreign investment (no tax, generous subsidies), but the kind of people, companies, and officials that it brings are not necessarily *čisti lica* (clean [face] people). Women working in the precarious textile industry (see Bonfiglioli 2014), for instance, described to me the inhumane treatment by "local" managers and the foreign owners of the factories—workers locked up and forced to fill impossible orders overnight.

One informant, whose gender I am concealing because revealing it could have violent consequences, spoke of foreign women kept in a dungeon, released only at night as sex workers. The owner of the nightclub was a "respected" man, and police and other *važni* (important) men regularly frequented the establishment. As the informant exclaimed, "Don't tell me they [police] don't know what's going on!"[8] Similarly, another person in fear for their life after refusing to cooperate with wrongdoings and seeking a visa to a foreign country, exclaimed, "What's the point? Nothing is done." While simultaneously proclaiming the presence of *rasipani lice* (rotten individuals), the informant described the distinctly Macedonian trait that I encountered in the mid-1990s, saying, "Macedonians are sheep" (i.e., they follow). There is often harsh judgment of *našite* (our [people]), as expressed by the expression "Our [people] don't do anything, they're scared of everything." Indeed, as the informant said, "We Macedonians are all spoiled [rotten]" (*Nije Makedonci site sme rasipani*).

Concluding Remarks

The forms of decay that rise to consciousness or visibility make it amenable to the idea of human agency. Indeed, the common notion of decay as a posthumous (linear) process of going from good to bad, or even bad to worse, suggests that a postmortem analysis may render possible the agentive capacity needed to redress perceived wrongs. Such a view is, by far, less threatening or ominous, even when repeated efforts at redressing wrongs may fail. Understandably, political and social actors seeking to mobilize action of some sort typically deploy such a conceptualization of decay. For scholars, "decay" has utility as a spectacle that is "good to think with," to paraphrase Claude Lévi-Strauss (1962, 89). Many theories presuppose that decay, the death of some prior forms of organizing or being, is necessary for creativity, innovation, and rejuvenation.[9] Though Clifford Geertz, for instance, is not concerned with decay per se, his depiction of a "world in pieces" or the "shattering of larger coherences" serves as an opportunity for anthropology to question or even to rejuvenate its theoretical and methodological premise: "Where does this falling apart into parts—let us call it 'disassembly'—leave the great, integrative, totalizing concepts we have so long been accustomed to using in organizing our ideas about world politics, and particularly about similarity and difference among peoples, societies, states, and cultures" (Geertz 2000, 221). The struggle between nature and the interventionists, agents of change, juxtapose the imperative for movement, rejuvenation, and innovation with the concerted efforts required to analyze, arrest, or leave behind decay in some way, lest there is regression, "involution" (Geertz 1963; see also Christakos 2010), or "degeneration" (Constable, Potolsky, and Denisoff 1999).

But such notions of linear decay are limited to the extent that they can illuminate either the process of prolonged death (analogous to the setting in of inevitable "rot") or the experience of a perpetually suspended state between decay and rejuvenation—incomplete and complete action that allows neither standing still nor movement, neither negotiation nor passivity. Though I may be painting quite a bleak picture here, it is an aspect of human experience, and "falling apart" is often deployed so as to explain personal and social events and actions and ill-fated positionalities. Furthermore, a *raspagjane* narrative points to the inability to train a microscope on some forms of its manifestation.[10] Struggling with navigating forever falling apart and the social decadence and paralysis that it can produce, you learn to take the next punch, the next hit, as best as you can. It is in this sense that the often used phrase *se krpime* (we stitch along), or an acceptance of fated positionality, merely intensifies the feeling of being in a perpetual state of falling apart. But, though there is the temptation, as Fabio Mattioli (this volume) describes, for the Skojani interlocutors to "embrace the abyss" where there is no hope and no decay, there is also the imperative to transcend, even if it is merely to "stitch along." The "long-standing hope kept alive," as Hirokazu Miyazaki (2004, 2) refers to it in the case of Fijians, is for many Macedonians a matter of believing against one's better judgment, knowing reality and yet still assuming that it can be changed. Loss of hope is a loss of self.

Notes

I would like to acknowledge the tremendously helpful comments and critiques of the people involved in the project of this volume, particularly Ghassan Hage, Michael Herzfeld, and Tamara Kohn. I would also like to thank the readers for Duke University Press for their thoughtful advice for improving the article.

1. Merriam-Webster Online, s.v. "decay," https://www.merriam-webster.com/dictionary/decay: "gradual decline in strength, soundness, or prosperity or in degree of excellence or perfection"; "a wasting or wearing away"; and "to decrease usually gradually in size, quantity, activity, or force." *Merriam-Webster's Learner's Dictionary* also includes the definition as "the process or result of going slowly from a bad condition to a worse condition."

2. I discuss in more detail elsewhere my fieldwork and the nuances of being an anthropologist who studies her own society (Schubert 2020). Briefly, as a native Macedonian, I spent the first eight years of my life in a remote village located along the southern border between Greece and the ex–Yugoslav Republic. Since migrating to Australia with my family, I've continued to be immersed in various ways with village customs. The main fieldwork site was in several different regions, predominantly in bands of villages surrounding the towns Bitola and Ohrid.

3. Many studies explore the significance of villages in shaping national imaginaries (see, for example, Herzfeld 2020 for Greece and Rogers 1987 for France). In the case of Macedonia, the depictions of villages in shaping Macedonian culture is notable—for instance, the media coverage of annual village festivals such as the Karnival celebrated on New Year's Day (according to the pre-Gregorian calendar).

4. Many rural reforms have been instigated since independence, influenced by international development organizations such as the World Bank (see Jaisaard et al. 2002).

5. I was particularly caught by the title of an article by Myron Weiner (1971), "The Macedonia Syndrome," which seemed to perpetuate the stereotypical depictions of a place of sickness, an affliction that requires triage.

6. There is a wealth of literature on the contestations of Macedonian national identity and the late nineteenth-century "Macedonia question." See, for instance, Daskalovski 2017; Cowan 2000; Brown 1998, 2003; and Danforth 1995.

7. On the significance of the house as symbolic of agnatic kinship identity, see, for example, Pina-Cabral 1992; Schubert 2005.

8. According to the UNHCR, Macedonia is a source, transit, and destination country for trafficking. See also US Department of State 2018.

9. Though beyond the scope of this chapter, it is worth considering the extent that social theory is generally framed around the idea of what is in decay or how rejuvenation comes from the death of some prior form of thinking or organizing. See, for instance, Arnold Toynbee's (1934) "death of civilizations" thesis, Karl Marx's critique of philosophy and capitalism (1954, 1969), or Anthony Wallace's (1949) religious movements and rejuvenation. Georg Simmel's treatment of "ruins" is also close to this conceptualization of decay as he refers to an "equalizing justice" with "the decay of those men and works of men which now can only yield, but can no longer create and maintain their own forms of their own" (1958, 385).

10. I borrow the phrase from Susan Navarette in the discussion of the nineteenth-century Decadent literature style: "The Decadent style was also the author's equivalent of the microscope, an instrument that by mid-century had fully exposed the otherwise hidden realms of the microbe and the bacterium and had thus made possible the disclosure of what Huysmans called 'la souveraine horreur'" (1998, 45–46).

2

TRASH AND TREASURE

Pathologies of Permanence on the
Margins of Our Plastic Age

Debra McDougall

In a viral video, a Costa Rican fisherman slowly removes piece after piece of plastic trash from the guts of a dolphinfish: lids, a comb, a lighter, the shredded remains of cups and bags, and small chunks of no-longer-identifiable objects. The video is one of countless digitally circulating images of how far garbage penetrates the world's ecology: dissected birds dwarfed by the plastic extracted from their digestive tracts, turtles tangled in plastic netting, desolate beaches coated in plastic rubbish. The image of imperishable plastic objects encased in the putrescible innards of the just-caught fish can serve as a memento mori of our plastic age—not a reminder that our living flesh will eventually decay, but a reminder that our garbage outlives our flesh.

Plastics are conjured from the decayed remains of ancient life, ingeniously transmuted into materials with uncanny combinations of malleability and durability. They can be shaped into anything, but this malleability is delimited in space and time; plastics are given form in factories, but then become difficult to recraft (Michaels 2013). Unlike substances such as the cement and steel of suspension bridges discussed by Akhil Gupta in this volume, plastic objects appear immune to the "tendrils of decay." They invite no maintenance. Nor do plastic objects show "the marks of time's passage" that Michael Herzfeld (this volume) sees as "a trigger of affect and nostalgia, of a conversion of decay into treasure" in the genteel dilapidation of Rome.

Plastic waste does, of course, decompose. Like nuclear waste, however, it decays within a temporal cycle not only far longer than a human life, but far longer than the duration of most states, empires—indeed, most human institutions. The spatial scale of decomposition is also confounding. The chunks of plastic objects that hold their shape through the digestive tracts of marine animals are only the most visible form of plastic in the world's waters. More worrying are the tiny microparticles and invisible toxic additives that are transforming oceans and terrestrial waterways into plastic "slurry" or "soup" (Gabrys 2013). These microplastics pose immediate danger to mollusks and amphibians, not the fish, birds, or mammals whose suffering is more easily seen by human eyes (Law and Thompson 2014).

The nightmare of our plastic oceans arose with the corporate-sponsored post–World War II dream of a plastic age. In a review of the new science of plastics published in 1941, V. E. Yarsley and E. G. Couzens looked forward to the day when a new plastic man would come to age in a shiny, clean, hygienic world, full of plastic surfaces, furniture, buildings, and playthings. At the end of his life, this plastic man wears plastic spectacles and dentures, then "sinks into his grave in a hygienically enclosed plastic coffin" (quoted in Thompson et al. 2009, 1973; see also T. Fisher 2013, 288). These technologically augmented bodies living in built environments free of decay, dirt, and mold would also have to learn to toss the miraculous material away. An editorial in *Modern Packaging* in 1957 enthusiastically observed, "Consumers are learning to throw these containers in the trash as nonchalantly as they would discard a paper cup—and in that psychology lies the future of molded plastic packaging" (quoted in Hawkins 2013, 63). The journal's editor sought to persuade the audience of the keynote address in a 1963 National Plastics conference that the "future of plastics is in the trash can" (quoted in Hawkins 2018, 98). Plastic pollution is not an externality. It was part of the corporate plan from the beginning.

How are we to understand this peculiarly abject state where treasures seem increasingly ephemeral but trash has a toxic afterlife, reappearing unexpectedly as fragments in fish guts or as chemical traces in our fat? I want to suggest that objects get their value—as trash or as treasure—in relation to humans and their bodies. And I begin not with the epicenter of plastics production in post–World War II Europe and the United States but in the rural southwestern Pacific.

"PLASTICS HAVE REVOLUTIONIZED our daily lives," declares a major overview of the effects of plastic on the environment and human health (Thompson et al. 2009). It is hard to argue with the evidence: 260 million tons per annum, increasing exponentially; 8 percent of global oil and gas production used as feedstock or energy for production; pervasive effects on environments and bodies regardless of their proximity to plastic production or access to plastic products. The authors' use of the first-person inclusive pronoun, a usage that pervades the literature on plastic, seems to include all humans in a common problem. Yet "our daily lives" also elides the way that the benefits and hazards of the plastic revolution, like all other sociopolitical or economic revolutions, are unevenly distributed.

The island of Ranongga lies in the far western reaches of the Solomon Islands, an independent state in the southwestern Pacific comprised of six large volcanic islands, about 900 smaller islands, and a linguistically and culturally diverse population of 670,000. When I first visited twenty years ago, plastic packaging was usually reused. Liter bottles of water were used for months, even years. Unlike aluminum kettles, which had long replaced bamboo tubes as water receptacles, they could be thrown into string bags or backpacks without spilling. Rice was sold in woven plastic bags designed for reuse: the ten-kilo bag came with a stitched-on strap that transformed it into a handy shoulder bag, and the twenty-kilo bag was easily repurposed to carry root crops or coconuts. Loose tea came in a plastic packet that, after the tea was gone, was handy for carrying the lime used for chewing betel nut. Instant noodles had recently become a widely used food, and their colorful wrappers were often folded and strung together with wrappers from other snacks for house decorations. Small bottles of Schweppes soda were transformed into fishing reels or used to hold small amounts of kerosene for lamps or to store coconut oil used for skin and hair. Plastic containers and packages had some value.

Over a generation, I've watched plastics proliferate and lose their use value. A generation later than their European and US counterparts, Solomon Islander consumers have learned the lesson taught by the pioneers of plastic: plastic is trash. Today, rural residents of Ranongga travel more frequently to provincial towns and the national capital city and buy more bottled water, which has become cheaper in recent years. Large packets of loose tea have been replaced by single-use packets of milk tea and milk coffee. The plastic covers of hardtack biscuits, ubiquitous even in the 1990s, are joined by packaging for an increasing volume and variety of salty snacks, cookies, candy, gum, ice pops (frequently drunk unfrozen), and cordial mix (sometimes licked from the packet). Packaging piles up. The shoreline of the village where I have lived—itself transformed by a massive earthquake that lifted and exposed the island's fringing reefs in 2007—is increasingly strewn with plastic bags, nets, packaging, and broken flip-flops. Women labor to keep paths and common areas clear of litter.

I am more repulsed by plastic packaging than my Ranongga friends are; they seem to treat it like any other food waste or plant litter that is out of place in the cleared space of a hamlet or village path. A few years ago, having joined in the village beautification efforts before a large church gathering, I delivered a grandmotherly harangue during the church announcements, scolding the children who were tossing their candy wrappers and ice pop sleeves all around the church building and grounds, areas that we (their classificatory mothers and grandmothers) had so painstakingly cleaned and decorated with flowers in preceding days.

In truth, though, the trash strewn amid the flower beds bothered me less than the rotted teeth of the children laughing back at me. In 1999, when my parents came to visit me during my first year of field research, they sponsored a dental tour of Ranongga, with my father (a dentist himself) assisting a Solomon Islander dentist. Because such a tour had not been undertaken for many years, most of the work was extractions. In the village that was my adopted home, however, my father screened all schoolchildren to send them for fillings in town. He was surprised by the stark variation in oral health. Some kids had teeth decayed to the root, whereas others had no cavities at all. "Do those kids brush?" he asked me. As I looked through his list of names and treatments, I realized that all the kids with the worst decay had spent much of their lives living in town or near logging operations where their parents worked for cash. Those with perfect teeth were from families with almost no money and certainly no toothbrushes. Today, though, the globalization of junk food and increasing access to cash means that even children whose parents are not in waged or contract labor have access to sweets that rot their teeth.

Those teeth are decayed because of refined sugar but also because of plastic packaging. Few of the tooth-destroying foods that also contribute to rising levels of high blood pressure, diabetes, cancer, and all other noncommunicable diseases would be a regular part of a rural Ranongga diet without cheap plastic packaging that allows small quantities of food to be turned into countable objects, shipped, and kept dry in a hot, humid environment. Gay Hawkins (2018, 99) observes that plastics were not simply substituted for existing containers made of glass, metal, or paper; plastic packaging opened possibilities for all manner of foods that could not otherwise exist, including culinary wonders like liquid cheese to be slurped from a tube and all the "junk" food available in an ordinary village canteen. These globally distributed cheap food commodities are big business precisely because even the world's poorest people can afford them (Gewertz and Errington 2010; Errington, Gewertz, and Fujikura 2013).

Plastic technologies that would help ameliorate the damage of ubiquitous junk food are noticeably absent in economically marginal places like rural Ranongga. I have rarely seen plastic tubes of toothpaste or toothbrushes. There is no dental equipment in the village clinics. Nowhere in the country are the amazing machines of plastic and metal that allows the bonding of new composite resins to replace the decayed tissues of the tooth. A cancer diagnosis here remains a death sentence. The wonders of plastics-dependent medical technologies are distant and difficult to access. The neatly packaged lollipops, though, are everywhere.

THE PATHOLOGY OF plastic emerges not only from the fact that it is disposed of but does not decay, but also from the way it quickens the decay of corporeal bodies—bodies that intentionally consume junk food encased in plastic or unintentionally ingest plastic's toxic remains. There is something decidedly strange about the way plastic is designed to be both durable and disposable. Plastic objects endure but are worthless; they invert a more conventional logic whereby what is durable is also valuable. Yet durability alone does not distinguish between trash and treasure: treasures really get their value in relationship to the human body.

Durable artifacts normally take a long time to make. My Ranonggan friends lamented that no one today is patient enough to make the shell rings of generations past, now that everyone is using light paper (recently, thin plastic) currency. The most important type of valuable, bakia, was constructed out of the incredibly hard fossilized shell of a giant clam, stuff from the ocean dug from deep under the earth. These heavy rings are exchanged primarily in transactions of land and persons. Old people told me that the time required to grind this harder-than-rock material into a perfectly even, round ring was the time required for a sprouting coconut to grow into a fruiting tree or a child to grow into an adult.

Traditional kinds of valuables are intimately connected to the human body. Some treasures *are* the body. After the flesh has rotted away, the ancestral bones are enshrined, anchoring past to present and future. Other treasures stand in metaphorical relationship to the corporeal body. Throughout the Austronesian world, houses are understood as the externalized bodies of persons who endure across generations as fleshy bodies are born, grow, die, and decompose. Others treasure extend or adorn the body. Carefully crafted shell, stone, metal, fibers, or wood are worn as jewelry and detached from the body as currency. Such treasures are inherited and exchanged in networks of relationships that are best conceived not as connecting discreet individuals but as constituting them as persons.

Consider the *taonga* held annually by New Zealand's poet laureate. This "treasure" (as the Maori word *taonga* may be translated) is a beautifully carved walking stick, a *tokotoko*. Symbolically, it extends the person who holds the stick. Like the Maori meeting house, it is conceived as a person itself. Over the period of the poet laureate's incumbency, the "parent" *tokotoko* gives birth to a "child," which the carving master designs for the poet to keep after her tenure has finished. In 2017, Selina Tusitala Marsh was named New Zealand's poet laureate, the first Pasifika woman to be honored in this way. Rather than leaving the parent *tokotoko* untouched behind glass in New Zealand's National Library as previous poet laureates had done, Marsh took it out to "tell its stories" (Marsh 2018). She composed poems in its honor. She took it on marches to preserve turtle habitat and other environmental causes. She passed it around primary school classrooms and academic conferences, including a meeting of the Australian Association of Pacific Studies in 2018, asking all of us to hold it and give it some of our sweat and our mana—our power, life-force, or efficacy. The *tokotoko* attracted other treasures, including a chiefly flyswatter, the traditional accompaniment for a chiefly walking stick, from a high-ranking Polynesian chief. Its mana was expanded in tandem with Marsh's as they traveled together to distant shores and were honored by new people.

Durable valuables like the Maori *tokotoko* or the Ranonggan *bakia* expand personhood, stretching beyond the limited spatial and temporal scope of a single human life. In her study of kula exchange of the Massim region of Papua New Guinea, Nancy Munn (1986) traced the creation of value through transactions embedded in the process of making persons through the production and exchange of food. Her ethnography is poised in time between the precolonial violence where persons were also violently unmade through regional warfare (Macintyre 1995) and postcolonial globalization that would propel the people of Gawa Island into more direct connections with others far beyond the kula ring. There are no traces of plastic in Munn's photos and text. Food is not purchased prepackaged from a shop but grown on matrilineal land. Life cycle rituals, which symbolically recognize the contributions of others to the making of persons, and interisland kula exchanges originate with this autochthonously produced food. Munn analyzes these exchanges in terms of their qualities—the movement of heavy, soft, decayable food against light, hard, durable objects like seafaring canoes and the necklaces and armbands of the kula. These decorated and storied kula valuables take on the quality of persons but without the limitations of a person's heavy and limiting corporeality. Kula valuables are courted by suitors using love magic; they are lured from their owner by the beauty of another valuable moving in the opposite direction. Years later, having traveled hundreds of kilometers, they are enticed back home, more beautifully decorated than when they left—like ancient Roman ruins, they are more valuable for sheen of age, the mark of having been passed through, caressed, and oiled by many hands. In Munn's analysis, the durability of these objects allows the fame and the name of the kula trader and his home place to transcend both the limited span of a human life and the limited scope of direct face-to-face relationships.

The possibility of expansion of value is haunted by an alternative vision of self, one emerging in ideas of witchcraft and sorcery. Like other monsters of the region—Ranonggan folk tales focus on greedy giant ogres who gobble gardens, animals, and people, even those they call grandchildren (McDougall 2016, 68–72)—the Gawan witch is driven by greed and engages in unfettered consumption, without consideration for others. Munn observes that witches cause all kinds of sickness and suffering, but "the ultimate aim of witches is to cause death so that they can appropriate and consume the corpse" (1986, 215). One vector of such sorcery throughout the southwestern Pacific is trash. A would-be sorcerer works his or her craft on the durable bodily waste of his victim, like fingernail clippings, hair, betel nut husks, or food scraps. Life-destroying sorcery and life-enhancing exchange follow the same logic: objects that were once part of a body, or worn on a body, continue to contain some aspect of that body. Just as the circulation of an object of bodily adornment extends the person beyond the physical body, ensorcellment of bodily leavings destroys the person to whom they belonged.

For those who fear sorcery, waste products that do not rot swiftly may pose mortal danger. Even for those of us who do not fear sorcery, these images and symbols can help us conceptualize the physical danger of durable waste and the moral danger of unfettered consumption. Plastics contain and emit toxics; we might also imagine that our plastic trash is "poisoning" us in the neo-Melanesian English sense of the word *poison*: it is cursing us. Plastic trash is the refuse of the promise of limitless consumption. It now generates death.

IN HIS INTRODUCTION to this volume, Ghassan Hage suggests that we live in a time of pathological decay. One aspect of the problem is premature decay: infrastructure that collapses in decades, not centuries (Gupta, this volume; Mattioli, this volume); the decaying bodies of prisoners locked away in toxic buildings (Kohn, this volume); soldiers with broken bodies and souls (Hage, this volume); First Nations people suffering from the untreated wounds inflicted by colonialism (Klein, this volume); and the white helpers who struggle to keep the decay away from their own bodies (Dalley, this volume). These forms of decay no longer seem to be leading to regeneration, where the decomposing matters of one generation are taken up anew by the next.

The pathology lies less in the speed of decay than in the fact that it does not reach its natural conclusion—it is a suspended or failed decay. Neoliberal capitalism, Hage argues, has a zombie essence; rather than collapsing and being transformed into something new, this is a capitalism that remains in a permanent state of decay without ever fully decomposing. It is also a capitalism made possible by petroleum. When burned, these ancient remains of life are causing catastrophic climate change; when transformed into plastics, they linger to choke the earth.

This essay has focused not on the rot that has become increasingly difficult to hide from view but on the trash that refuses to rot—the durable excrement of the modernist promise of endless growth. As material and as metaphor, plastic helps to focus attention on what dies when our cheap commodities exist in perpetuity. Valuables should travel across the ocean and land on distant shores, generating value and multiplying relations, giving and enhancing life. Yet modern rubbish withstands sun, wind, and water to land unwanted on a stranger's shore. Surely one of the challenges of our time is to return to some semblance of normal human life—where our treasures circulate to generate value beyond the fallible human body, and our waste stays in place to decay.

Note

I thank my friends in Ranongga who have helped me understand the human condition and the pathologies of our times over more than two decades. I am grateful to Ghassan Hage for the invitation to write beyond my comfort zone. I thank Cameo Dalley and Akhil Gupta for their suggestions in the last phase of revisions; and I thank all other contributors to *Decay* for their critical readings of earlier drafts.

3

INFRASTRUCTURE AS DECAY AND THE DECAY OF INFRASTRUCTURE

Akhil Gupta

There are two interlinked registers in which to think of infrastructure and decay. One concerns how infrastructures decay over time due to their materials rusting and wearing out; the other points to the ruination caused by the infrastructures of the Industrial Revolution, which, in turn, were literally fueled by decaying organic matter. Maintenance keeps infrastructures functioning, staving off decay, but maintenance is seen as unglamorous and uninteresting compared to the heroic masculinized activity of invention and construction. What would be implied for the ruination engendered by the infrastructures of the Anthropocene by giving priority to the loving care of maintenance?

The infrastructure instrumental in the rise of industrial capitalism, such as the steam engine, was operated by decayed matter, the ruins of past biological processes, in the form of peat, coal, petroleum, and natural gas. In the Anthropocene, it is thus possible to renarrativize the Industrial Revolution to emphasize colonial plunder, the reliance on decaying matter, and ruination rather than traditional, Whiggish themes of economic enrichment, growth, and spectacular civilizational achievement. From the perspective of the Anthropocene, the Industrial Revolution was the period when stored hydrocarbons were utilized to bring the planet to the brink of ruination. Unearthed and unleashed, deposits of past biological organic matter created climate change, which now threatens to ruin life on the planet. This darker, dystopian narrative about the Industrial Revolution emphasizes how infrastructure built from the ruins of organic matter in turn brings about ruination. However, in most scholarly and popular discourse, it is still uncommon to describe the Industrial Revolution in the language of decay and ruination, rather than the language of progress, growth, civilization, and the birth of a new era of well-being, safety, and prosperity. These ideas are now sedimented into the common sense of development discourse, and they exist in uneasy tension with an acknowledgment of the "risks" of climate change and efforts to mitigate the adverse impacts of a warming planet.

Infrastructure plays a central role in this larger dialectic of civilization and ruination, development and destruction, and construction and decay because it is the key technology that converts stored hydrocarbons into the sources of energy that have given us the era of capitalist development. Susan Leigh Star remarks that although infrastructure is commonly seen as an invisible "system of substrates," the critical relationships that they enable are often missed (1999, 380). The larger societal and civilizational processes between (re)generation and decay are mediated by infrastructure, which have been obscured in part by the rhetoric of the civilizing mission, the political story about the rise of the West, and the lofty economic goals of global development.

I am suggesting that we think of infrastructure and ruination in two interlinked registers. Infrastructures ruin in their capacity to act, and it is only because they ruin that they can act. Some examples will help make this clear. Building a large coal-fired power plant involves the destruction of the natural environment because the site itself may require the clearing of forests, the leveling of land, the drawing of water from the ground or rivers, and so forth; raw materials such as steel, iron, and wood need to be supplied by mining ores or by harvesting timber from forests; the equipment used to construct the plant may itself be run using gasoline or diesel engines, and so on. Thus, infrastructures cause destruction in their very creation. However, the connection to the larger issues above have to do with the fact that the running of the power plant and the production of electricity requires the excavation of coal, and the production of carbon dioxide, sulfur oxides, nitrous oxides, and other pollutants. This infrastructure can only act through ruination, and what it enables (electricity that supplies power to factories, offices, and homes, creating growth and development) cannot be separated from the destruction it causes. McDougall makes a similar argument about the destruction caused by plastics created from hydrocarbons (this volume). Infrastructures create progress, civilization, growth, jobs, and human development alongside and at the same time as different forms of decay—destruction, ruination, climate change, and pollution. Those two outcomes are different sides of the same Janus-faced process. It is only by paying attention to infrastructure that we can understand how those two historical processes have been conjoined in the modern history of the world.

We can study the dialectic of construction and ruination in infrastructure in another register too, however—one that respects the relative autonomy of the infrastructural (Gupta 2018). In this perspective, infrastructure becomes the object of study, not simply inhabiting the background to reach other goals or objectives, but occupying center stage and entering the limelight.[1] Usually infrastructure escapes notice until it breaks down (Star 1999, 382). However, by paying attention to decay throughout the life cycles of infrastructure, we may begin to theorize the work of decay at the heart of modern capitalist practices. The Enlightenment belief in humankind's mastery over nature may have prevented a more complex understanding of infrastructure as always existing in a relationship with (natural) decay, rather than as a means of conquering it or eliminating it altogether.[2]

What lies between infrastructure's construction and ruination? In the poetics of infrastructure, the drudgery of maintenance pales when compared to the heroism of construction and the romantic pull exerted by the elegiac in ruination. Using the example of the ancient core of Rome, Michael Herzfeld (this volume) distinguishes between two different forms of ruination: one exhibits the genteel decay worthy of elegiac rumination; the other, *degrado*, connotes breakdown and disorder, a form of ruination that is simultaneously physical and social. In this essay I propose maintenance as the third term inserting itself between the poles of creation and decay. To the extent that infrastructures project solidity and endurance, it is because the overlooked activity of maintenance keeps decay at bay.

The temporality of infrastructure focuses on the process of construction. There is a great deal of attention paid to infrastructures in the planning stages and during the periods of construction, which may extend over several years or even decades. During this time, what is often privileged is the heroic overcoming of obstacles, both natural and social. A bridge with a span that defies what was thought technically possible, or a railroad that traverses treacherous, mountainous terrain, inspires the kind of awe that was previously reserved for the sublime in nature. An example of the former is the Golden Gate Bridge in San Francisco; an example of the latter is the Rhaetian Railway in Switzerland. Today the Golden Gate Bridge is appreciated largely for its aesthetics, but most engineers even today know that it was a technological marvel: both the longest and tallest suspension bridge in the world at the time of its construction during the Great Depression (1933–37).

Plaques and tourist brochures often encode these narratives of heroism and the conquest of impossible odds. They reshape the experience of that infrastructure for subsequent generations, and reinvoke danger and impossibility for people who might otherwise fail to experience such feelings in encountering the object. Aesthetic or technical virtuosity in the design and construction of buildings might similarly invoke feelings of the sublime.

Taking the example of the Golden Gate Bridge again, a visitor today who has seen longer suspension bridges, or someone who knows nothing about bridges, might fail to be impressed by the bridge as a technological achievement. Even an appreciation of the bridge's aesthetic beauty might be diluted by anticipatory experiences of seeing countless images of the bridge as a symbol of San Francisco and California. For example, residents or visitors to Lisbon may have seen its copy (25 de Abril Bridge) before experiencing the original. The encounter with the bridge today is highly mediated by the circulation of its image: it is experienced through its image, the icon through the symbol and vice versa, so much so that the bridge itself becomes a simulacrum of its images.[3] But—and here is the important point—this dizzying, saturated world of the bridge's images make it impossible to experience it as an aesthetic or technological sublime.

Most often, the story of the arc of infrastructure ends when the ribbon inaugurating the structure is cut and the infrastructure (highway, bridge, building, airport, train station) is declared open. Paradoxically, infrastructure dies as an object of debate, contention, and often appreciation, at the very moment that it becomes useful. Even before it is completed, infrastructure starts to decay. The work of maintenance that prevents infrastructures from ruination—the staving of decay—is thus essential to the temporality of infrastructure. Maintenance keeps that which is constructed from decaying, or at least decaying faster than its "lifetime." Yet the very concept of the "lifetime" of an infrastructure presumes the work of maintenance that is often forgotten in the stories about how that infrastructure got built. Maintenance is routine work: it is unglamorous, and it does not appear to push the borders or boundaries of technology or aesthetics. Maintenance partakes of a general devaluation of the routine in the project of modernity. In this view, innovation and novelty are ends in themselves, and they end when the object has been built. What is most important socially, or what contributes the most to the life of a community or family, is less valued than what is novel. In the modern world, innovation has become an end in itself—the most prized and valued human activity. In this world, maintenance suffers by being the equivalent of feminized labor in the household (Russell and Vinsel 2016). Maintenance is considered dull, routine, everyday work. However, without the caring labor of maintenance, the beauty of heroic, "masculine" construction would never last. What we would see is "premature" decay (that is, natural decay, the degradation of materials at varying rates). The awe-inspiring (infra)structures of modernity would decay much faster than those that have been carefully maintained.

On Tuesday, August 14, 2018, a highway bridge named after its famous architect and lauded for its design, the Ponte Morandi, collapsed in Genoa, Italy, killing forty-three people. It was one of the larger infrastructure failures in a large, industrialized nation-state and revived a debate about crumbling infrastructure. The fear is that other bridges in Italy and elsewhere in the global North are more than fifty years old and that tens of thousands of bridges in the older, industrialized countries are beyond their designed life spans (Pianigiani, Povoledo, and Pérez-Peña 2018). Hailed for its innovative design when first built in the 1960s, the Ponte Morandi was an architectural marvel, soaring "light and airy" over gritty parts of the city.[4] An architectural historian lauded it as "one of Italy's most important bridges" (Glanz et al. 2018). The beauty of the bridge lay in its simplicity, with three A-frame towers three hundred feet high holding up the roadway using twelve supports or stays. The problem with the design, it turned out, was that the entire structure became vulnerable if even one of the supports gave way (Glanz et al. 2018).

It was not a classic struggle between aesthetics and function so much as a conflict between aesthetics and maintenance. The bridge ultimately collapsed because the design did not have a way to incorporate routines of maintenance. Usually the price for ignoring maintenance routines is not so high: Brand reports that one-fifth of designers of high-rise buildings had not considered how the windows in their buildings would be cleaned (1994, 112).

Normally, a bridge like the Ponte Morandi would incorporate exposed steel cables that hung from the top of the support structures to the sides of the roadway. Morandi's innovation was to encase the cables in prestressed concrete. He believed that doing so would protect the cables from the elements and thus be less vulnerable to corrosion in the sea air.[5] However, cracks developed in the concrete shell almost immediately, allowing water to enter, and the steel cables inside started corroding by the time the bridge opened to traffic in 1967. By the late 1970s, Morandi himself inspected the bridge and concluded that it had seriously degraded (Glanz et al. 2018). In the late 1990s, the supports for one of the three towers were completely replaced, but no action was taken on the other two towers. A professor of engineering at the University of Genoa opined that "degradation and corrosion went at an unthinkable pace here. . . . Well-designed bridges last 100 years and then need maintenance, not after less than 40 years" (Pianigiani, Povoledo, and Pérez-Peña 2018). Estimates in 2016 concluded that maintenance expenses probably exceeded the cost of building a new span (Pianigiani, Povoledo, and Pérez-Peña 2018).[6]

The problem lay with the fact that the concrete encasing the steel cables prevented an inspection of the degrading parts. Gary Klein, an engineer in the United States who studies structural failures, said, "There's nothing more imprecise than trying to evaluate the condition of internal cables. . . . It's a very imperfect science" (Glanz et al. 2018). The designer created the conditions that resulted in a fatal accident by not considering how the bridge would be inspected and maintained.

In 1999, in a wave of neoliberal outsourcing, the government of Italy gave the Benetton company, Autostrade per l'Italia, a contract to maintain and build highways and motorways, including the Morandi Bridge. Despite an internal report in 2011 warning of intense decay, the company failed to repair the supports for the other two spans (Pianigiani, Povoledo, and Pérez-Peña 2018). Although Autostrade had decided to repair the stays on the other two towers, the work had not yet been scheduled (Glanz et al. 2018). After the collapse, the government charged the company with failing to maintain the bridge while making millions off state contracts, whereas Autostrade steadfastly held to its view that it had complied with all regulations regarding maintenance. What complicated matters was that one of the two parties in Italy's antiestablishment ruling coalition, La Lega (formerly called Lega Nord, or the Northern League), had received a €150,000 donation from Autostrade and had voted to renew the company's license in 2008 (Glanz et al. 2018).

Stephen Graham and Nigel Thrift (2007) argue that catastrophic failure of the kind witnessed in the case of the Morandi Bridge hides the importance of a larger process of routine breakdown and failure. Acknowledging decay and breakdown as an expected part of infrastructural systems enables a reexamination of the distinction between innovative creation and routine maintenance, in which the latter are not considered secondary to the former (Graham and Thrift 2007, 5). In fact, maintenance is how societies learn, because that which is maintained is never simply restored to an original condition but is altered during repair (6). Maintenance and repair often result in innovations that enable infrastructures to function for periods far beyond their designed life span and to take on new functions that were not even envisioned when the project was built. For example, the design for the Morandi Bridge might have worked had a technology for inspecting internal cables been developed between the time that the bridge was first constructed and the time before it seriously degraded, but that did not happen.

The Golden Gate Bridge, for instance, requires thirty-eight painters: they work on it year-round to maintain its "international orange" color and prevent corrosion from the salty air. Similarly, it was discovered that the belief that the bridge had been engineered to withstand a major earthquake was false, and new scientific evidence led to a major program to retrofit the bridge, given its proximity to the San Andreas Fault. The retrofit cost almost USD$400 million and was a complex engineering challenge because it had to be accomplished without disturbing the heavy traffic that goes over the bridge every day. A complex lift system was custom-built to transfer the load from the existing bridge to temporary supports while the necessary changes were made. Similarly, the approach road to the bridge through the San Francisco Presidio was deemed structurally unsound in the case of a major earthquake and was demolished in 2012. It was replaced by a new USD$1 billion road called the Presidio Parkway.

Thus, maintenance involved the constant work of reproduction, but also new construction, and the replacement of degraded parts, or parts that were considered unsafe. It was therefore much more than simply keeping the structure "the same" as before. And what does it mean to keep something "the same" when the materials are rusting, warping, and degrading? Despite its associations with organic life, decay is inherent to inorganic materials and to human plans—in short, to the assemblages that constitute infrastructure. The tendrils of decay reach into every part of the infrastructural assemblage.

Maintenance is not just about the infrastructural object; it is also about the social relations enabled and created by infrastructure. Jessica Barnes reminds us of the redistributional consequences of maintenance (2017). In the case she analyzes, the maintenance of irrigation canals serves to reinforce the Egyptian state's control over water distribution, and therefore of the land and the peasants. Maintenance is not a neutral, technical function that only changes the materiality of the object being maintained; it also reinforces or alters the relations of power and inequality embedded in infrastructure. It is an eminently social task, not merely a technical one. For example, when the Morandi Bridge collapsed, it narrowly missed falling on low-income housing below. Over six hundred people were evacuated from their flats, and the Italian government had to find replacement housing for them.

But how does one study maintenance? What methodologies might we employ to understand the work of maintenance, its redistributional consequences, its importance for daily routines, and the work of innovation embodied in it? I want to suggest that ethnographic methods are especially attuned to the temporalities of decay and maintenance. The temporal rhythms of decay and maintenance are gradual and patient, unfolding slowly and sometimes imperceptibly, but are always consequential. The accumulation of the process of decay might result in a spectacular collapse like the Ponte Morandi, but the problem built up unhurriedly over a long period. Maintenance must attend to decay's temporality, whether the material involved is organic or inorganic. Ethnographic work is singularly suited to studying such processes because it too involves very patient, methodical research that unfolds over a long period. Ethnographic work privileges the experiential, the phenomenological, and the relational: how people inhabit infrastructures, how they experience them, how they feel about them, and how they see them as enabling or inhibiting the relationalities that mark their lives. These relations could be between people, but they could also be between people and objects, or between people and nonhuman beings. The question of the role of maintenance in creating different vectors of inequality is best answered by the patient methodology of ethnography, by long-term, close observation of how changing infrastructures through maintenance alters peoples' lives—their relations to one another and to their infrastructural environment and to nonhuman companions and adversaries. The work of studying and understanding maintenance, therefore, as a processual and meaningful activity depends on the deployment of a methodology that is attuned to the processes of change, not just one that provides snapshots of the before and after.[7]

In this chapter I have conceptualized infrastructures as both creating decay and experiencing decay. They are the causes of destruction because of the despoliation that must occur for them to exist as well as for the consequences that ensue from their use. Nothing illustrates this point better than the role played by the steam engine and the internal combustion engine as the motors of the modern capitalist world. But infrastructures experience decay themselves in that they are subject to dissolution, degradation, breakdown, and change. The art of maintenance is what keeps them functioning even as they change and decay. Maintenance, therefore, plays a critical, and easily overlooked, role in the existence of infrastructure. Much more of our attention is drawn to the creativity and ingenuity of construction and design than to what is seen as "mere" maintenance, routines of upkeep that are seen as requiring less skill, mental ability, or training. Such a view is entirely mistaken: maintenance is that critical third space between construction and decay, between building and degradation, and between the future and the past. Attention to maintenance allows us to conceptualize the work of repair as a creative and critical function that enables innovation and discovery so that infrastructures can function even as they degrade. It is not merely routine work. Working against one strand in the literature, I think it would be a mistake to celebrate and romanticize maintenance as yet another heroic act (Jackson 2014, 233). Steven Jackson warns that "repair is not always heroic or directed toward noble ends, and may function as much in defense as in resistance to antidemocratic and antihumanist projects" (2014, 233). For this reason, we must see how maintenance may serve to exacerbate existing inequalities or perhaps even create new vectors of inequality.

Decay plays a very different role in infrastructure than in other domains of social and economic life. For instance, infrastructures are maintained because it is presumed that they are supposed to last; by contrast, the plastics that McDougall studies (this volume) are manufactured to be discarded. The problem of decay in the two cases are polar opposites: while infrastructure decays and its decay is a problem, plastics do not decay fast enough, so the problem is their lack of decay and persistence in the ecosystem. Infrastructural decay could be compared to Dalley's case (this volume), where bodily decay is symptomatic of decay in the body politic; infrastructural decay that leads to failure like the Ponte Morandi functions as a sign of the breakdown of the social contract. Finally, unlike Herzfeld's analysis of decaying buildings, infrastructure on the whole does not gain aesthetic value the more it decays: functionality takes precedence over aesthetics, and a rusting bridge is seen as a source of danger, not as an object whose beauty is enhanced by the fact that it has rusted.

Notes

I am grateful to Ghassan Hage for leading this project, and to Cameo Dalley, Michael Herzfeld, Elise Klein, Bart Klem, Tammy Kohn, Fabio Mattioli, Debra McDougall, Monica Minnegal, and Violeta Schubert for comments on an earlier version of this essay.

1. The phrase "entering the limelight" draws attention to an infrastructural technology of the stage that is largely forgotten and ignored.
2. I am grateful to Bart Klem for this insight.
3. I would like to thank Michael Herzfeld for suggesting these ideas to me.
4. An image of the Ponte Morandi, accessed December 15, 2020, can be seen at https://upload.wikimedia.org/wikipedia/commons/a/a2/Genova_Ponte_Morandi.jpg.

5. The information in this paragraph is taken from Glanz et al. 2018.

6. A new bridge was built to replace the Ponte Morandi in record time and inaugurated on August 3, 2020. See Pianigiani 2020.

7. I am particularly grateful to Michael Herzfeld for suggesting that I explore the relationship between maintenance as a topic and ethnography as a method.

4

THE WATERFALL AT THE END OF THE WORLD

Earthquakes, Entropy, and Explanation

Monica Minnegal, Michael Main, and Peter D. Dwyer

It was late February when the earthquakes came. Within six weeks of the first massive upheaval, there were more than two hundred aftershocks. There were terrifying landslides everywhere. The inner walls of the Mount Sisa crater collapsed, and earth, rocks, and vegetation spilled into the upper reaches of the rivers that radiated from the summit. One landslide buried eleven men, women, and children who were sleeping in a house near the tiny Edolo village of Fau (Dwyer and Minnegal 2018).

People were traumatized. At night, as they tried to sleep, they could hear the land falling apart. Houses collapsed. People were injured. Many gardens were destroyed. Travel was dangerous, the threat of more landslides the new normality. But gradually, abandoning former hamlets, they assembled at the only two villages where it was possible to communicate by radio with the outside world, to let others know of their plight. And the quakes continued. Day after day, sites and tracks that embodied the social and ecological lives of those who inscribed them were lost in the chaos of the falling land.

FIGURE 4.1. "The ground was moving under us, the trees were shaking above us."
Photo by Sally Lloyd, April 2018.

A Huli Eschatology

The Papua New Guinean earthquake of February 2018 occurred when movement of the Australian tectonic plate activated a major fault system in densely forested mountains to the immediate southwest of the land of Huli-speaking highland peoples. This process has been underway for millions of years, deforming the boundaries of continental regions and, at critical thresholds of tension, triggering swarms of earthquakes that had the incidental outcomes that mineral resources might be enriched and oil and gas might accumulate in pockets between folds in bedrock (Zahirovic et al. 2018). Indeed, the epicenter of the February earthquake was only a few kilometers from gas fields that feed the vast, multi-billion-dollar Papua New Guinea liquefied natural gas project.

The geological processes that drove those earthquakes may be understood within the frame of the second law of thermodynamics (Kastens 2010; Main and Naylor 2010; Regenauer-Lieb, Yuen, and Fusseis 2009). This law states that all processes tend toward decay and disintegration—that the disorder or entropy of a system always increases. "As entropy increases, the universe" tends naturally to move "from a state of organization and differentiation in which distinctions and forms exist, to a state of chaos and sameness" (Wiener 1950). Living systems may appear to find a way out of this inevitability, doing so by feeding on free energy in the form of sunlight and nutrients, but any reprieve is temporary.

This view of decay pervades Western thought. Without constant vigilance and labor to keep things in their place, order immediately begins to break down. Weeds must be rooted out each day if our gardens are not to become jungles; patches of rust or mold must regularly be scrubbed away so that our possessions can shine as they should. And the struggle to hold our bodies in shape, to at least delay the "return to dust" that is our fate, is continual as we diet and exercise and fight off microbes, and vaccinate to build our defenses. Only with death does that struggle cease. Death itself—an abrupt yet inevitable outcome of, and surrender to, decay and disorder—may enable the release of nutrients for other bodies to harness in their effort to build order. But to focus on this renewal of life merely distracts from the inexorable decay that frames those successive lives. Similarly, a temporal perspective based in geological rather than cosmological understandings may emphasize the way in which earthquakes constantly recycle the planetary crust to produce "a lush, habitable planet" (Broad 2005). But this replenishment merely delays the inevitable.

The tempo of decay may vary. Its effects may be resisted, even reversed locally though always temporarily. They may also be exacerbated, disintegration hastened through lack of care or deliberate action. And they may at times reach a crescendo, with systems going through a phase-change as disorder accumulates—bodies die, buildings fall down, landscapes collapse. But such events are merely episodes in a longer trajectory of decline. People may influence the pace, but they do not drive the process of decay itself.

Huli people would not disagree with this understanding. Or, at least, in the years before colonization they would not have disagreed. To these people, climatic and geological instability—evidenced by times of drought, floods, and earthquakes—were concomitants of the continual decay and dissipation of the fertile substances that sustained life (Ballard 1994; M. Main 2018). So it was, as well, with social instability. As men and women grew old and died, the knowledge and skill handed down by ancestors were eroded and lost. People's moral failures and failing health were reflected in the "skin" of the land.

The decline of the world—of the fertility of land, of the moral and material well-being of people—was inevitable unless people themselves took action. To this end, from time to time they countered inexorable decay by instituting fertility rituals at the local level of clans or at a more embracing regional level. These rituals, however, were merely provisional; they postponed, but did not eliminate, the inevitability of a final collapse. Indeed, Huli recognized that knowledge of the necessary rituals, and the discipline to perform them, also declined through time. As symptoms of decay intensified, therefore, Huli ritual leaders pursued more drastic remedies, seeking to bring about the end of the existing order in the hope that what emerged in its place would be stronger, more resilient. They attempted to bring about a "time of darkness"—like that actualized centuries earlier by a fall of volcanic ash (Blong 1982)—that would restore health and fertility to the land and the people.

In these Huli understandings, both material and social order are understood to decay through time, but people have the knowledge and the power to inhibit (or exacerbate) that decay, to replenish fertility temporarily or even, perhaps, bring about a new world of greater productivity.[1] Thus, people were deeply implicated in declines in material or social well-being and were responsible for the continuance of human life and place. Like Duna, their immediate neighbors to the north, they believed "that moral behaviour conserves fertile substance, and that immoral behaviour sees it depleted and will ultimately bring about the world's end" (Haley 2007).

From the early 1950s, however, the world changed for Huli. The Australian colonial government established permanent bases; built airstrips, roads, and bridges; and introduced money and the material paraphernalia that accompanies Western ways of living. Missionaries of multiple denominations settled at different communities from which they proselytized. Other outsiders came exploring for minerals and oil. Gradually, the rituals through which people had both comprehended and managed their world were abandoned. Gradually, past certainties were lost. Now, as people were confronted by disastrous events, there was confusion and anxiety as they sought for explanations in a mix of remembered pasts, reconstructed myths, and possibilities inherent in the storytelling of Christian-, corporate-, and science-minded outsiders.

Causes and Consequences

To the south of the places where the Huli people live, the land spills down rugged, rainforest-clad mountain slopes to the undulating hills of the Great Papuan Plateau before rising again to the rim of Bosavi, an extinct volcano that reaches an altitude of 2,500 meters. The crater, four kilometers across, lies fifty kilometers south of the epicenter of the February earthquake. To the Edolo, Bedamuni, and other people who live nearby, and to those who view it from a distance, Bosavi has been always a place of mystery, a place inhabited by spirits who, if treated with disrespect, might be aroused and attack intruding hunters "with terrific tropical rainstorms and cause huge rocks or trees to roll down the mountainside" (Schieffelin 1976). After the earthquake, it was stories of Bosavi that were the first to capture the imagination and spread. The cloud cloaking the summit of the mountain was seen as smoke. Messages relayed by radio, mobile phone, and Facebook gave credence to an idea that the earthquake would be followed by a massive volcanic eruption. It was not easy to dissuade frightened people. Some fled their villages on the slopes of the mountain, relocating to lower-altitude valleys.

Many attributed their own survival, as the land fell apart around them, to God. As one said: "We should have died. The ground was moving under us, the trees were shaking above us. The rivers are thick. The fish are dead. Nothing is safe. God brought us through." To others, elsewhere in the country, the earthquakes and the deaths and damage they caused were themselves acts of God: a punishment because God was angry, because people had turned from his ways, or because the national government was corrupt. Newspaper correspondents offered warnings: "If we do not make adjustments in alignment with divine directives from above, who knows what will happen next in our country" (*Post-Courier* 2018a). Some religious groups went further. The chair of the Body of Christ in Papua New Guinea said the earthquakes were God's curse on the country for its failure to support a US decision to move its embassy to Jerusalem. He referenced the Bible: "If you bless Israel, I will bless you and if you curse Israel, I will curse you" (Salmang 2018). The Church of Scientology sent volunteer minister disaster specialists into stricken villages, where they strove to soothe anxiety and stress by teaching "the Triangle of Life" and to relieve pain by a technique they called "touch assist." They declared the remote Edolo village of Huya—surrounded by landslides, overflowing with refugees from elsewhere—to be "a lost land," and they had been instructed to investigate a rumored "depression," with possible supernatural connotations, in the region of the epicenter of the quake.[2] Religion-affiliated NGOs dedicated to providing relief food and facilitating medical evacuations were hard-pressed to counter expectations generated by rampant rumor.

The most persuasive causal explanation attributed blame to ExxonMobil, the lead company in the joint venture that held responsibility for the liquefied natural gas project. It was the petroleum companies that had drilled deep into the ground, close to the epicenter of the February earthquake. It was the companies that had, since May 2014, extracted millions of cubic meters of gas and exported it in purpose-built tankers to China, Japan, and Korea. Some people argued that by disturbing rocks deep below the surface the geologists had destabilized the ground and triggered the earthquake. Some suggested that fracking—opening fissures in subterranean rocks by injecting liquids at high pressure—had caused the disturbance, though this technique had not in fact been used. Others observed that the haste with which petroleum companies withdrew their own employees from the area was in itself evidence of their knowledge and complicity. And all Huli people knew that deep within the mountain ridge that now supplied gas there was a perpetual fire—a fire strong enough to light up the whole world. They were aware, too, of a long-standing prophecy that one day outsiders would come and try to take the fire from those who rightfully owned it. Now, it seemed, fulfillment of that prophecy was having disastrous consequences.

The liquefied natural gas project had been predicted to provide huge financial benefits to the Papua New Guinea state and to people who owned the land from which gas was extracted and across which it was piped. By 2018, those expectations had not been realized (Flanagan and Fletcher 2018). Many landowners were frustrated, and from time to time, violent protest erupted (M. Main 2017). With the earthquakes, however, it seemed that the project was not just failing to deliver benefits but was causing actual harm. The state was concerned; it could not afford excessive disruption to the project. It commissioned a report from Geoscience Australia, an agency of the Commonwealth Government of Australia. The report concluded that "the size of the earthquake and intensity of the ground shaking . . . are consistent with the regional plate tectonics that have formed the New Guinea Highlands over millions of years" and that the "earthquake is highly unlikely to have been triggered through mining or hydrocarbon exploration and extraction activities" (*Post-Courier* 2018b). This was no surprise to any geologist. But it did not satisfy people who lived on the ground who had been shaken or whose houses and gardens were destroyed or whose relatives were buried in mud. The Australian response had been too rapid. It was a desk job. No one had come and looked for themselves. One writer expressed the doubts of many: Geoscience Australia "is an arm of the Australian Government that works lock step with the mining and gas industry" (Anda-Harapa 2018). The governor of Hela province—the homeland of Huli speakers—demanded an "independent inquiry," one in which his own government would set the terms of reference.

Neither myth nor religion nor science offered an accessible, readily acceptable explanation of what, to many people, appeared frighteningly like the end of days. The earthquakes continued for months. Many were minor, some were large, and it was impossible to know when they might cease. The land continued to decay, and with it the paths and places people had known. Many people desperately waited for support that their government failed to provide. In a May editorial the *Post-Courier* captured an important truth. "It is true," the editor wrote, "that Papua New Guineans are resilient in restoring their lives following devastating natural disasters," but there are some forgotten communities "that might just not make it." Those people do not have the information needed to interpret what was happening. "For them the earthquake was out of the normal and beyond the paranormal" (*Post-Courier* 2018c).

The Waterfall at the End of the World

The hills and valleys of the Great Papuan Plateau are home to people of several language groups: Edolo, Bedamuni, and others. Some of those groups have fewer than a thousand speakers; one has more than ten thousand. All live as small, widely dispersed communities, reliant on a mix of gardening, arboriculture, processing palms to extract sago flour, and hunting and fishing in the forests and from the streams and rivers that are their homelands. These are remote communities, far from the mainstream of modern Papua New Guinea, all now deeply influenced by decades of contact with Christian missions that have promoted health, education, and religious teaching in a region that receives little support from government. These are people who have abandoned many past practices, have hopes for future development, and seek always to accommodate memories of earlier beliefs to the "truths" they learn from outsiders. All Edolo communities and eastern Bedamuni communities were seriously impacted by the earthquakes (Dwyer and Minnegal 2018).

Bedamuni origin stories tell of Dunumuni, an ancestral woman whose dismembered body and bodily fluids were the source of the physical and social landscape within which all known people live. It was at the time of her death, as the landscape was created, that codes of moral behavior were laid down. In a small lake near the center of Bedamuni territory a man named Asagoi holds one of Dunumuni's tendons. That tendon stretches beneath the ground to the northeast, beyond Bedamuni territory through the land of Edolo people, to the head of a waterfall on the river known as Sewa. If the people fail morally then Asagoi may pull on that tendon, and "if he does, the cliff over which the waterfall tumbles will collapse, there will be earthquakes, the ground will break and 'men and women will finish'" (Dwyer and Minnegal 2000).

As with Huli, then, a possible catastrophic end of the world is a consequence of the failure of people to act appropriately as moral agents or as custodians of the land. For Bedamuni, however, the decay that renders the structure of the world unstable and leads to eventual collapse is not somehow "natural," happening inevitably unless people intervene. Rather, human action is understood to directly induce decay. Indeed, in some domains of existence this was as it should be: those actions were thoroughly appropriate. Among men, for example, it was understood that processes of aging and death—of irreversible decay—were a consequence of personal sacrifice, of ensuring the growth and maturity of youths and young men through gifts of the seminal fluids that were necessary to reproduction of both biological and social worlds (Kelly 1976). By contrast, any attempt to accumulate vitality for oneself, by withdrawing it from others, induced physical decline and ultimately death of those others. Such actions were strongly sanctioned. Among Edolo, Bedamuni, and related peoples, moral failure and the associated decay of sociality was tangibly expressed as acts of sorcery that led to illness and death. Deaths were always sources of great anxiety, indications of evil being active within society. But again, in this region of Papua New Guinea there were practices that reduced the likelihood that this moral decay would bring the world to an end, that Asagoi might find it necessary to bring about collapse of the waterfall on Sewa. At séances, a medium communicating with spirits could sometimes diagnose cause and direct attention to the likely sorcerer. Killing the sorcerer would, at least temporarily, restore harmony to the community (Knauft 1985).

These practices are gone now. Sorcery remains a source of great concern, but accused sorcerers are very rarely killed. Men still age and die, though they have not sacrificed bodily fluids as their forebears did in the recent past. Disastrous events still affect the lives of people, but whatever their cause, resolution seems beyond the control of the people themselves. In 1997, an El Niño–induced drought threatened life and well-being across much of Papua New Guinea. Among Bedamuni and Edolo, many people were hungry, and some died. The drought came at a time when anxiety was heightened by rumors that the year 2000 heralded an end to the world. But, as many expressed it, "the Australian government saved us, they brought relief food." They gave no credence to the efficacy of their own efforts to survive.

At the end of February 2018, the ground shook in ways that no living person had previously experienced. The waterfall on Sewa collapsed, spilling rock and mud into the river, turning it into a stinking slurry of decaying prawns, fish, turtles, and crocodiles. The water was unfit for drinking, washing, cooking, or harvesting. People were left wondering: Was this God's handiwork? Had the geologists destroyed the ground? Or had Asagoi pulled on Dunumuni's tendon and destroyed the waterfall at the end of the world?

Agency and End Times

The Bible's Book of Revelation and the second law of thermodynamics both teach that the world as people know it will end. To some thinkers these endings—one an outcome of divine intervention, the other an outcome of natural processes—are disparate and may never be reconciled. Others strive to bring them together, positing, for example, "the principle of entropy as an existential dynamic of the Fall" and thereby "reasserting the universality of original sin" (Bradnick 2009, 67; see also P. J. Davis 2011).[3] An understanding of evil as an analog of entropy, of the former as the inexorable, accumulative and dissipative fate of human beings from the time of the Fall, of the latter as the inexorable, accumulative, and dissipative fate of all matter from the beginning of time, underlies a reading of both as processes of decay that culminate in terminal collapse (R. J. Russell 1984). Our position is both more modest and ethnographic. We find commonality in the ways these philosophies of life and the cosmos may be experienced. It is of little consequence that they may not be understood in ways that their authors, translators, or disseminators intended them to be understood.

The Book of Revelation predicts a time of cataclysmic events that destroy the natural and human order. There will be many signs of its imminence. "And the temple of God was opened in heaven, and there was seen in his temple the ark of his testament: and there were lightnings, and voices, and thunderings, and an earthquake, and great hail," and "in the earthquake were slain of men seven thousand: and the remnant were affrighted" (Rev. 11:13, 19, KJV). The Apocalypse will happen: that is guaranteed. No person may prevent it, though all may prepare for it. But the timing is uncertain. As Chris Ballard wrote, the Christian Apocalypse "is both terminal and fundamentally non-negotiable"; it renders Huli history "plastic to the will of God" and offers no place for agency (Ballard 2000, 219). Knowledge of that forthcoming apocalypse induces "a severe loss of autonomy" and "confusion about the destiny of the cosmos." As one man expressed it: "Jesus has said that, when he returns, the earth will end: When Jesus comes back, will we be consumed by fire or drowned in the flood as in Noah's time? We no longer know" (Hiluwa-Irugua, cited in Ballard 2000, 220).

Science, too, it seems, tells of an inevitable end to all that is and to all that might have been. That is the prediction of the second law of thermodynamics. Life and sociality, earthly and cosmological existence, will be reduced to chaos. This understanding is fundamental to all sciences, both in theory and in practice. We are surrounded by signs: living things die, their bodies decay; soils lose their fertility, mountains erode, volcanoes erupt, earthquakes happen. Like the Christian account, the promised certainty of the second law of thermodynamics "is both terminal and fundamentally non-negotiable"; it renders Huli history plastic to the will of science and offers no place for agency. "What will happen," we were asked, "when all the oil and gas is taken from the ground?" That was four years before the quake. "Will the ground fall in? Will the ground be finished?" The friend who asked us did not himself know. He had no way of knowing.

Christianity guarantees an end to the world but offers salvation. It holds out a promise of eternal life in another place. It asks only that you believe. Science too guarantees an end but, in the interim, may hold out a promise of great wealth. The minerals, oil, natural gas are there to be taken. It asks only that you trust, that you subordinate your cultural understandings to others who assert they know best. To many adherents, Christianity offers imagined earthly pleasures in Heaven; analogously, science offers Heaven on earth. Each system of thought imagines it has so much to offer to those who believe or trust. Each offers an understanding of processes of decay, framed by a vision of an inexorable end that is without human cause. Neither comprehends what it may take away from those who are asked to believe or trust, for in the final analysis both negate the possibility that people can act as agents of cause and control concerning questions about the meaning and end of existence.

Notes

1. In different ways, in their contributions to this volume, Ghassan Hage, Michael Herzfeld, Bart Klem, Fabio Mattioli, and Violeta Schubert reveal ways in which people in diverse settings—Lebanon, Rome, Sri Lanka, Macedonia—may understand their experience of societal decay as an outcome of moral failure that is expressed within the community rather than being imposed from outside. They do not, however, describe ways in which a rhetoric of moral failure may be overcome, as Huli imagined to be possible, by community-level action. Schubert argues that, as Macedonia is engulfed

by urbanization, residents of rural villages may experience decay as an inevitable and permanent state of being; as, in a sense, locally entropic. Writing of Rome, Herzfeld links understandings of urban decay both to a perception of moral collapse in society as a whole and to ideas about original sin.

2. An interest in investigating rumored depressions is evident in the teachings of the Church of Scientology, which tell that when billions of Thetans were brought to earth they were first stacked in the craters of volcanoes and then blown up. Their immortal essences attached themselves to the souls of people, where now they manifest as evil.

3. Herzfeld (this volume) similarly points to the sense of inevitable decay implicit in the idea of "original sin," as distinct from the decay instigated by everyday sins; the former can at best be arrested, but the latter should be reversed.

5

"VILE CORPSE"

Urban Decay as Human Beauty and Social Pollution

Michael Herzfeld

In Verdi's opera *Attila*, the Roman general Aëtius (Ezio) rhetorically demands, "Who can now discern Rome in the vile corpse?"[1] The magnificent imperial capital was collapsing into ruins as economic neglect and military failure—as well as the corrupt habits of its ruling class—ravaged the social fabric and thereby also hastened the neglect and consequent putrescence of the city itself. That older decay, however, has by our time morphed into a condition of romantic ruination; at the same time, new forms of physical corruption—accumulating garbage and potholed paving, to which less tolerant residents would add the often carelessly daubed graffiti that seem to proliferate everywhere—are today seen as the signs of a moral corruption that its critics bitterly contrast with the heroic grandeur of the ancient past but that perhaps corresponds much more closely to the reality of the decay that Aëtius so angrily denounces on the operatic stage.

In contemporary Italian understandings of past and present, the image of decay has deep roots in Catholic doctrine about original sin—ideas constantly evoked by images of winged skulls and other reminders of the "corruption of the flesh" adorning the city's ubiquitous churches. It is the material consequence of the weakness of Adam and Eve and their expulsion from the eternal joys of Eden—a weakness that is also understood as the source of pleasures both carnal and aesthetic, and thus of the extraordinary beauty its admirers constantly attribute to Rome. It is thus also, at least implicitly, an important element in the local archaeological understanding of the concept of conservation.

The link between the theology of sin and archaeological conservation becomes palpable as one walks through the streets of the *centro storico*, the part of Rome officially designated as its ancient core, where I conducted fieldwork during the preparations for a jubilee year and their realization in 1999–2000 (see Herzfeld 2009).[2] Virtually no conservation is allowed to look too pristine, too much like a *restoration* to some putative original appearance. Restoration here is the antithesis of conservation: residents and conservations experts alike usually treat it as an unjustifiable intrusion into the lived reality of the city's historic fabric. At best it may be treated as a preventive measure (the architectural historian Cesare Brandi's "preventive restoration") designed as a "conservative vision" that "includes all maintenance procedures able to limit degradation and thus avoid or postpone any restoration" (Natali 2008, 108); Brandi understood that the aesthetic and the historic were always to some extent in competition with each other and feared that an anachronistic aesthetic might irreversibly remove the evidence of historical change (Brandi 1977; see especially Carbonara 2009, 32). In limiting the accumulated physical degradation of the city's material fabric, conscientious conservation also sustains the visible traces of time's corrosive passage, and this satisfies tourists' somewhat voyeuristic appetite for the picturesqueness of gently restrained decay.

Perhaps the most prominent form of such ideologically acceptable decay is a generalized architectural patina that has become the object of effusive romantic enthusiasm in its own right.[3] The discolorations of patina, or more generally the marks of time's passage, are a trigger of affect and nostalgia, of a conversion of decay into treasure.[4] In Rome, at least, such discolorations are not always viewed with approval by locals,[5] but in foreign observers, heirs to the Grand Tour and the enthusiasms of Goethe, they clearly excite an aesthetic appreciation of Rome's delicate and unceasing balance, occasionally upset by violent irruptions of concrete modernity, between fragility and durability.

In some streets, notably the magnificent Via Giulia, one might be forgiven for thinking that one had wandered into a landscape designed by the engraver Giambattista Piranesi[6]—a landscape in which a riot of vines and other creeping plants entangles the ancient masonry in embraces perhaps more fitting for the nymphs and deities of the neoclassical imagination than for the robotic rush of modern life. In Rome, ruins are everywhere, reminders of mortality at every turn. As in Piranesi's prints, however, much of the impression of natural encroachment on human creativity is artfully controlled; it is an aesthetic practice in its own right.

This architectural version of decay—we might call it "arrested decay"—is part and parcel of the daily experience of ordinary Romans. For some, its romantic visual effects are a source of wealth, attracting generous infusions of tourist lucre. It is not the architectural equivalent of planned obsolescence; rather, it suggests a provisional halting of the inevitable. In this sense, it harmonizes with a more cynical perspective: the view that temporary (and usually illegal) fixes are actually more or less permanent, since the legal process of dismantling or removing an illegal architectural addition is often expensive, lengthy, and of uncertain outcome.

In short, Romans live with a deeply embedded and thoroughly material understanding of the fragility of anything made by human hands. The artfully ravaged beauty of their houses does not stop Romans from complaining about unhygienic and uncomfortably cramped conditions, and the frequent efforts of ordinary citizens and real estate speculators to create greater comfort are easily identified in a landscape dotted with illegal structures, often concealed under large umbrellas during construction (see Herzfeld 2009, 128). The target of their ire and evasion alike is the Inspectorate of Cultural Goods, because this bureaucratic institution has the power to restrict their ability to make changes they consider necessary for modern living. For its part, the inspectorate argues that its interventions are necessary to stop the further decay of these antique houses. With the creeping (but now rampant) commoditization of historicity (many people in Rome would like to own a house in the city's historic core), an uneasy and frequently disrupted truce obtains; its effect is to arrest further destruction to the aging fabric of the city as seen from the street, but to permit the radical restructuring of house interiors. A curious result of this situation is that artfully decaying exteriors often now conceal the luxury that gentrification brings to interior decoration and spatial arrangements.

In these circumstances, the outward signs of decay are visible but arrested. Visitors experience the sensory impact of gentrification, with elegant restaurants emitting attractive odors that compete and combine with those of furniture polish, church incense, and rainwashed or sundrenched masonry. This is the odor of a carefully conserved antiquity (and often also of sanctity), a smell that differs dramatically from the stink of rotting refuse that assails fastidious nostrils during the frequent breakdowns in garbage collection. Not all decay resembles the putrefaction of the flesh that punishes those who too easily identify with otherness, as Dalley describes in this volume; some forms of decay are comforting zones of cultural and social intimacy, their odor a nostalgic whiff of childhood memory or perhaps a reminder of the perfumes, redolent with ill-got or invented prosperity, that conceal quotidian messes and stenches.

The city's insistent invocation of decay—the elegant and the disgusting alike—speaks of the human imperfection at the core of Catholic theodicy. History, viewed in these terms, is a story of the inevitable decline we call mortality. It tells of Sisyphean attempts to push that process back—all doomed to failure, but all ennobling in their very futility and, at the same time, much more generic in character than the attempts to explain and appease divine anger with which, for example, the Huli people of Papua New Guinea confronted natural disaster (Dwyer, Main, and Minnegal, this volume).

Romans' sense of sinfulness does not arise from events in the immediate here and now. Rather, it expresses an abiding sense that humans—or at least Romans—are perpetually condemned to atone for sins that they are equally condemned by their amiably flawed nature to repeat over and over again. Thus, the two now heavily gentrified parts of Rome—Monti and Trastevere—that contain the largest numbers of medallions and icons of the Madonna were long considered to be the most steeped in petty crime; Monti, for example, was, until a couple of decades ago, the home of petty protectionist rackets, including the practice of stealing bicycles and holding them for ransom, and it was also the preeminent red-light district for much of the city's history. At the time of my fieldwork, there was at least one loan shark impudently defying the displeased authorities and the ire of some reformist residents.

In Italian religious culture, the Madonna has long fulfilled the role of the indulgent Mother who intercedes with the divine Father, usually understood as a severe and remote figure, to spare the spoiled child—a model for local understandings of masculinity as something to be indulged in its aggressive self-regard even when it descends into petty criminality (see Herzfeld 2009, 102–5, 141; 2015, 28–29). This model also serves to explain how actions condemned as sinful endlessly recur and as endlessly lead to redemption: prayers before the medallions of the Virgin are sufficient to alleviate the burden of sin—until the next round. In Monti's streets, the formal ideology of the church is upstaged by the practical piety of those it has defined as sinners, and their imperfections are mirrored in the stained stucco, chipped ornamentation, and faded paint of the walls, and by the weeds and vines that constantly threaten them with further decomposition while simultaneously enhancing their enervated elegance. The *centro storico* is truly historical in this sense, a carefully curated testimony to the mortality of carnal existence. The Eternal City is, paradoxically, a monument to the impermanence of everything human, and indeed of everything humane, everything that beauty turns into the object of desire.

So much for the decay embodied in the physical fabric of the city, a decay that reflects and intensifies the mortality of its inhabitants while also paradoxically participating in their ceaseless search for an elegance that calls on deep historical foundations. But there is another decay that concerns some Romans more persistently, and that is an imagined *social* decay—a decline in cultural standards, in a country where on the one hand governments repeatedly boast of the primacy of the Italian cultural heritage but where, on the other, most non-Romans view with a jaundiced eye what they see as the provinciality of their nation's capital. This decay, which represents a loss of control over that more genteel patina of the romantic imagination, is not an aesthetically pleasing form of visual decadence but something that discontented citizens call *degrado* (degradation). It is a sign of loss—of a lost battle to maintain the impoverished elegance of the ancient imperial capital. Moreover, it has acquired unpleasantly racist implications. The term is especially popular among supporters of the more right-wing parties and expresses their disgust at breaches in their conservative aesthetic and ethics. Increasingly, however, it also appears in the speech of Romans of most other political orientations who similarly feel that their city is now being invaded by sources of decay that they are powerless to arrest. The old decay, for which there seems to be no generally accepted specific term, was stoppable; indeed, every act of conservation seemed to pause it. In a sense, it resembled the blue cheese of Claude Lévi-Strauss's famous analysis, in a strange way recalling Tamara Kohn's fine-grained evocation—at once tragic and heroic—of the same image in the very different context of prison rot (this volume); it represented a tenuous but enjoyable moment of control over the forces of nature and especially over the putrefaction of human life and civility (see Lévi-Strauss 1969).[7] The new decay, in the newly alarmist vision, threatens irreversible, catastrophic collapse; the use of the single slogan-like term *degrado* invests it with a sense of impending universal doom completely lacking in the more diffuse language of elegant, highly localized architectural ruination. I will argue, however, that the change is not as radical as its exponents claim—that, indeed, what is now denounced as degradation has a great deal in common with the fossilized ruination of the conservators—and that a far greater threat is posed by racists who employ denunciations of *degrado* as their rhetorical weapon of choice. Perhaps the common ground lies in the use of *degrado* to describe the condition of the classical remains during the Middle Ages, a period often equated in the modern imagination with the barbarism of otherness.[8]

What discontented Roman citizens see around them is an accretion of waste, graffiti, rowdiness, vomit on the streets, the threat of petty violence. None of these things is new to Rome. But disaffected Romans like to rehistoricize them as the product of current social problems—of in-migration, poverty, a lack of discipline in the schools, the corruption of the many police forces, the inefficiency and laziness of arrogant municipal functionaries. They subsume all under the generic name of *degrado*. For those of a far-right orientation, it is especially easy to blame these things on immigrants, people who are assumed to lack the cultural refinements of true Italians. As a result, the term *degrado* seemed for many years to be a rightist slogan. But such complaints are increasingly spreading to people who hitherto had avoided supporting the rightist parties; the charge of *degrado* has become a general expression of dissatisfaction with the sense of physical and moral collapse in society at large, visibly reproduced in the increasingly dilapidated condition of the city.[9]

The current mayor of Rome (at the time of writing), Virginia Raggi, is a member of the populist Cinque Stelle (Five Stars) party. For her party and its erstwhile coalition partners in national government (2018–19), the explanation for *degrado* is easy: undisciplined youth and especially immigrant youth. At the same time, she has been accused of failing to take effective action over one of the commonest and most visible (and smelliest!) manifestations of this kind of decay: the rapidly accumulating mountains of uncollected garbage that I have contrasted with the genteel odor of carefully controlled architectural decay.

For many Romans, including at least one architect who waxed eloquent on the topic, urban beauty results not from careful planning and observance of all the relevant laws but, to the contrary, from continual sinning against the formal order of church and state. The riotous glory of the Roman baroque, for example, suggests a besetting absence of disciplined planning. To Romans, who have defied the bureaucratic authority of the Vatican for nearly two millennia, disobedience to the law is written into the landscape; flaws, including the inevitability of the collapse of dilapidated (*fattiscenti*) buildings, are part of the human condition, a consequence of original sin and the architectural equivalent of mortality. The permanence of these conditions resembles the "falling apartness" described by Schubert (this volume) for Macedonia: brief moments that appear to rescue society from this ongoing dilapidation turn out to be occasions for its renewal or perpetuation. Ironically, perhaps, the "Eternal City" is the site of some of the most decisive rejections of permanence and perfection, whether in its preferred modality of historic restoration or in its insistence on ignoring every master plan that has ever been written for it.

But the crucial question is this: At what point does an inherited condition of glorious (or perhaps simply cheeky) insubordination and illegality transmute into degradation and decay? When is the romantic ruin reconceptualized as *degrado*? Is it when it has fallen so far into ruins that there is no hope of recovering any sense of its ancient appearance? Is it when the graffiti scrawled on its antique walls usurp the role of officially regulated decay to the point of no return? The current anxiety about degradation, much of it motivated by racist hostility to migrants who are bringing about significant changes in the uses of public space,[10] plays a central role in effecting this transformation. In a city famed for its durable and visually impressive monumentality, the damage wrought by time is "our" damage and, as such, is equated with the inevitable decay of all things human rather than with the intrusive decay associated with a contaminating otherness.[11] It is permanent, inevitable, and divinely ordained imperfection.

Degrado is another matter. *Degrado* is the effect of a "foreign" source of decay, one that cannot be absorbed into the city's abiding aesthetic because it cannot be controlled. Hence the appeal of neofascist concepts of "order" (*ordine*)—a term that for anthropologists conjures up the taxonomic regularity that Mary Douglas (1966) saw as the basis of social stability and authority, but that in the Italian (and more broadly European) political vocabulary reverberates with more unpleasant memories and inclinations of fascist public discipline and racist fanaticism. Neofascists reject what they see as the degradation of Western civilization, a degradation that they find exemplified in the graffiti-laden walls and garbage-infested streets of Italian cities. In this material degradation they also find an urgent metaphor for the "contamination" of Italian society by foreign migrants and their culturally unfamiliar ways.

Discourses about decay in the streets of Rome and other Italian cities thus serve to encode concerns about more sensitive matters, especially questions of race and immigration. The romanticism of a Piranesi print or of an elegantly aged and faded palazzo facade clearly datable to the Renaissance or earlier is not *degrado*. On the contrary, it is a mark of *civiltà*—of a way of life associated with "urbanity" in the double sense of "urban living" and "suave savoir-faire."[12] These values do not necessarily embrace the laws of municipality or nation-state, but they do focus on the importance of what in English we usually call "civility," the ability to get along together and to accept a certain degree of human imperfection as the sometimes surprisingly pleasant price people must pay for the culturally intimate pleasures of sociability. If this is "decay" in any sense of the English word, it is a "genteel decay"—a mark of cultural superiority and of the respectability conferred by the visible signs of a long history.

This decay is the result of the inevitable imperfection of anything produced by human hands, and it is embraced with the affection accorded to the familiar, timeworn accoutrements of everyday life and especially, as we have seen, to widely shared standards of personal elegance. The other variant, *degrado*, is a diseased condition induced, so those who use the term insist, by unwelcome externalities. While we may label both varieties as decay, recognizing the contrast between them helps us to understand how Romans navigate the enormous and accelerating social changes now transforming their urban experience, and how they deal with the sensation that the genteel physical decay of their familiar spaces is exhibiting clear signs of yielding to the more radical decay of the social fabric—to what they see as disfigurement by mostly brief textual graffiti scrawled everywhere without respect for the dignity of the ancient city, to the collapse of social and moral values, to the corruption of the polity by greed and self-interest, and, above all, to the breakdown of amiable cohabitation. A static condition of controlled decay yields, in this perception, to an uncontrolled plunge into anarchy and annihilation.

This change has its roots in some painful realities. The anxiety about Roman identity has been particularly enhanced in recent years by an increasingly evident spate of evictions from the city's ancient core. Right-wing politicians exploited the anger and sadness that the evictions generated by contrasting these tragic events with the influx of large numbers of migrants bearing strange languages and potentially dangerous religions. The Chinese are thought to write in code; how could anyone possibly imagine that the Chinese characters are actually a standardized writing system? Muslims, especially those from the Arab world, are constantly suspected of terrorist intentions. Rightist politicians play on such assertions, creating moral panic among those least equipped educationally to resist what is as much an assault on their sense of security as it is on the status of the migrants themselves.

Thus, the commoditization of living quarters—the spate of evictions followed by the massive replacement of the earlier population by a combination of wealthy families and impoverished migrants—has in turn intensified local hostility both toward the intellectuals and professionals who are bringing it about and benefiting from it and toward the migrants who are displacing the evicted as workers and residents.

Such reactions are locally channeled through cultural assumptions, which in Rome are in turn shaped, as I have already indicated, by citizens' long engagement with the doctrines and attitudes of the Catholic Church. Deep cosmological roots, consisting of ideas about identity and the sinful condition of the human race at large and of Roman citizens above all others, underlie the current turn toward a racist and embittered populism throughout Europe and beyond, inflecting that broader perspective with a cultural specificity that is constantly reinforced by living amid the city's architecture. Rome may offer a rather extreme case by Italian standards, but this is what makes it anthropologically salient: I am concerned not with "typicality," but with an extreme that reveals a larger, national, or even transnational pattern of interpretation.

That pattern also has a historical dimension that we must take into account: the collapse of "cohabitation" (*convivenza*) between social classes vastly differentiated in terms of wealth and education, and the resurgence of the inequalities that sustained that ideal but that were also to some extent restrained by its rhetoric. Resentment of those inequalities has replaced the prevailing sense of controlled decay with an abiding and disturbing sense of uncontrollable "chaos" (*caos*)—of cosmological anarchy, realized economically as precarity and socially as disorder and uncertainty about the future. The elegant decay of the past has been replaced by aggressive and uncivil confrontation among people who no longer feel able to rub shoulders with their neighbors with the conditional but comforting ease of yesteryear.

In Roman society, the prevalent belief system holds that all human beings are sinners and that those in high office are often the worst of all. Whereas older models of social "accommodation" were treated as a cultural ideal, however, the new decay—*degrado*—is a metonym for the entire range of perceived social and cultural failures of a system. The collapse of this system can no longer be understood as a charmingly picturesque conceit analogous to the insouciantly controlled decay of a sixteenth-century palazzo or, indeed, of the equally insouciant mien of the Renaissance courtier to whose privileged life the present-day Italian establishment claims to have succeeded.[13] One could see the Roman conservators' refusal to restore buildings to an arbitrarily determined original form as an insouciant demonstration of their self-confidence in accepting the mortality of the present, and especially of its beauty.

But that insouciance wears thin when disfigurement outpaces maintenance. Rightists blame that change on a swelling tide of alien migrants, reacting to the newcomers with the ugliness of violence both symbolic and physical. Others respond to the obvious racism with varying degrees of indignation.

There are historical antecedents to both attitudes. Romans generally pride themselves on having always lived in a multicultural society. The population of ancient Rome boasted enormously varied origins, and differences of skin color and other phenotypical traits were represented in art but apparently without any appreciable hint of discrimination. Discrimination was social rather than racial; slaves, captives from all over the known world including much of Europe, intermarried over time with free workers, and intermarriage occurred at other levels as well. In medieval and Renaissance times, to be sure, discrimination and exploitation of internal others, especially of the Jewish community (which had ancient roots in Rome), were cruel and persistent, and in the twentieth century the Fascist regime, after an initial period of relative tolerance, brought with it "racial laws" that imitated those of Nazi Germany.

Yet these attitudes have waxed and waned over time, hostility to outsiders alternating with bouts of inclusiveness. Romans, like other Italians, are aware of having suffered discrimination in the United States on the basis of their darker skin, and even strongly right-wing Romans acknowledge the central role of the Jewish community of Rome in ensuring the survival of a local and predominantly working-class culture that they see as contrasted with the upper-crust affectations of that of the other major Italian cities. Their stereotypical evaluations of present-day migrants also suggest an attitudinal hierarchy. In this schema, Filipinos, who are predominantly Catholic, are gentle and untroubling, while Spanish-speaking Catholics from Latin America, whose Romance language renders them both understandable and yet also almost too clearly alien to many Romans,[14] must also face the ambivalence of a church hierarchy that converted their ancestors but is unsure of the outcome (see Napolitano 2016, 4–5). Muslim Bangladeshis have more or less taken over the kitchens of some of the most traditional restaurants and are viewed as excellent and cooperative workers. The Chinese, on the other hand, are in direct competition with Italians over silk and textile production, although their capacity to run coffee bars has endeared them to working-class patrons of those establishments in at least one major city.[15] Other migrants, especially Rom from Eastern Europe, are viewed with deep suspicion, while certain groups—Nigerians and Albanians prominent among them—are assumed to be involved in prostitution and other forms of human trafficking. The major criterion operating in these evaluations appears to be the extent to which the migrants show signs, not so much of assimilation as such, as of a capacity or willingness to operate within the looser framework of *convivenza* and cultural accommodation or adaptation. Given that Romans stereotype themselves as "accommodating" (*accommodanti*), and that their notion of being *civili* has more to do with reciprocal acceptance than with obedience to the law, this is hardly surprising; but its limits appear in rightist denunciations of *degrado* as the result of the presence of foreign immigrants.

The Roman attitude to decay can also usefully be understood in relation to different kinds of nostalgia. As long as the institutionalized decay that marks the *centro storico* remains more or less in balance, it corresponds to what I have elsewhere (Herzfeld 2016, 139–64) called "structural nostalgia." Such nostalgia is structural because it reproduces itself from generation to generation; it is the logic of parents who tell their children, "In my young day we were much politer to our elders!"—and know full well that their parents told them the same thing, with the same pattern repeated in every generation. It is also structural because it points back to an Edenic situation of mutual trust and reciprocity, an imagined state of perfection before the corrosion of time set in, when interactions between people of different means and backgrounds supposedly did not produce overt expressions of hierarchy—the logic, again, of that "cohabitation" of different social strata in a single street or district in which Romans express nostalgic pride while perhaps temporarily forgetting that living together did not, in the end, automatically mean complete class harmony or economic and social equality. Such imperfections of cohabitation, moreover, could be implicitly blamed on the inherited original sin that had initially, in the religious cosmology, begun the corrosion of that trust and that reciprocity and started humanity—and Rome in particular—on the downhill course toward the awfulness of modernity. It is indeed cohabitation that today, in the view of many Romans, is most threatened by the rapidly intensifying decay that Romans call *degrado*, a perceived condition that leads those who can afford them to seek secure, separate, and well-guarded dwellings. Such a theodicy is dangerous to the extent that it exempts even racists from ultimate responsibility for their own attitudes and allows them to represent their refusal of cohabitation with migrants as an implicit consequence of inherited wrong.

Degrado, to be sure, is in the eye of the beholder. Today, perhaps because many of the graffiti that adorn the walls and buildings of Rome are expressions of disaffected and rebellious youth and, often, of migrants' protest against racism as well as far-right expressions of that same racism, it has become clear that cohabitation is no longer working as well as it once did (or is that view, too, an expression of structural nostalgia?). Some graffiti are sometimes acceptable even to the most fastidious, but that acceptability, as I have already implied, always depends on political orientation and on a willingness to see the most inventive graffiti as art. The more usual contempt for graffiti contrasts tellingly with the pride and excitement that virtually all such cultural conservatives would express at the discovery of ancient specimens of graffiti, of which my favorite example—because it encapsulates the paradox of arrested decay as well as the realization that too much decay spells collapse—comes from Pompeii:

Admiror, paries, te non cedidisse ruinis
Qui tot scriptorum taedia sustineas.

I am full of wonderment, o wall, that you haven't crumbled into ruins,
with all those writers' tedious nonsense you have to bear.
(see Voegtle 2012)

Not all historically interesting graffiti, however, are automatically considered worthy of preservation. In its eagerness to erase the signs of *degrado* and to establish itself as the guardian of urban decorum, the present, right-leaning city administration set out to remove graffiti from all the walls of Rome. In so doing, however, the functionaries made a dangerous mistake: they erased an inscription by a social-democratic group contesting the first free post–World War II elections in 1948. While this erasure may not have been a deliberate attack on a sacred object of the democratic left-wing groups, it understandably provoked howls of outrage from leftist commentators, and the historic political graffito was restored—possibly a unique act in the annals of historic conservation in Italy, both because modern graffiti are rarely treated as serious historical relics and because the very act of restoring an original seems to contradict the prevailing philosophy in which conservation *excludes* restoration. In this unusual situation, a deliberate act of destruction had to be undone so as to suggest that it had never happened.[16]

The right-wing assault on *degrado* presupposes a bourgeois ethic of *decoro* (decorum)—the term officially and institutionally invoked by the Rome administration in its attack on graffiti. This concept is not unlike that which motivates conservative planners in other parts of the world—Thailand under bourgeois-leaning military rule is an excellent illustration (Elinoff 2017; Herzfeld 2017)—and is related to policies hostile to the presence of impoverished ethnic minorities in major city centers and to the ongoing right-wing hostility to migrants of all varieties. The political right wing attempts to pin the cause of urban decay on the migrants, often associating this calumny with an attempt to stoke fears of miscegenation, in contrast to the usual left-wing view that immigration helps to maintain a population threatened by a declining birth rate.

To these right-wingers, the decay of the city is the mark of a decline in civility. We should note, however, that there are two, mutually opposed varieties of civility (see Thiranagama, Kelly, and Forment 2018)—and, we could argue on congruent grounds, two kinds of *civiltà*. One is the mutual tolerance and acceptance that are implied by the Italian notion of being *civile*—that is, able to share an urban space comfortably with people who are manifestly different in appearance and behavior. This is an open-minded civility, and may, as often happens in Italy, be opposed to the sometimes repressive or impossibly complicated formality of the state bureaucracy. The other kind is the repressive conservatism that, while it may not favor the violence of the extreme right, generates the values that the extremists then claim to "defend" in the name of national, cultural, racial, religious, and even gastronomic purity. Such a vision of static order has little space for difference of any kind. Further expropriated by ultra-rightists, moreover, it excludes the provisional imperfections of *convivenza*, a shift that strengthens its capacity to justify violence as a cure for *degrado*.

The irony, however, is that it participates in, and indeed exemplifies, this more drastic form of decay—a decay that, unlike that of historic houses, is rooted in a vision of perfect order sustained by the most horrible forms of genocidal authoritarianism the world has ever known. Most of us, faced with that vision, would probably prefer a decay—the urban chaos Italians call *degrado*—that at least creates a space for the play of humor and irreverence and for the irreverent but generous civility that offers humanity a future. The *degrado* of today is indeed not very different from that denounced by Verdi's Aëtius. At the same time, from a more leftist and diversity-oriented perspective it might well look like the continuation, rather than the antithesis, of the joyful sinfulness that seems to be enshrined in Roman conservation practices and their respect for the glorious architectural rebellions and disobediences of yesteryear.

Conversely, would we not regard a descent into racist violence as the ultimate decay of human decency—of inclusive civility, indeed of *civiltà*? It would be a consequence of inherited hostilities that we have failed to overcome and that ironically threaten instead, with their language of purification and order, to reduce humanity to the ultimate degradation of cultural, racial, religious, and social hatred. That is not the genteel decay enforced by today's intellectual heirs of Piranesi, nor yet the often culturally and socially productive confusion that inevitably accompanies diversity. In denouncing *degrado*, this racist ideology, this brutal incivility that seeks to revive and perhaps exceed the evils of the Fascist era, reveals itself as something that aims far beyond the gentility of aesthetically contrived decay or even the aesthetic blasphemy of total architectural reconstruction. It seeks instead a deliberately planned finality: the extirpation of the living cultural diversity that is the historically attested heir to the ancient traditions of Rome.

Notes

I would like to acknowledge the truly genial critiques of many people involved in the project of this volume—Cameo Dalley, Ghassan Hage, Elise Klein, Bart Klem, Tamara Kohn, Fabio Mattioli, Debra McDougall, Monica Minnegal, and Violeta Schubert—and to express my pleasure at having tackled so potentially unpleasant a topic in the company of such a remarkably astute and enjoyable group of colleagues. Many thanks, too, to the readers for Duke University Press, especially for the suggestion to mention the issue of patina.

1. "Roma nel vil cadavere / chi ravvisar or può?" See *Attila: Dramma lirico in un prologo e tre atti*, accessed December 15, 2020, http://www.librettidopera.it/zpdf/attila_ts.pdf, 17.

2. Much of the ethnographic material adumbrated here is explored in detail in that monograph. The detail presented there is essential for understanding the practical dynamics of managing the kinds of decay I describe here, but for the purposes of this essay, I focus more closely on the conceptual relationship between the very evident forms of decay (including the physical degradation of the city's material fabric) and the pervasive sense of human corruption and its theological explanation.

3. See, for illustrative examples, Fiona, "Patina of Rome," Lilyfield Life (blog), June 22, 2017, http://www.lilyfieldlife.com/2017/06/patina-of-rome.html, the "original wooden ceilings and patina walls" described by Amanda Eberstein and Rebecca Holland (2017), or "the cobblestone medieval lanes, with their peeling terracotta patina" (Aldern 2018). Patina even became a metaphor for the Fascist burnishing of its own concrete architecture with the aura of the classical authority it so notoriously claimed in the concept of romanità (Romanness); see Gwynne and Marcello 2015, 338. Not all patina is treated as romantic or beautiful; the justification for the corporately funded cleaning of the Colosseum was conducted to "remove a dreary, undignified patina of soot and grime" (D'Emilio 2016). As we shall see, decay and stability are kept in a tense balance; when decay is perceived as lacking in gentility, it becomes degradation.

4. Perhaps the most extensive treatment of these aspects of patina, albeit in a very different setting (post-Katrina New Orleans), is Dawdy 2016.

5. For example, in my film *Monti Moments: Men's Memories in the Heart of Rome* (Berkeley Media LLC, 2007), a taxi driver points to where a family emblem had been largely erased, muttering unhappily about its discoloration. Keeping a refined decay in place is a permanent balancing act!

6. On Piranesi and his relevance to the aesthetics of conservation in Rome, see especially Jokilehto 1986, 93–94.

7. The richly complex implications of blue cheese as a metaphor for putrefaction and control in human relations partly derive, as Kohn suggests, from the impressive array of blue cheese varieties and the status hierarchy that organizes them.

8. For an example of this rhetoric, see Rendina 2003. On the status of the medieval in modern times, see Fazioli 2017.

9. For its physical manifestations, a good place to start on the extensive documentation is RomaToday, "Segnalazioni" [a section for reporting examples of urban decay], accessed December 23, 2020, https://www.romatoday.it/social/segnalazioni/degrado-urbano/.

10. One example is the alleged takeover of the Piazzetta, the symbolic center of Monti, by Ukrainian and Romanian Catholics who allegedly used the excuse of the presence of a Uniate church on the square to gather regularly and engage in heavy drinking and riotous and sometimes hostile behavior (Herzfeld 2009, 230).

11. Compare the racist rejection of the new prostitutes from Eastern Europe and farther afield, as explicitly contrasted with "our" prostitutes, who walked the streets of Monti from antiquity until very recently (Herzfeld 2009, 8–9).

12. The first serious discussion of this concept in English appears in Silverman 1975. See also Herzfeld 2009, 3–5, 182.

13. The allusion is to Baldassare Castiglione's ([1528] 1910) treatment of *sprezzatura*, aristocratic disdain for the consequences of one's actions, embodied in a gestural system found throughout the country. For a comparable Greek instantiation of the same principle (although detached from any pretensions of aristocratic identity), see Malaby 2003, 134–35.

14. Spanish and Italian share a Latin origin and are to a considerable extent mutually understandable.

15. On the conflict over the textile trade in Prato, see Krause 2018; and over silk in the Comasco, see Yanagisako 2002. On Chinese coffee bars in Bologna, see Deng 2018.

16. For an account of this event, see Eleonora Carrano, "Cronaca: Roma, a rimuovere la scritta storica è stato il servizio di decoro urbano. Che beffa!," Il Fatto Quotidiano (blog), March 20, 2019, https://www.ilfattoquotidiano.it/2019/03/20/roma-a-rimuovere-la-scritta-storica-e-stato-il-servizio-di-decoro-urbano-che-beffa/5050922/.

6

DECAY OR FRESH CONTACT?

The Morality of Mixture after War's End

Bart Klem

Pollution of the Mind

Having completed a long week of interviews in hot and dusty villages, I decided to treat myself. It was September 2011, and I was doing fieldwork in Trincomalee, eastern Sri Lanka, studying the societal changes taking place after the end of the separatist war. I had seen a new sign down the road from my guesthouse that read "Herbal Spa." Calvinist instinct had inhibited my indulgence in a massage, but on second thought, I told myself this could be ethnographically relevant. After all, it was only a few years ago that this locality on Trinco's northern fringe had marked the end of relative safety. Beyond this lay a landscape of insurgency with army checkpoints, badly damaged villages, displacement camps, and roaming cadres of the rebel Liberation Tigers of Tamil Eelam (LTTE). After the 2009 defeat of the LTTE, hotels had sprung up along Trinco's shores, and tourists had returned. And now a massage parlor had sprung up—common in other parts of Sri Lanka, but a first in the more conservative east, a region predominantly inhabited by the Tamil and Muslim minorities.

Thankfully, my excuse for indulgence turned out to have some merit. When I walked up to the *tuk-tuk* (autorickshaw) that had arrived to collect me, I saw—to my surprise—that a woman was driving it. Noting my puzzlement, the masseuse explained that it was a better service to pick up clients in person. Sithara (as I will call her here) was a Sinhalese woman of twenty-six. I was struck by her assertiveness and self-confidence. She told me that she had worked in some well-reputed hotels down south but wanted to start her own business. So she got on her motorcycle and rode to the place where new markets were blooming: in the former war zone of the northeast. She showed me her slick facilities, handed me a towel, told me to get naked, and started her routine.

I was taken aback. Everything about Sithara was considered unthinkable in Trincomalee, where young women are expected to be chaste, shy, and family oriented, particularly in their mid-twenties, when marriage prospects are impending. They are not supposed to walk about by themselves beyond given public spaces, let alone drive a rickshaw, set up shop in a different region, lay their hands on naked foreigners, and earn more money than a senior civil servant.

Sithara was the personification of the significant changes that engulfed Trincomalee after the end of the civil war. New phenomena like this massage parlor caused concern. One of my Muslim friends, a senior bureaucrat, summed it up nicely. Having been to other places, he knew that "sometimes they do the second part of the massage also. Now, if people are talking about a massage, we immediately think about the second massage. Actually, massage is a need for the body. But it is bad if ladies are massaging a man or the other way around, and these things happen." He could not ascertain whether there was back-alley prostitution in Trincomalee, but the very idea polluted the mind.

In this chapter, I will posit that the raft of societal changes that take place when a war ends result from a sudden increase in circulation. The dissipating strictures of the war newly expose the region to the world. The heart of the essay concerns the cultural narratives with which this increased circulation is interpreted, and the political work vested in these narratives. The dominant narrative that I encountered centers on the notions of decay and purification, a set of terms I borrow from Jonathan Spencer (2003): new forms of influx bring about the decay of sociocultural composition; mitigating such unwanted mixture warrants intensified efforts of purification. While this perspective is heuristically powerful, it also legitimizes a conservative, exclusivist, patriarchic, and potentially xenophobic political positioning. I thus close the essay with a contrarian perspective, adopted from Karl Mannheim (1972), that increased exposure breeds fresh contact. Building on this contrarian perspective, I will argue that the interpretation of postwar change as cultural decay has analytical merit, but we must interrogate the political work that this trope is made to do.

The Postwar Predicament: "The World Is Closer to Us"

The arrival of self-confident Sinhalese women like Sithara and the emergence of massage parlors were but one new form of the influx in postwar Trincomalee. This welter of rapid changes and influences was attributed to the sudden opening up of the region after the end of the war. And for some, this gave rise to moral anxiety. With the arrival of Sinhalese and foreign tourists and the entrepreneurs catering to them, "so many cultures will come," one of my respondents anticipated. "We may lose our cultural values. We may have new problems, like narcotics or child abuse." A man from Muttur, a small town near Trincomalee, explained why people were so concerned about new exposure. "Cultural-wise, Muttur was very isolated during the war. Earlier, there was also no internet connection. No mobile phones either." After the war, almost everybody has one, he said, and they spend lots of money on it. "We used to protect our own food. Now there is an open market. We buy our things from [elsewhere]." He argued that these new opportunities posed a threat to the local custom and culture, the basic things that defined them as a community. The social fabric was affected: "People are thinking to work individually now." People's habits were changing, particularly among the youth. "They are taking alcohol. Most of them are. They are even smoking. Because they are connected to the other areas. People are worried about this, but we can't control that."

During the LTTE insurgency, none of this was happening. People could not just go anywhere, and very few people from the outside came in. Children were with the family, under the control of their fathers. Youngsters were recruited for military training: youth from Sinhalese border villages joined the army or vigilantes; Tamil youth and children as young as ten were recruited or forcibly conscripted by the LTTE. In the areas under LTTE control, where the movement ran a de facto sovereign administration, there was a tight regime of discipline and surveillance (Klem and Maunaguru 2017, 2018; Thiranagama 2011). Their rules prohibited alcohol, theft, or prostitution, and this regime was enforced through harsh punishments. Many people I talked with felt this had created a sense of safety amid the lurking dangers of military violence. It was widely acknowledged that, unlike in army-controlled areas, women could walk around freely after dark in LTTE-controlled areas without worrying about harassment. And alcoholism, a common problem among the rural poor elsewhere, was virtually absent. Outsiders were, by and large, kept out by the LTTE. One interesting side effect of this curtailment of public life was that new religious movements did not gain a foothold in these Tamil villages. The charismatic evangelical Christian preachers who had swept across Sri Lanka in the previous decade or two, spawning a significant amount of controversy (Spencer et al. 2015), did not percolate into the society ruled by the LTTE.

Sri Lanka's northeast, and particularly the territories ruled by the LTTE, had thus been severed from certain kinds of globalized circulation since the escalation of the civil war in the 1980s and 1990s. With the defeat of the insurgency, first in the east (in 2007), then in the north (in 2009), LTTE surveillance collapsed, frontlines and checkpoints disappeared, and infrastructure and telecommunication improved rapidly. With the lifting of the region's wartime isolation, the metaphorical floodgates to the world were opened. Mainline churches (Catholic, Methodist) in rural villages formerly ruled by the LTTE saw an exodus of their congregation to evangelical movements, which had newly gained a foothold in these areas and impressed the inhabitants with spectacular healing practices, big loudspeakers, and lots of animated chanting. There was a rapid upturn in alcohol consumption, cigarette smoking, and—it was whispered—drugs. And unlike in the war-ridden past, the youth were hanging around playing with their cell phones. A backwater like Muttur witnessed the arrival of a contingent of Chinese engineers and laborers who were deployed to build roads and bridges. The locals watched these newcomers with fascination, and fried chicken became a common dish overnight.

Many of my respondents, who were typically well-employed adults and usually male, witnessed these changes with apprehension. Of most significant concern were those influences that touched on questions of intimacy: the conduct of youth (particularly girls), the unraveling of traditional gender roles, and the erosion of family cohesion, lineage, and sexual morals. With the increased mobility of youth, partly linked to the massively improved access to urban education, new opportunities for socializing and escaping parental surveillance emerged. Similarly, access to the internet represented a combined opportunity and cultural threat. One Muslim father told me he was concerned about pornography—he didn't utter the actual word but used the suggestive, indirect phrasing that characterized conversations about these topics: "I can't control my son not to use the internet. I teach him to use it for his future. But when he goes out, I don't know what kind of internet he's using. What kind of pages he is watching. In Tamil [the language spoken among Tamils and Muslims in Sri Lanka], we say, we can't see the other side of the wall. We are thinking, maybe that is better. However, we are trying to see what is on the other side. Muslim youth may also want to see what's on the next page."

The postwar years were a time of major unresolved political issues (i.e., minority rights, ethnic divisions, failing justice, stagnant state reform) and an increasingly authoritarian government (which effectively militarized the northeast) (Goodhand 2010; Klem 2014, 2018). But what concerned some of my respondents most was not their political plight but the impending danger of losing their traditions and cultural purities. And interestingly, this was a concern shared among Sinhalese, Muslims, and Tamils—ethnic communities that were typically pitted against each other.

For these people, the postwar moment was the harbinger of cultural decay. They would rarely actually use this word, but the way they verbalized the changes that were engulfing them resonated with precisely this notion. They talked about these social changes as threats to cultural purity, which they attributed to the rapid increase of outside exposure that then spoiled the cultural fabric within. It was not a demise caused by being left behind, a problem of isolation and stasis. On the contrary, the erosion of cultural norms was directly attributed to the process of opening and being reconnected.

One Sinhalese Buddhist monk phrased it with elegant simplicity when he said that after the war, "unnecessary [bad] things come. We are closer to the world. So those things are also closer to us." Increased circulation caused people and principles to become unfixed and posed a threat of disintegration. Social harmony and cohesion became undone, and people who considered themselves part of a tight-knit cultural community were at risk of "becoming singular," as one of my respondents called it. The social order did not simply collapse—that is, it did not undergo an irreversible process of falling apart due to the exertion of force. Instead, its decay was caused by the *easing* of the war's forceful grip on society, which then germinated changes from within because of new forms of exposure.

Cultural Decay: Disintegration Due to Circulation

In the above rendition, decay comprises the disintegration of the cultural fabric of norms, positions, and hierarchies, a process that is attributed to increased human circulation and exposure and results in the perceived demise of tradition, harmony, and cohesion. This interpretation of cultural decay is not a new phenomenon, of course, nor is it unique to Sri Lanka or postwar contexts. The idea that movement stands at the root of cultural erosion manifests itself in a particularly pronounced form during the postwar transition, but it actually has widespread purchase. I am drawing here on an incisive essay by Jonathan Spencer (2003), which illustrates that the perception of human movement as a threat to purity and a source of both moral and material failure has been remarkably resilient throughout history. One of the critical recurring issues, Spencer posits, is that human movement troubles the conception of the nation-state as "the same people living in the same place" (2003, 2–3; the phrase was inspired by a fragment from James Joyce's *Ulysses*). This discomfort with human movement, Spencer posits, is visible throughout colonial aspirations of order, the process of postcolonial nation-building, and contemporary concerns over refugees and labor migrants.

In Sri Lanka, efforts to regulate circulation abound, both historically and in the present: in colonial attempts to settle and civilize roaming populations; in the cultural reproduction of caste hierarchies and boundaries between nature and society; and in the public perception that labor migration to the Gulf states has caused fragmented and morally disoriented families (Spencer 2003, 4–5, 13–15). These efforts are most clearly manifest in the deeply engrained opposition between wet rice farming (*paddy*) and shifting cultivation (*chena*). The former represents the treasured cultural space of "property, fixity and hierarchical ties to landlords and political authorities" (Spencer 2003, 8), a space managed by people of character with well-documented histories and a great capacity for planning and enduring commitment. The latter represents a deplorable practice that stands at the root of material and moral failure. Slash-and-burn agriculture, so the reasoning goes, is a space of avoidance, a careless practice for people whose economic unsettledness is matched by their cultural character: loose, coarse, and impressionable (Spencer 2003, 8–9).

Unfettered circulation, in other words, yields cultural decay. It is a threat to moral integrity and social cohesion. Continuous purification work is required to stem such threats and protect the bounds of community. In the same way that dirt is matter out of place (Mary Douglas's [1966] famous dictum), people out of place cause cultural confusion and discord (see also Goodhand, Klem, and Korf 2009; Korf 2006; Korf and Hasbullah 2013). The moral narrative about postwar change that I have begun to sketch above matches Spencer's argument almost seamlessly. The civil war was characterized by military surveillance, tightly knit communities, and significantly restricted circulation—in cultural terms, it was a time of upholding boundaries, preserving traditions, and curtailed circulation. The years after the war were a time of rapid opening up and increased circulation. Curfews were lifted, lots of people were on the move, phone and internet connectivity spread like wildfire, and evangelical churches embarked on a proselytization spree.

Those who considered themselves proponents of fixity and guardians of cultural character were particularly worried about people whom they thought would be more prone to new exposure—and thus in need of protection against it. They saw youngsters and uneducated people as more impressionable. Women and children were seen as most in need of being sheltered from new, foreign, or modern corrupting influences. And they considered it logical (if deplorable) that the conversion spree of evangelical churches mainly took place among poor communities of *chena* cultivation and daily wage laborers, while well-established *paddy* planters clung to the religious order of their local Hindu temple.

Reconstituting Tamil Purity after the War

The notion of decay as cultural disintegration due to increased circulation thus legitimizes a continuous effort of purification. This becomes particularly manifest in the maintenance of caste-based hierarchies, which propel a contrasting conception of a *fixed* community of rice cultivators who had sufficient moral fiber to resist the erosion of social norms versus *loose* communities of wage laborers, shifting cultivators and fishers who lived day by day and were thus more susceptible to cultural decay. Evidently, this conception was particularly common among those who identified as the former, though many were only cultivators in name (or by caste) and had assumed an office job of some kind. The *paddy* fields they continued to own were, in part, a keepsake—family heritage to visit after office closure, cultivated by daily wage laborers, and with little significance for their sustenance.

The contrast between those who claimed to uphold purity and who were portrayed as prone to cultural decay came to the fore during return and reconstruction after the war. After almost three decades of war, displacement, and struggles over ethnic territory, the 2009 defeat of the Tamil insurgency marked a watershed moment where people set out to reconstitute the positions, boundaries, and moral fiber of their community.

I observed this process quite closely in and around Sampur, a well-known settlement just south of Trincomalee. Sampur is a very old (its inhabitants would say "ancient") village of Vellalahs ("high-caste" cultivators) with a renowned Hindu temple. It is considered significant as a "pure Tamil" space in the ethnically mixed Trincomalee district. During the war, Sampur was strategically important as the main LTTE hub in the Trincomalee region and a model village in the movement's vision: a constituent of the aspired independent Tamil state. In 2006, however, Sampur was conquered by the government military with an overwhelming artillery barrage. The entire population was displaced or killed, Sampur was razed, and the area was declared a special zone, accessible only to the Sinhalese military. A "pure Tamil" space had effectively become a Tamil-free space. The Sampur survivors, however, resisted government attempts to relocate them. After a whole decade of living in displacement camps and engaging in legal battles and public protest, the special zone was eventually lifted, and in 2016 the community returned to their lands in Sampur (see also Amirthalingam and Lakshman 2009; Fonseka and Raheem 2009; Klem 2014).

When I interviewed some people who had just returned, in 2016 and 2017, they were living in temporary shelters on a makeshift demarcation of their plot, while masons worked tirelessly on more permanent structures. They were happy and proud to be back, but with all the losses and the erased landscape that they called home, their victory was a muted one. They expressed a strong desire to reconstitute Sampur as a pure Tamil space. Clearly, this had been part of the reason they had been so insistent on their return and the reason they had received legal and political backing from a suite of powerful actors: Tamil politicians, Colombo-based lawyers, and even international figures. Preserving Sampur (a Tamil concentration in a multiethnic landscape under encroachment by the Sinhalese majority) represented a Tamil "national" interest that transcended the individual desire to return home. It soon became clear, however, that reconstituting a pure Tamil space encompassed more than an ethnic claim to the territory. It also involved efforts of differentiation and purification *within* the Tamil community.

Attachment to the land not only pivoted on Tamil ethnicity but also concerned the reconstitution of a caste geography and the placement of kinship clans (*kudi*) within that. "High-caste" cultivators pride themselves on having good land with natural wealth: fertile soil and clear, nonsaline water that is suitable for drinking and cultivation. As with other Vellalah settlements, the senior *kudi*s among the land-owning caste live at the core, alongside the Hindu temple, which plays a central role in reproducing caste hierarchies. One may find middle-caste communities surrounding these areas, like *Tattar* (goldsmiths), *Kurukulak Karaiyar* (teachers who are historically linked to the fishermen caste), and *Thimilar* (raiders). The paddy fields and the reservoirs needed to cultivate them lie interspersed with these settlements, and beyond that, we find uncultivatable scrub and less-respected communities. In Sampur's case, these are the Indigenous *Veddah* (or *adivasi*), who were "forest dwellers" till a few decades ago but now make a living through agricultural labor and small-scale fishery. Relocation, whether because of war, tsunami, or a special zone, upsets this cultural geography. The better-off Sampur respondents found it utterly unsurprising that some of the people from the *Veddah* fringe settlements had accepted government offers to relocate to a different place. They considered this offer out of the question. "Sampur people won't go to the jungle," a leading community member told me sternly. "They are cultivators."

Evidently, this was not simply about preserving a livelihood of rice cultivation. It was also about avoiding becoming what they called a "mixed community." When my respondents used this phrase, it was very clear that mixing was seen as undesirable. "Mixed" was effectively an antonym of "pure." "Sampur is a very rigid place," one respondent explained to me. Its community not only opposed erosion of the caste and clan hierarchy; it also objected assaults on its religious constitution. Sampur was not only a "pure Tamil" place, it was also an exclusively Hindu area, and recent attempts by evangelical churches to make inroads into their community were met with stiff opposition. In the surrounding *Veddah* villages as much as half the population had joined these new churches with their charismatic leaders. To prevent people with "weaker" character from being converted, rules were imposed against Christian activities in Sampur.

Reconstituting a cultural community in Sampur thus involved a broad range of purification agendas. In sync with the above-discussed concern with movement and circulation, mixing was seen as a source of cultural decay. Reconstituting Sampur as a pure Tamil space involved protecting ethnic (Tamil) territory, religious (Hindu) space, and social hierarchies (subservient to the *Vellalah* caste and its internal clan arrangements).

Postwar Circulation as Fresh Contact

Our central concern so far has been the conception that circulation and mixture yield cultural decay. This is a recurring historical theme (as Spencer shows), and it is a contemporary ethnographic finding in postwar Sri Lanka (as illustrated above). But it is also a political position advocated by particular people, and as such this rendering of decay deserves critical interrogation. Elsewhere in this volume, Herzfeld interrogates the political positioning apparent in the peculiar Roman paradox of simultaneously cherishing the degradation of the past (manifest in its ruins) while fulminating against the perceived degradation of the present (the perceived social and moral demise, which is then attributed to human circulation: to migrants). The political work of rendering change as decay, which I have described above, is remarkably similar. After all, the insistence on "pure Tamil" space (however understandable for a minority undergoing the postwar settlement dominated by the Sinhalese majority) could quickly degenerate into a xenophobic, son-of-the-soil ideology. And purification efforts within the Tamil community pivot on cultural conservatism, patriarchy, caste hierarchy, and gerontocracy. The tropes of decay and purification help stabilize the social position of relatively well-to-do families and delineate more marginal roles and places for lower castes and Indigenous *Veddahs*, for women, and for youth. They portray changes to these delineations as an externally induced threat that needs to be opposed. In effect, this perspective embraces an almost stifling nostalgia that defies the centrality of circulation and renewal to human society.

This is particularly fascinating, and ironic, when we remember that social emancipation was a central plank in the Tamil insurgency. The plethora of Tamil militant movements that sprang up in the 1970s and 1980s (including the LTTE, which coercively prevailed over the others from the mid-1980s onward) had a secular Marxist signature. These groups combined Tamil national liberation with class struggle, women's emancipation, the advancement of youth interests, and a rejection of the caste system and other "backward" traditions. The LTTE prided itself in having female cadres and instilled in its fighting force a horizontal kind of kinship that replaced the hierarchical, gerontocratic, and gendered kinship trappings of the traditional Tamil family (Thiranagama 2011, 183–227). The conservative narrative of circulation, decay, and purification negates these emancipatory agendas.

There are also, however, subaltern and progressive perspectives on postwar societal change. In closing, I will engage with these perspectives to turn on its head the biological metaphor of decay because of mixture and exposure. After all, circulation and exposure are associated not only with rot but also with freshness. Water that does not flow loses its biodiversity. Poorly ventilated spaces become musty. Circulation breeds life. In a similar vein, we could conceive of social circulation and human mobility as a source of renewal rather than decay. From that perspective, the sudden opening to the world in postwar Trincomalee after several decades of militarized curtailment represents a moment of "fresh contact."

I am drawing this phrase from Karl Mannheim's ([1927/1928] 1972) famous essay "The Problem of Generations," where he coins the notion of fresh contact as the defining feature of a generation. Mannheim describes fresh contact as "a changed relationship of distance from the object and a novel approach in assimilating, using, and developing the proffered material" ([1927/1928] 1972, 293). The notion of fresh contact has broad sociological relevance, he posited, and is directly tied up with human movement. It occurs when "an adolescent leaves home, or a peasant the country-side for the town, or when an emigrant changes his home, or a social climber his social status or class" (293). In each of these cases, fresh contact results in a "striking transformation of consciousness" (293). It is like "beginning a 'new life'" (293). But it is particularly significant for the phenomenon of generations who, by coming of age at roughly the same time and place, engage the world afresh, with new experiences, newly interpreted memories, new interests, and new adversaries. The emergence of a new generation enables "the constant 'rejuvenation' of society" (296). By the same token, the demise of a previous generation "serves the necessary social purpose of enabling us to forget" (294).

Mannheim's ideas help shed light on the winds of change in postwar Trincomalee and on the sense of disorientation they produced. Like Mannheim's adolescents, peasants, migrants, and social climbers, Trincomalee's inhabitants were exposed to a radically new context, which resulted in new experiences, changes of consciousness, and friction around assimilation. What is arguably different is that these changes occurred not primarily because Trincomalee's inhabitants moved out to a new context (though more than a few did), but because those who stayed became exposed to a new context coming in. The whole region arguably experienced fresh contact.

Fresh contact was especially manifest among youth. Nearly ten years after the LTTE defeat, a central feature of postwar Tamil society is the emergence of the first generation of youngsters who have little or no memory of the war and who do not have to worry about being recruited by the LTTE or being held up at an army checkpoint. It is these youngsters who use their freedom to hang out with peers and play with their phones, who escape parental supervision by moving to the urban centers for education or work, who have little appetite for a life organized around rice cultivation and caste hierarchies, and who may well end up challenging the practice of arranged marriage.

Clearly, it would be a mistake to assume that all Tamil youth are modern subjects who abandon tradition and pick the fruits of globalized circulation. During my fieldwork I met youngsters who were staunch Tamil nationalists, devout Christians or Hindus, and ardent defendants of cultural tradition. Some of them professed nostalgia to a time they had never experienced—"appropriated memories," as Mannheim would have it ([1927/1928]

1972, 296). Fresh contact, as Mannheim makes clear, does not merely mean shedding a traditional past and embracing a modern future. It marks a renewed engagement with past and future, and different social groups within the same generation may engage with these in highly diverse, even antagonistic ways.

A "Fresh" Take on a "Rotten" Trope

Both "fresh contact" and "cultural decay" denote processes of change that are associated with human movement and generational rifts. Both could be seen as biological tropes, but with opposite associations. Both freshness and decay are typically the consequence of exposure but depending on whether this exposure is deemed good or bad, it is associated with being either rejuvenated and pristine, or rotten and degraded.

This opposition is heuristically useful. On the one hand, the notion of decay offers us an insightful lens on postwar changes and anxieties in Trincomalee and Sri Lanka more broadly. It provides a narrative that threads together a wide variety of social changes (ranging from youth practices, to proselytization by evangelical churches, to land struggles and caste hierarchies), and it gives us analytical insight into the causal background that these changes are attributed to: the sudden opening up after the war and the resulting increase in circulation and exposure. Without the narrative of decay, it is difficult to understand the moral panic and the increased readiness to police cultural boundaries and the fixation on purification.

On the other hand, the angle of fresh contact usefully sheds light on the political work conducted by the trope of decay. Mannheim's notion of fresh contact offers us an alternative, more progressive vantage point. It takes issue with the conservative politics underpinning the narrative of purity. And it debunks the assertion of ethnic exclusion, patriarchy, caste hierarchy, and gerontocracy. Instead of naturalizing tradition and preservation, fresh contact naturalizes change.

Diagnosing social and political processes as decay renders those processes negative. It implies a contrast to a supposedly less rotten past, a suggestion that—insightful as it may be—smacks of nostalgia: a nostalgia, moreover, that longs for a time when people also lamented the decay of tradition, thus relegating us ever further back to a mythical past. The trope of decay also externalizes responsibility from those who are supposedly subject to it. It connotes changes that *happen to* people but tells us little about active participation and deliberate strategy, which are present too. Interpreting the welter of postwar changes as cultural decay resulting from increased exposure offers us an insightful lens, but we must interrogate the political work vested in these interpretations.

Note

Parts of this chapter are based on collaborative work with Urs Geiser, Shahul Hasbullah, Thiruni Kelegama, Alice Kern, and Benedikt Korf, as part of a project funded by the Swiss National Science Foundation (grant number PDFMP1-123181/1). I am grateful to them, as well as to my colleagues at the University of Melbourne (and Ghassan Hage in particular), for the productive collaboration in this collection. Some of my earlier work (Klem 2014; Klem and Kelegama 2020) developed ideas related to this chapter, and a small part of the empirical material used here appears in that text as well.

7

SEEDS OF DECAY

Fabio Mattioli

Surviving a traumatic blow can be a question of sheer luck. Recovering from it, however, means relying on the human body's mysterious capacity to heal. Molecular processes regenerate bones, cartilages, and vessels at a microscopic level. Sometimes this biological algorithm of subsistence traps invisible pieces of crushed tissue beneath layers of new bodily matter. Unable to be purged from the body or to be fully restored, these fragments of past matter linger on, englobed by new cells, asphyxiated by regenerated matter, reduced to tissue out of place—a source of silent pain and haunting friction; small arthritic cysts that, over months, years, or decades can reverse the process of healing into one of rot. These zombie cells, planted like kernels, exist in the limbo between life and death. There they become seeds—not of growth or renewal, but continuous decay.

In the case of physical fractures, surgical operations can identify and remove rotting shards of tissue and avert their material decay. Things get slightly more complicated with psychological damage. During healing, misplaced fragments of traumatic experiences are often steamrolled deep into the unconscious under a new narrative tar—a porous foundation for reconstructing our selves. But beneath that existential infrastructure, fragmented voices from an unsettled past create small ripples that disrupt the surface of our conscious narration. Here seeds of decay become neurosis, slight cognitive dissonances where the inability to either forget or unearth the trauma infects one's enduring present. When dealing with these immaterial splinters, no pill or technological operation can immediately remove the attrition. Discovering and removing damaged pieces of our persona requires a careful, long work of digging through layers of self: the archeology of our very souls, where the many past versions of ourselves are rearranged as we consider (different?) futures in what can only be a poetic, intimate, and suffering relation. Some people call it therapy, others faith or even friendship.

But what happens when the invisible seeds of decay are fragments neither of bones nor of one's self, but splinters of collective hopes for the future—impalpable, yet omnipresent imaginaries shattered by history's violence? What happens when it is not a physical or a mental matter that gets destroyed and trapped, but the very idea that the future can be better, the sense of forward motion that permeates the social fabric of (most) modern societies? How do citizens react when the myriad dreams that constitute the very foundation of their *sense of hope* are shattered and thrust in the most disparate depths of their being—neither entirely removed nor fully healed?

This essay understands decay as an existential condition generated by the continuous encounter with one's failures. In the mundane descriptions of workplace failures provided by Macedonian workers, the very idea of hope, understood as future improvement, is recursively proven to be unreachable, to the point of becoming itself a seed of decay. The metastasis of hope into decay is couched in the dramatic process of socioeconomic upheaval caused by the transition from socialism. Broken ladders and rusty Yugo cars demonstrated Macedonia's stuckedness—unable to reach for its socialist past or to build a better future in its (neo)liberal present. Macedonians understood this stagnation as proof of their quintessential failure, a consuming process where hope itself stopped being an incentive to motion and became a self-defeating, purulent wound to their capacity to think of progress. My interlocutors found themselves wishing to give up when faced with this kind of decay—to abandon hope and be numb to the historical forces that pushed them to fail over and over again.

The essay suggests that turning the hope for progress into a seed of decay was mostly the consequence of the traumatic transition from socialism. In 1989, the collapse of the Berlin Wall marked the destruction of the very economic and political foundation of socialist societies, promising a new era of democracy, freedom, and prosperity across the Iron Curtain. In the former

Yugoslavia, however, and especially in the Republic of Macedonia, these new hopes were crushed by the geopolitical tragedies that accompanied the introduction of free markets. Balkan wars, economic embargoes, and financial collapses shattered, one by one, the dreams of development that had been dangled as the goal of the transition. Just like splintered bones and fragments of personalities, these crushed dreams nested below a reality of postsocialist survival already saturated with discourses and images of decay (see Schubert, this volume)—splinters of hopes that started to rot beneath new layers of making-do.

For many of the workers and middle-class professionals of Skopje, living in postsocialist Macedonia felt like a process of continuous decay. Urban Macedonians, who had seen their economic and political fortune collapse, found it impossible to move forward not just as individuals, but as members of the new republic. My interlocutors described how they consumed themselves to keep afloat, to pay their bills, to complete their jobs, to obtain adequate healthcare or education. Skopjani resented the improvised fixes and loopholes to which they often had to resort. It bothered them that their actions were contributing to a perverse spiral of moral and economic rot—both their own and that of fellow Macedonians.

Unlike other contributions to this volume, the "seeded" form of Macedonian decay is not caused by an absence of hope or action, and the work of maintenance does not counter it. In postsocialist Macedonia, decay stems from an abundance of agential attempts at mending and navigating the impossible conundrums of the transition. Stagnant efforts to survive have forced Macedonians to confront, day in and day out, their failure to progress—a painful robbing of the present against shattered memories and past desire that drives Macedonians to despair. Seeds of decay cannot be healed, reasoned my Macedonian interlocutors, because their attempts at fixing the present only produced more failures, friction, and rot. In the twilight of certainties generated by the transition, *hoping for* a better future had only led to more failures, deepening their sense of moral degradation. To stop their collective decay, urban Macedonians felt that they had no other choice but to give up that hopeful approach to the future—to give away their agency and to find peace in the oblivion of hope.[1]

The Ladder

On Skopje's construction sites, October afternoons have a peculiar warmth. Yellow rays of sunlight accompany the slow gestures of workers moving between jobs. As I watch the light change, the building too seems to age, each new shade of light bringing out a new tonality of the many kinds of paint used over the several years of construction time.

That day had been both hectic and tedious. The biggest jobs had been completed long ago, yet the building could not be inhabited because there were no pipelines for sewage or running water. Early in the morning, the brigade had been mobilized to dig these infrastructures, only to realize that it made no sense because the municipality had not done their work, and without the right connections, the pipelines had nowhere to go.

By the midafternoon, workers alternated between muddy earth and clean apartments, with questionable results. Dragi, the warehouse manager, attended to sledgehammers, spare parts, and buckets—not the first choice for someone who always dreamed of being a waiter on cruise ships but had bills to pay and a family to feed. Instead of banquet halls, Dragi reigned over the container-made warehouse, where he arranged wrenches and pinches like fine pieces of silverware. There were, however, some positive sides—loopholes in his stagnant job. He could stop at any time, extract two instant, tubular, 3-in-1 coffee packets from his overalls front pocket, and *wham*, one gesture landed powder, hot water, and sugar at the bottom of two plastic cups. A pragmatic master of ceremonies, Dragi mixed the murky liquid with what remained in the plastic tube. Silently, we sat and drank our coffee. Sugar? Sure. Acts of sociality, the construction way.

By the end of the coffee, we could see other workers emerging from their working stations scattered along the nine-story building. Gorast appeared carrying a once-yellow ladder whose wooden frame seemed kept together only by a patchwork of metal nails and plaques—the ladder equivalent of a zombie. "You see," panted Gorast, picking up a hammer from the toolbox, "this ladder should have been thrown away years ago. But no, here I am fixing it, once again. This, my friend, is Macedonia."

Macedonia, a decaying ladder. Gorast's diagnosis dimmed his mood, bringing back the vestiges of Yugoslav, industrial glory, the hope of progress conjured by the transition, and the experiences of economic devastation that had ensued and saturated the landscape around us. I followed his line of sight around the workplace, as his eyes jumped from the decrepit Yugo car used to transport heavy items between construction sites, to the trash that had accumulated since his employer had stopped paying the truck driver, to the sewage lines they were digging (by hand), which were clearly undersized for the needs of the new neighborhood.

To an extent, Gorast's state of mind reflected the feeling that his employer, a small construction firm I will call Construx, was slowly morphing into a zombie company—kept alive by extraordinary measures that could only prolong its economic decline. The first of these measures had been reducing and then delaying salaries for Gorast, Dragi, and other employees—sucking the life from their work schedules and transforming them into zombie-workers who roamed the site hunting for jobs to complete. Despite these savings, the company continued to struggle. More delays accumulated. Subcontractors were abandoning jobs half-finished, leaving the uninhabited building to age without dwellers to care for it—economic stagnation that turned into physical decay.

As long as Construx half-lived, however, workers felt that their lives were intertwined. Yes, the managers' excuses smelled like a rotting fish. But Construx was *their* undead—and a gentle one at that, when compared to other construction companies. Where construction sites were booming, workers were often not paid decent wages nor pensions and other benefits. Workers who were well into their fifties, such as Gorast, had little bargaining power.

Since its independence from socialist Yugoslavia in 1992, Macedonia had lost most of its industrial production and had experienced a very high level of unemployment (Mattioli 2020). Small companies could not afford state-of-the-art machinery; large companies could afford not to buy it and instead forced workers to struggle with rusting tools and makeshift solutions. In this foul landscape, Construx was an exception. It had (almost) always paid taxes and benefits on workers' full salaries and had, whenever possible, provided mechanical support to alleviate their most physical tasks. Combined with paternalistic human resource management, the company's quasi-socialist approach to labor had embodied a beacon of hope for disgruntled workers. Now that uplifting connection had turned into a chain that tied workers and company tighter and tighter as they struggled against the quicksand. In a sector dominated by oligarchs and strangled by an authoritarian government, Construx was haunted, forced to scavenge for resources, contracts, and even clients. A slow, painful social putrefaction.

For Gorast, the last in a long family line of builders, that paralyzing embrace was tragic. Gorast's relatives had been among the workers who had helped Macedonia enter the twentieth century, transforming an agrarian society into a socialist experiment. Had he been born in the 1950s, Gorast would have built new roads, hydroelectric canals, gigantic housing blocks, futuristic university complexes, or modern hospitals. As a Macedonian builder, he would have been a hero—one of those brave people who had resurrected Skopje after a devastating earthquake in 1963. Not to mention the individual benefits! He would have had preferential access to low-interest loans, competitive pensions and salary—guaranteed even when the company encountered turbulent economic conditions by a social safety net that was determined to push even the unwilling parts of society into the new millennium.[2]

Instead of building bridges to a better future, Gorast was stuck repairing, yet again, that crumbling yellow ladder for a company that was slowly falling apart. A part of him knew that the patchwork of metal and wood was a testament to his inventiveness and resilience. Yet when he looked at the ladder, he did not see a comrade of many battles with whom he could reminisce and be proud. Every stroke of his hammer evoked distinct despair, as if bending through the metal had unearthed a scrap of past never forgotten—a hurting, indescribable splinter of social memory that suddenly had gone back to grind against his moral self, painting the world around him in dark tones. Where was the future that the transition had promised? Would he ever reach it if steps kept on breaking, no matter his efforts?

Lacking a perspective for the future projected a sense of futility on the tasks that workers such as Gorast found almost unbearable—much more painful than the simple absurdity of their working conditions. Yes, workers wanted to be paid, to have benefits, and to have access to mechanical lifts instead of carrying payloads on their shoulders. But, more importantly, they wanted to feel, once again, at the heart of a social project—one they could propel forward, with their knowledge, muscles, and experience. That mere idea, today, was out of the realm of possibility. Workers actively tried to erase it, banishing thoughts of equality and progress to a space of nostalgia or cynicism. Below layers of acceptance, however, fragments of those past aspirations continued to scratch their pretended compliance, infecting workers' everyday attempts at navigating postsocialist workplaces with a sense of despair.

The Name

A pungent smell of cigarette mixed with the stale aftertaste of car deodorant whispers "Skopje" more than any of the gigantic signs chaining hills, fields, and mountains to the legacy of Alexander the Great. As we drive past the airport, my eyes feel as if they could fill the landscape like a well-worn glove. I can almost predict, by memory, the turns of the highway and the succession of grapes, grains, and tomatoes on the honey-colored slopes. Inevitably, smooth, ripe hills give way to a string of factories, where locals "enjoy" working on buses, car components, and catalyzers that they will never be able to afford, let alone use. After we pass these parachuted prefabricated buildings, the ruins of socialist dreams begin to clutter both sides of the road.

Like drawings from a dystopian future, crumbling silos, decrepit housing, and even a once-towering hotel remind inhabitants that a better future has not superseded the past. Block after block, these ruins persist, undaunted by the logics of urban speculation.

Below an urban landscape that seems to endure, unchanged,[3] a few telluric transformations have shattered the political land on which Macedonians stand. In 2018, the center-left government that took power after a decade of authoritarian rule by the right-wing VMRO-DPMNE struck a landmark deal "that would open the door to the future, Macedonia's European futures" (Reuters 2019; see also Neofotistos 2021; Mattioli 2021). Known as the Prespa agreement, from the town where it was signed, the treaty saw Greece agree to avoid vetoing Macedonia's entry in the European Union, in exchange for the country's name.

Since its independence in 1992, the Republic of Macedonia has had a contested life. Perhaps its most troubling issue revolved around the use of the name "Macedonia." Under Ottoman rule, "Macedonia" was an administrative region that included parts of today's Greece and Bulgaria, together with the Republic of Macedonia (Neofotistos 2021; Todorov 2013). With the Ottoman Empire's collapse and nation-states emerging in the Balkans, that region was divided between Greece, Bulgaria, and Yugoslavia. In this increasingly polarized nationalist climate, defining, appropriating, or recognizing "Macedonia" became a burning issue. Was there a distinct Macedonian identity, language, culture, or even territory—or were "Macedonians" just converted people who used a dialect and exhibited a "corrupted" identity proper to other states?

Greeks, for instance, claimed the monopoly over the geographical designation of Macedonia, which they utilized to identify its own northern region, while refusing to recognize the presence of Slavic-speaking Macedonians in the areas around Thessaloniki.[4] Bulgarians, on the other hand, claimed that any Slavic speaker in the former Ottoman region of Macedonia was, in fact, a Bulgarian national. While the geopolitical power of socialist Yugoslavia forced the issue into hibernation during the Cold War, Macedonia's contested status flared up again in 1992. When the former socialist Republic of Macedonia voted to become independent, it also started to revitalize its nationalist arsenal—setting itself on a collision course with its much more powerful southern neighbor, Greece.

What ensued were several blockades from Greece, including two economic embargoes in the 1990s, which contributed to precipitate the already precarious economic condition of the landlocked republic. Factories closed, goods could not be sourced, and basic state functions, including running rudimentary healthcare, were on the brink of collapse—to the indifference of the European Community. When that hard form of embargo was lifted, Greece continued to pressure the former socialist republic in diplomatic arenas, slowing down and then vetoing its accession to NATO and the EU. By 2017, while most countries (including the United States) recognized the state as the Republic of Macedonia, some utilized the (much-hated) acronym FYROM (Former Yugoslav Republic of Macedonia). For Macedonians, that name constituted a constant reminder of its forgone past—a splinter of a future that they could never materialize.

The Prespa deal struck in 2018 was supposed to solve this stalemate. The Greek government promised to lift its vetoes to NATO and the EU. For Macedonians, though, this possibility of moving forward in the political arena comes at a high price. According to the agreement, Macedonians will have to change the constitutional name of their country to North Macedonia. Yet it remains unclear what, if any, direct benefits the change will provide. At the time of writing, there is no concrete road map for joining either NATO or the EU—in fact, in 2019, France vetoed a European Parliament resolution to set a date for beginning the accession talks. Bulgaria threatened yet another veto in 2020. More importantly, it is increasingly hard to see the benefits of joining the two organizations. While accessing the EU has been heavily promoted as the only route to lift Macedonia out of its economic stagnation, very few impartial analyses have been offered to back up how further integration in the EU market will help a small economy like Macedonia—and its economic tissue of small, rural, informal producers.

Despite the decision's importance, voices critical of the agreement have been labeled as pronationalist—signs of the deep hold that the moral rot of the VMRO-DPMNE authoritarian regime had inflicted on Macedonia's society. In late 2018, the government promoted a consultative referendum to confirm the agreement, which failed to reach a quorum, demonstrating a very significant opposition to the agreement. But despite these failures, the government barreled ahead. After what some describe as "buying" the support of MPs from the opposition, possibly in exchange for dropping corruption charges, the government changed the constitution and the country name to the Republic of North Macedonia.

As the name change had been ratified only a few weeks before my travel, I asked my driver what he thought about the government's decision to ignore the referendum. "Abe vidi" (You know), he began, speaking with a tone that invited resignation. "The deal is total bullshit. But do you think we have a choice?

SEEDS OF DECAY | 93

There is nothing we can do about it; it will go ahead with or without us." I told him that, certainly, that was a reason to vote against the change—to at least signal that he disagreed with what had been decided. As it turns out, the two things seemed disconnected. Most of the people I spoke with in the following weeks and months hated the agreement. A few were even doubting the usefulness of joining the EU. Yet they had voted for the agreement in the referendum.

I remember stopping midway with my coffee when one of my closest friends, a critical intellectual, told me he had done the same. Why?, I asked. He replied that he was not a nationalist. I suggested that there were other reasons to oppose Macedonia's entrance in the EU and NATO—especially now, after years of suffering, in a moment of crisis. "Yes, of course," he agreed. "But do you think we have any other choice? It is all already decided. Do you think the new prime minister has a choice? At least this way it will be quicker."

A thick silence fell over the table as we sipped our drinks. By the last drop, I realized that most of my conversations with friends and acquaintances were couched in a conspiratorial tone—an admission of powerlessness that turned toward cynicism. Rather than veering toward an occult economy of accusations,[5] these theories evoked a distorted scenario, where Macedonia's hope to be recognized on the world stage was turned against itself (see Graan 2013). It was as if every powerful country or syndicate in the world had its eyes suddenly pointed at Macedonia—not to help its cause, but to deny it agency and confine it to the boudoirs of history.

Some of it was true, of course. Macedonians had less influence than Greece. Indeed, given the turbulent transition from the authoritarian regime of former prime minister Gruevski, the new government was on life support, and it was international actors who had their fingers on the switch. Their backing of Prime Minister Zaev was conditional to his commitment of integrating the small country into NATO, a move that Brussels considered paramount to shield the Balkans from Russian influences.[6] Yet none of those facts meant that Macedonians *had to* capitulate. Quite the opposite: it meant that international partners had every interest in keeping the Macedonian government at least half-alive—which meant that Zaev had some room to negotiate, domestically and internationally.

Conspiracy theories radically denied that possibility. Their world was not one populated by cutthroat dealings—a map of dangers that, as much as they were exaggerated, could be sidestepped to reach safe shores. In the schemes I heard, the fight was over, with a sense of relief. Gone was the arduous task of balancing on the shifting floorboards of a country at the mercy of geopolitical waves. For conspiracy theorists, the abyss had won. There was no chaos in the plots my friends evoked—not even the kind of chaotic, mean debate that amuses online trolls. No, what they wanted their convoluted intrigues to do was to concede, give up, and bring the fight to an end. No more standing up, stuck in a continuous, meaningless roll of events. They had done it, year in and year out, for almost thirty years now. And for what? Every new road had taken them to yet another swamp, leaving them with the sour taste of defeat. An independent country? Stuck in the limbo between recognition and ethnic conflicts. A new economic system? Stagnant, without new inflows of capital or markets to flow into. A new political class? Decaying into networks of undead oligarchs and ghostly intelligence agents.[7]

A conspiracy theory was, in fact, a big "fuck you" to those hopes that kept on infecting their lives with decaying, half-living offspring. Enough of those seeds of future that keep turning into disappointing plagues! Conspiracy theorists enlisted—no, begged—the listener to help them imagine a world where they had no hope, no voice, no freedom, so that they could finally stop their half-lives as zombies of the Western world. Take our name, Europe. Devour our soul, and let it be a new dawn, or the endless night.

Into the Abyss: Giving Up Hope to Stop Decay

Most of the books that describe the social landscape post-1989 paint scenes of chaos and disarray (Shevchenko 2008; Verdery 2003). Yet in exceptionally marginal societies like Macedonia, the transition did not emerge as a shock. Rather, it was a series of continuous, endless nosedives. Socialism was no Eden, no doubt. But what came next was an endless fall.

That sense of being stuck in a perpetual plunge was particularly taxing for urban Macedonians, not (only) because it entailed difficult working and living conditions. Indeed, the fall forced Skopjani to embrace makeshift working routines and approaches to living—an inexorable process of maintenance that kept on destroying future possibilities. Their crushed hopes of progress did not disappear, however. Instead, the desire of moving forward came to be nested in Skopje's collective imaginary, until mundane attempts at fixing broken ladders, instant coffees, and botched referendums brought them back. Through these failures, Macedonians reflected on the contrast between what they hoped for and what they had been able to achieve—a mirror that did not restore an image of modern, liberal subjects but displayed a putrid portrait of zombies, drowning slowly in a stagnant landscape.

This sense of decay, in Skopje, was not the opposite of hope (Hage, this volume). Instead, it ensued from a particular configuration where hope had been shattered, but not completely erased from citizens' social memory. In the experience of Macedonian working- and middle-class urbanites, decay was precisely the consequence of deposited and irretrievable hope. It constituted a process of reevaluation where Skopjani perceived their misery as an abnormal, protracted half-life, unable ever to achieve the forward movement that they had imagined would follow socialism.

In this scenario, there was never a single culprit who "let the rot in" (Hage, this volume). Instead, decay was everywhere and nowhere, directly inscribed into the very history of Macedonia's collective consciousness and propagated through the precarious acts that allowed citizens to survive the hardships of the transition, including the fundamental action of naming, and calling into being, their country and their collective identity. Only a radical excision could, potentially, address such a pernicious source of decay—not by changing their everyday condition but by removing all hope of progress.

That event, that existential excision, came about in 2018, when Macedonians were asked to change their name to appease Greece and, potentially, enter the European Union. My interlocutors did not believe that forsaking their past and taking on a new name would suddenly solve their problems. Yes, there was a remote possibility that, with the new name "North Macedonia," citizens would suddenly reach a Nietzschean bliss—able to finally shape their own world and decide their future, equals among equals.[8] But that did not matter. Very few people expected their material lives to improve and their political future to look any brighter. Quite the opposite: conspiracy theories and other passive reactions to the Prespa agreement signaled a wish to give up—a desire to stop having to fix, appropriate, or navigate the impossible context of their never-ending fall from socialism. Ladders would continue to be broken, they reasoned. But perhaps, if they managed to get rid of their hope of progress, they could stop feeling so terrible about it.

In this essay, I have used the word *decay* to indicate two kinds of phenomena. *Decay* refers first to mundane moments where my interlocutors felt that the "proper" order of working life fell apart. Broken ladders and rusty Yugos, however, did more than suggest a breakdown of morality. Instead, they pointed to a more profound experience of decay, a form of collective stagnation caused by the repetitive failure of the hopes of progress unleashed during the transition from socialism. This paradox suggests that the relationship between decay and hope is far more complicated than we often presume. One is not the negation of the other. Instead, unrealized, frustrated hope can itself become infected—can turn into a purulent testimony of failure, a seed of decay. Nestled deep in the individual and collective imaginary, seeds of decay contaminated my interlocutors' everyday actions, in a process so morally painful that they wished they could abandon any hope of progress and change to stop it.

Unlike the militiamen observed by Hage in this volume, Skopjani's discourses of defeat, which identified everyday fixes or blocked geopolitical transformation as inherently flawed, were not aimed at forging a space of meaning and recovering symbolic agency as victims. Instead, Macedonian urbanites I spoke with felt that the only way to stop their process of decay was to remove the debris of hope from the deepest recess of their collective imaginary. For many, that meant giving in to the geopolitical forces that had been such a crucial component of their sense of self-determination, letting them extirpate their long-standing imaginaries of future progress. Accepting the name "North Macedonia" felt like thrusting themselves on a spike, a symbolic self-impaling that could bring an irrevocable end to their half-lives. Finally, they would give up their dreams of autonomy and replace them with an unconditional surrender. Absorbed by a careless EU, Macedonians would finally be absolved for their failure—their last deposits of hope removed and replaced by the nothingness of empty sovereignty. In their embrace of the abyss they would be immobile, without either hope or decay.9

Notes

1. This suggests a counter-Nietzschean movement (Nietzsche 1964, 1996). For Nietzsche, religious hope promotes a sense of self-effacement that ultimately denies one's agency and naturalizes oppression while waiting for otherworldly rewards. This kind of hope should be rejected for a different one—an approach to the present and future which ultimately culminates not in waiting for heaven, but in demiurgic action. What we observe in the case of Macedonia is the failure of demiurgic hope—and the paradoxical attempt to erase hope, not in order to regain agency but in order to stop one's existential suffering.

2. Of course, not everybody wanted to embrace socialist modernity. While Yugoslav socialism was often more moderate compared to its Soviet version, it still encouraged citizens to conform to a modernist, secular understanding of social life—a process that sometimes exacerbated interethnic conflicts (Mattioli 2014; Dimova 2013; Neofotistos 2012).

3. Some of the factories opened or closed after I began approaching the city in 2008. Yet the feeling of placid out-of-time-ness of Skopje's decaying urbanism remains.

4. For some of the complications of this history, see Karakasidou 1997; and Danforth 1995.

5. The speculative dimensions of capitalism are often rendered vernacularly through languages of occult, where winners and losers are transposed as perpetrators or victims of witchcraft—often couched in a landscape of moral and material decay (Comaroff and Comaroff 2001).

6. In 2018, Macedonian intelligence agencies released a series of reports detailing the activity of Russian's operatives to stir anti-NATO and EU propaganda (Belford et al. 2017) in what many feared could evolve into an attempted coup similar to what had taken place in 2017 in Montenegro (see Mattioli 2020).

7. The dramatic waves of privatization that swept across Eastern Europe in the 1990s paved the way for well-positioned individuals to capture significant share of wealth from former socialist companies and public agencies. Many of these emerging oligarchs were former directors of socialist enterprises, or well-positioned officers of the intelligence agencies (see Dawisha 2014).

8. In *Thus Spoke Zarathustra*, Nietzsche (1964) suggests that humankind has to overcome three different "stages," exemplified by different animals. First humankind behaves like a camel, which accepts the weight of tradition and other people's decisions. Then humans turn into dragons who destroy the morals and the law, only to realize that this position, too, is limited by what they are set to destroy. Only the last existential stance, that of a kid, allows humankind to be truly free—demiurges of their own destiny, which they create with playfulness.

9. See Gökarıksel 2017 for a broader discussion of how nihilism resonates across postsocialist contexts.

8

DISCOURSES OF DECAY IN SETTLER COLONIAL AUSTRALIA

Elise Klein

In the last ten years, addressing the disadvantages of First Nations people has been the focus of Australian government policy. This has led to the national policy framework Closing the Gap, which aims to reach seven goals including increasing the rates of First Nations formal employment, life expectancy, numeracy, and English literacy. These seven goals direct government funding priorities. Yet each year, government reports to Parliament on the progress made toward those goals, which have shown how policy efforts continually fail to meet the set targets (Commonwealth of Australia 2019, 2020). There are various explanations as to why there has been such a chronic failure to reach the set targets, including the suitability of the goals, which omit important aspects of overcoming disadvantage, such as land rights, self-determination, and settler colonialism (Kowal 2008; Altman 2014). Instead of addressing these critiques of the program's goals, policy-makers have largely shifted the blame for Closing the Gap's failure onto First Nations people through the "social decay discourse," where individuals and communities unable to close the gap are labeled dysfunctional. The social decay discourse is about a morality in decay, and often draws on racialized tropes that have been around since European invasion: tropes that interpellate a decline or deficiency in social norms, often from the assumed use of drugs, alcohol, unemployment, and irresponsible behavior (see Baxendale 2018, 1; Hutchens 2017). For example, in making the case to government for a more punitive approach to Indigenous policy in regional Australia, billionaire Andrew Forrest, in his federal government–commissioned *Forrest Review: Creating Parity*, a policy review of Indigenous employment and training, claimed that "communities, especially remote first Australian communities, are desperate to stop the incoming tide of drugs and alcohol [enabled by unconditional state benefits]. They have exhausted every possible option in the search for effective methods for restricting the flow of cash to harmful uses and redirecting it to paying for essentials while in temporary and occasionally difficult circumstances, such as unemployment" (Forrest 2014, 102).

The social decay discourse legitimizes punitive intervention by governments that would not be acceptable for settler middle-class Australians (Garond 2014; Watson 2009). For example, the social decay discourse was a major enabler of the Northern Territory Emergency Response in 2007 and operated through policy-makers' claims of endemic social dysfunction and decay in remote First Nations communities across the Northern Territory (Lovell 2012). The minister for Aboriginal affairs at that time, Mal Brough, likened Aboriginal communities to that of a "failed society," where "normal community standards and parenting behavior [had] broken down" (Lovell 2012, 205). The intervention was justified in Parliamentary legislation as an enabler to "break the back of the violence and dysfunction in Aboriginal communities" (Lovell 2012, 205) and involved the suspension of the Racial Discrimination Act to enforce of a raft of policies targeting Indigenous individuals and communities across the Northern Territory (Altman 2010). The intervention included measures such as attempted bans on alcohol consumption, bans on pornography, quarantining of welfare money, highly regulated tenancy arrangements that disallowed different residential arrangements, compulsory acquisition of township leases from the legally recognized owners to facilitate governmental controls, and the appointing of government business managers with legal rights to monitor the meetings of community organizations and to hold absolute powers in townships (Altman 2007).

In this chapter I will draw on field-based research in the East Kimberley between April 2016 and November 2018 to argue that this social decay discourse continues to be a key aspect of contemporary Australian settler colonialism, particularly in the making and maintenance of punitive Indigenous welfare policy. This discourse has both affective and material consequences for people's lives and livelihoods, further producing the disadvantage that Closing the Gap targets purport to deal with. For example, Maramanindji scholar Darryl Cronin argues that punitive measures impoverish and oppress communities and lead to the deterioration of people's livelihoods: "Many Indigenous people regard their poverty and disadvantage as a condition formed upon them by the dominant society. They know that the management and control of their lives, particularly their exploitation and their dependence on welfare income and welfare programs are connected to matters of control and assimilation, and that there are many interest groups in society who profit from the structures and institutions that have been created to keep Indigenous people in a subordinate position" (2007, 198). This chapter exposes how settler colonial processes underway in the East Kimberley are obfuscated by the social decay discourse, including the depoliticization of settler-created disadvantage, the further legitimization of punitive policy, policy abandonment, and accumulation by dispossession.

The Making of Disadvantage and Inequality in the East Kimberley

The East Kimberley is a largely remote region of Australia often targeted by settler policy makers for what they see as an ongoing failure to meet Closing the Gap targets. Disadvantage in the East Kimberley disproportionately falls on First Nations peoples: 47 percent of First Nations people living in the region live in poverty (Markham and Biddle 2018, 18).[1] This number increased by over 2.5 percent between 2011 and 2016. Many of these First Nations households are reliant on government payments, which are notoriously well under the national poverty line. Poverty is also exacerbated in that the cost of living in the Kimberley is 15 percent higher than that of Western Australia's capital city, Perth (Kimberley Development Commission 2013). Poverty is a major cause of ill-health in the East Kimberley, and First Nations people have a life expectancy twenty years lower than that of non–First Nations people (Empowered Communities 2019).

Yet material poverty for First Nations people in the East Kimberley is linked to settler colonialism (as elsewhere in Australia), where wealth has been generated through the expropriation of First Nations labor and land. The development of the major town in the region Kununurra in the 1960s was contingent on the flooding of Miriuwung country to create the Ord Dam and Lake Argyle, the largest lake in Australia. The damming of the Ord River flooded more than half of Miriuwung country, including songlines, and hence constitutes one of the most recent acts of dispossession, displacement, and occupation in Australia's history (Coombs 1989, 1–20). Yet, as Grudnoff and Campbell (2017) reported, despite $2 billion spent on the Ord River Scheme, limited benefits have been enjoyed by a few: the scheme has only resulted in 260 (predominantly non–First Nations) jobs (Grudnoff and Campbell 2017, iv).

Unpaid First Nations labor built the pastoral industries of the East Kimberley, and many families suffered through Stolen Generation policies: their children were taken and used as slave or indentured domestic labor in settler households. Although work on stations included thousands of First Nations people, they were not paid. Their forced labor was essential to the economic success and expansion of the pastoral industry, which was never viable without First Nations unpaid labor (Standing Committee on Legal and Constitutional Affairs 2006, 29). As Shaw states, "Without Aboriginal stock workers it is unlikely that such European enterprises would have become viable" (1992, 17). Indeed, in the 1970s, with the introduction of equal wage legislation for First Nations people; the increase in technology on stations, such as helicopter mustering; and the global recession, First Nations people were forced again off their land as the stations claimed they could not afford to pay for their First Nations labor (Skyring 2012). This period "broke the back of the feudal relationship between station managers and Aboriginal families" (Yu 1994, 19). Settlers then forced First Nations people off the stations, leading to a refugee crisis of enormous proportions as people moved to the town fringes of Kununurra, Wyndham, and Halls Creek.

The 2006 Senate inquiry into First Nations stolen wages also acknowledges how unpaid First Nations labor in the Kimberley was extracted to build the very industries that generate private profits in the East Kimberley today (Standing Committee on Legal and Constitutional Affairs 2006, 29). The inquiry noted how this exploitation of labor has clear links to the material poverty many First Nations peoples currently experience.[2] Material poverty in the East Kimberley is therefore relational; it is a persistent "consequence of historically developed economic and political relations, as opposed to 'residual' approaches which might regard poverty as the result of being marginal to these same relations" (Mosse 2010, 1157). Yet these explanations of how First Nations disadvantage was settler made is conveniently silenced in contemporary policy making. Instead, First Nations behavior has become a target of intervention, which in turn intensifies disadvantage.

Policy Assemblages in the East Kimberley

The settler state has intensified its punitive policy approach through its focus on promoting socially responsible behavior and getting people into what it calls "real jobs." Settler job creation initiatives are underpinned by capitalist waged labor norms and limit what policy-makers understand as work. Many First Nations people in the East Kimberley engage in productive work "on country" undertaking customary (nonmarket) work for livelihood, but this work is not valued by the state. These First Nations collective norms and productive work have endured over a decade of critique by politicians, business leaders, policy-makers, and some First Nations elite, who describe this work as outside the "real economy" and promote social decay narratives about First Nations passivity, dysfunction, and nonparticipation in "real" work. Also not valued through such discourse is how First Nations people engage in other productive activities, such as unpaid care work: according to the 2016 census data, 38 percent of First Nations respondents in Kununurra provide unpaid childcare, whereas only 29 percent of non–First Nations people did the same. Instead, all these types of work and First Nations collective norms are overlooked, and bodies are passed off as unproductive, unemployed, and wasting away. They are then forced onto punitive welfare schemes that, under the language of behavioral change, target First Nations collective norms while denying self-determination and resources for collective survival.

A major part of this punitive behavioral approach in the East Kimberley is the cashless debit card (CDC) trial. The CDC is a type of income management that enforces the quarantining of 80 percent of state benefits received by all working-age people. Quarantining payments limits the amount of cash that can be withdrawn to just 20 percent of the total money received. The stated aims of the federal legislation (the Social Security Legislation Amendment [Debit Card Trial] Bill 2015) are explicitly to "encourage socially responsible behavior."[3] The CDC trial commenced officially on April 26, 2016, and was originally implemented for a year in the East Kimberley. However, in 2017, 2018, 2019, and 2020, the federal government extended the trial without any credible analysis that the card fulfills its aims (Hunt 2017).

The trial impacts First Nations people disproportionately—80 percent of people on the trial are First Nations peoples (Australian Human Rights Commission 2016, 91–92), despite government claims that the CDC is not a racialized measure. The CDC trial stems from an Australian government-commissioned review led by mining billionaire Andrew Forrest into Indigenous employment and training (the *Forrest Review*; see Forrest 2014). The various recommendations proposed in the *Forrest Review* went far beyond the original remit of employment and training, ignoring forms of productive work—such as care of country and community—that fall outside narrow understandings of paid work, and including recommendations for paternalistic interventions in early childhood development, housing, school attendance, and welfare reform (Klein 2014, 1). This was the second "Forrest review" in Australia's policy history; the first was published in 1884 by Andrew Forrest's great-great-uncle John Forrest, who provided a report in response to requests by settlers for government assistance to deal with the "Aboriginal problem" (Smith 2000, 79).

Like other income management programs in Australia, the Cashless Debit Card brings hardship to people's lives (Klein and Razi 2017, 7–9; Orima Research 2017, 72, 79, 82, 100). This is because there are very real problems related to the deficit assumptions underpinning the trial: that most welfare users have drug and alcohol problems; that the overuse of alcohol, illegal drugs, and gambling is caused by excessive access to cash; and that there is a collective behavioral deficiency limiting people's ability to find a job. Instead, most people receiving welfare do so because there are limited numbers of jobs in the Kimberley (Kimberley Development Commission 2013, 18–21), not because of any issue with addiction. Further, the Royal Australian and New Zealand Society of Psychiatrists (2017), among other mental health professionals, has argued that trauma and addiction (for people who do experience them) are made worse, not better, through punitive measures. The policy underpinned by these incorrect assumptions has induced hardship such as making the management of money hard for people on the card and through restricting people's access to buy essential items such as food, transport, rent, gifts, and secondhand goods (Klein and Razi 2017, 7–8).

There has been pushback against the card in the trial site. When the trial started, there were various protest meetings, and a petition circulated for the government to stop the trial, because many saw the card as an extension of the government's ongoing desire to regulate and control First Nations lives. Some people just never picked up their card and thus cut themselves off from state payments to avoid being subjected to the trial, furthering financial pressure on families of already limited financial means. Within weeks of the rollout, the card was given an entirely new name among those it was being forced on: the "white card." At no stage has the card been white. The card is silver. When asked, both those on the card and government workers reflected that the card was nicknamed the "white card" because it was imposed by white people. People have also said that using the CDC is like "taking us back to the ration days" (Klein and Razi 2017, 90). Rations were used in the East Kimberley (and elsewhere) before the 1970s, "to control Aboriginal movement and labor, as well as to try and discipline people out of 'Aboriginal' behaviors" (Gibson 2012, 63).

Intersecting with the CDC are other programs that try to engineer collective norms. For example, the remote work-for-the-dole program titled the Community Development Program (CDP) also targets the cohort of people subjected to the CDC. Whereas the CDC places conditions on how people must spend their payments, the CDP places conditions on what people must do to receive economic security. The program is an extreme attempt to further achieve employment parity—a key focus of Closing the Gap—requiring working-age participants taking a state payment to attend manufactured "work-like" initiatives, for up to twenty hours a week for a payment well below minimum wage (Altman 2015). The requirements for CDP are harsher than the government's nonremote and mainly non–First Nations JobActive program because of its rules and because of the remote setting; as a result, breaching rates for the CDP are much higher than those for nonremote programs (Fowkes 2016, 1). The consequences for people not turning up is that welfare money is withheld and families go without (Klein and Razi 2017).

While there are such extreme efforts in getting people into "real work," there has been limited success in doing so. People subjected to the CDC and the CDP are regularly left with significantly reduced payments, or no payments at all, furthering poverty and disadvantage. Specifically, the incidence of poverty experienced by First Nations peoples in very remote areas such as the East Kimberley has increased since the CDP and the CDC have been operational (see Markham and Biddle 2018, 18).

This punitive policy-making in the East Kimberley is also accompanied by the abandonment and negligence of the settler state (Povinelli 2011, 131–45). The decay of social housing infrastructure in the East Kimberley compounds settler-made poverty and displacement. Social housing is notorious for overcrowding, placement waiting lists of eight to twelve years, and the state's failure to make needed repairs on the dilapidated housing stock. Tess Lea's (2015) work on First Nations housing has revealed that families in state housing are held responsible by the state for the dirty, moldy, and decaying houses they inhabit. This decay of housing is blamed on First Nations people, who are accused of not looking after the housing stock "gifted" by the settler state. The transitional housing program has been put in place in the Kimberley to tackle assumed behaviors not conducive to settlement, where people are given a state house only if they have shown a willingness to assimilate into settler society—such as through engagement in the formal labor market and sending their children to school (Klein 2020). Not only do these racist assumptions overlook the lack of employment for everyone, but they also ignore how the houses decay but because they are poorly designed and neglected, receiving minimal state maintenance (Lea and Pholeros 2010, 189–92). In fact, in an inventory of state housing stock for First Nations families across 132 communities, of the 71,869 items assessed as requiring repair, 65 percent of problems were due to lack of maintenance, 25 percent was due to faulty installation or design, and only 10 percent was because of occupant damage or misuse (Torzillo et al. 2008, cited in Lea and Pholeros 2010, 192). This has led Lea to conclude that the "edifice is intimately dependent upon both reasserting slots for intervention with a predefined array of solutions and locating the cause of decay as culture-bound—many livelihoods depend on this circularity. . . . What is of interest is how, using similarly strategic repressions, decaying material forms are interpreted as cultural effects and given the salience of (alterable and human) cultural difference, ignorance or pathology" (2015, 383).

Both punitive welfare policies and abandonment contribute to the disadvantage faced by First Nations, and this has real impacts on people's health, well-being, and life expectancy. These impacts can be understood as what Lauren Berlant (2007) calls a "slow death" and further described by Jasbir Puar as a "population marked for wearing out, a gradual decay of bodies that are both overworked and under-resourced" (2015, 7). But in the case of the East Kimberley, it isn't just First Nations bodies that are forced to suffer under settler intervention. Collective First Nations norms are also forced to endure the necropolitics of the settler state through its constant enforcement of settler norms on First Nations people—particularly regarding what counts as productive work. Under the guise of addressing the seemingly commendable policy project Closing the Gap, the settler state masquerades as improving First Nations lives, while actually contributing to the destruction of bodies and collective norms. While death and elimination are repelled through the sheer endurance of and resistance by First Nations people, there is still a toll on bodies and collective norms; under the state's sustained attacks, First Nations people are never allowed to fully flourish and self-determine (Moreton-Robinson 2009). Puar (2015, 2017) makes a similar finding in her debility formulation, examining the Israeli settler process of maiming Palestinian bodies in Israel's ongoing war against Palestinian resistance. Instead of *shooting to kill*, Israeli forces *shoot to maim*, creating debilitating injuries, not death, to avoid violating global humanitarian norms (Puar 2015, 7–9). The Australian settler state engages in *social debilitation* through policies such as the CDC and CDP, where First Nations collective norms are not killed outright but are maimed so they are unable to self-determine and flourish. Social debility means that First Nations collective norms are excluded from finding their own modernities and pluriversal possibilities, maimed to a point where they can survive but not self-determine.

This social debility offers another possibility for settler colonialism—an ongoing process largely understood as attempting to eliminate First Nations peoples to access their land (Wolfe 2006, 402; Coulthard 2014, 4). Elimination, even in the form of outright killing, continues today in the form of death in police custody and settler induced suicide. Elimination also continues to be attempted through assimilation, where First Nations subjectivities and collective norms are targeted for alignment to settler subjectivities—through behavioral conditions placed on the use of state benefits, for example (Altman 2018, 349). Alongside the attempted assimilation, we also find social debilitation—a process where the self-determination of First Nations collective norms are denied without being completely erased.

Accumulation by Dispossession

There are various ways that the social decay discourse enables settler accumulation by dispossession (see Coulthard 2014). First, the social decay discourse provides opportunities for the employment of non–First Nations people who come to Kununurra to work in the service industry that is largely set up to mitigate Indigenous dysfunction. Western Australia Police, legal organizations, and government departments and agencies such as Child Protection, Housing, and Social Services employ a workforce of hundreds of staff—disproportionately non–First Nations people. These employment contracts are often accompanied by lucrative sweeteners such as guaranteed employee housing, cars, and high salaries. Second, the social decay discourse also legitimizes the continued attempts by both government and corporate entities to access First Nations land for what they call economic development. The white paper titled *Our North, Our Future* (Commonwealth of Australia 2015) sets the current twenty-year agenda by the Australian government to bring prosperity to northern Australia, including the East Kimberley. Referred to as "developing the North," this agenda has both bipartisan and state government support; it backs projects based on private enterprise, the extraction of resources from First Nations land, and the proletarianization of First Nations labor. Third, settler-made disadvantage also facilitates First Nations subjectivities as *the territory* of accumulation by dispossession. Indue, the private company that has been contracted by both the Department of Social Services and the Department of Human Services, has been harvesting a new industry to accumulate wealth on the business to trying to socially engineer aboriginalities. They acquired over $10.8 million of the $18.9 million spent on the trial (up until April 2017) for operating the card during the trial (in both Ceduna and the East Kimberley) and for building the technology.[4] Indue owns elements of the intellectual property from the trial for commercial purposes, but it has not been disclosed which specific elements. Further, First Nations people are purposefully left to endure the income management trial and the punitive work-for-the-dole programs, while bogus evaluations are circulated that are profitable for universities and private companies: these entities receive multi-million-dollar contracts, only to provide methodologically and analytically flawed analysis (Hunt 2017, 1–16).

Conclusion

Since Europeans arrived in the East Kimberley, First Nations people have been killed, managed, disciplined, and maimed to get out of the way of settler expansion. Regardless, First Nations people have endured and continue to resist settler colonialism and the long histories of social decay discourses that have legitimized both violent and banal attempts of elimination (Lovell 2012). The analysis of the affective and material impacts of the social decay discourse in the East Kimberley offers a small contribution to further understanding these contemporary settler colonial processes that First Nations are forced to endure. Social security or "welfare," often regarded as a mechanism to stop or reduce hardship, is actually (and has been for a long time, given the role of rations) an important aspect of this hardship. Income management is ongoing, established as a "trial" with no end date set for over four years, and no credible evaluation results to inform us about any outcome of the trial (Klein and Razi 2017). Both CDC and CDP programs compulsorily include the largely First Nations unemployed, even though full employment is not a viable goal in remote labor markets. These policies are implemented in the name of advancement and improvement possible under liberal frameworks of interventions designed to improve individuals while still subjugating them and debilitating First Nations collective norms. Until these structures and processes are deconstructed and First Nations' self-determination and sovereignty honored, the disadvantage and dispossession will continue.

Notes

I would sincerely like to thank all those in the East Kimberley that wish to remain anonymous for their insights for this project. I would also like to thank Bev Walley, Lawford Benning, and Jon Altman for their generous teachings over the years. I am indebted to Ghassan Hage for giving me the opportunity to contribute to this project and for his generous input on this chapter, which significantly sharpened any theoretical contributions it makes. This chapter has also had benefited from the wise insights of Sarouche Razi, China Mills, and the other contributors of this collection. I am also grateful for the conversations between Jasbir Puar and the participants of her 2019 masterclass hosted by Warwick University.

1. Markham and Biddle (2018, 2) use the conventional relative poverty line of 50 percent of the median national equivalized household income, meaning that the Aboriginal poverty rate is a measure of the economic situation of Aboriginal Australians relative to the entire population of the country.

2. For example, Professor Anna Haebich stated: "Aboriginal people played a major role in building the state economy in the pastoral and rural industries in the north and south of the state. It was the state government's discriminatory employment system that prevented Aboriginal workers from benefiting from the Australian labour system, which was hailed around the world as an exemplary model for protecting workers' wages and rights. Instead, Aboriginal people were subject to a disabling system which denied them proper wages, protection from exploitation and abuse, proper living conditions, and adequate education and training. So while other Australians were able to build up financial security and an economic future for their families, Aboriginal workers were hindered by these controls. Aboriginal poverty in Western Australia today is a direct consequence of this discriminatory treatment" (Haebich 2006 cited in Standing Committee on Legal and Constitutional Affairs 2006, 29).

3. The Social Security Legislation Amendment (Debit Card Trial) Bill 2015, Bills Digest no. 27 1015–16, p. 4, https://parlinfo.aph.gov.au/parlInfo/download/legislation/billsdgs/4123233/upload_binary/4123233.pdf;fileType=application/pdf.

4. Contract number CN3323493-A1 awarded to Indue operational contract, $7,939,809; contract number (CN3290604) awarded to Indue for the information technology build contract, $2,870,675.50 (The reference numbers for these contracts are published on AusTender, www.tenders.gov.au.).

9

DECAY AS DECLINE IN SOCIAL VIABILITY AMONG EX-MILITIAMEN IN LEBANON

Ghassan Hage

Michel, Tony, Toufic: Mold and the Stench of Death

It's February 2002. There are strong winds and heavy rain outside. I am in the top-floor apartment of an old five-story building. Huddled around a gas heater are six former members of the banned Lebanese Forces, the militia that saw itself as embodying "Christian resistance" during the Lebanese civil war.[1] Their ex-captain, an engineer who has resumed his career working in Saudi Arabia, has provided the apartment, where they gather, drink coffee, play backgammon, watch television, and chat. They are all in their mid-forties and unemployed at that time, though they perform a variety of casual jobs for a living. These ex-militiamen enjoyed a certain form of prestige and recognition during the war—some of them more than others, of course. But unlike their superiors, who were invariably better educated and had university degrees, they were not able to maintain their income or their status. They share a bundle of real and imagined complaints and suffering: they are unhealthy, they are poor, they are depressed, and as they all agree, they are defeated.

The Lebanese civil war ended with the Syrian army entering Lebanon as a peacekeeping force. They see it as a Syrian/Muslim occupation. Their leader, Samir Geagea, is the only military leader from the war era in jail. As they rub their hands around the heater on this exceptionally cold and wet winter day, one of them, Tony, looks at a corner of the ceiling and says, "Look, it's moldy." Michel replies, "You're moldy." Everyone laughs except Tony. In the years after the war, his right hand and forearm became paralyzed, and they've atrophied. He takes it personally. "Ayreh Feek" (Fuck you), he says to Michel. Michel puts his arm around him and says: "I didn't really mean just you. We are all moldy [*m'affaneen*]. We're rotting [*'am nehtereh*]." He points to a photo of Geagea in jail hanging on the wall and says: "Look at him. He's rotting." Then he looks at me as if I am always the person to whom one communicates grand declarations, and he says: "This is the price of defeat. Defeat is eating us from the inside."

I had heard many other ex-militiamen speak of defeat since the war ended. It is usually associated with a more generalized conception of Christian decline grounded in a comparative imaginary. Saudi Arabia's financing of postwar recovery has meant the growth of Sunni capitalism and the decline in Christian economic power. The power-sharing formula between the Christian president, the Sunni prime minister, and the Shi'a head of Parliament that forms the basis of Lebanese institutional politics has been modified to give more power to the prime minister and the head of Parliament. This generated a sense of Christian political decline. Hezbollah's Shi'a militia, which spearheaded the resistance against Israel with the help of Iran, are fully armed, while the Christian militia has had to disarm. This has translated into a sense of military decline. Defeat, in the way the militiamen talk about it, is often articulated as linked to this decline. While the social tendencies that make up this sense of decline are real enough, the relation between them and the sense of defeat is not always expressed rigorously or coherently: sometimes defeat is seen as a sign of this decline, sometimes it is seen as what initiated it.

Thinking decline with and through the militiamen did not only mean accessing it through the prism of defeat. It also meant accessing it through an articulation of defeat in connection to socioeconomic, psychological, and bodily decline. As in the reference to mold above, decline was often expressed in a language that conveyed a sense of decay directly or metonymically. Perhaps one of the most direct formulations I encountered was by Toufic, an alcoholic with serious kidney problems, whose wife left him soon after the war ended and who, while explaining to me how his health was deteriorating, said: "We fighters get so used to the smell of death we stop smelling it. We might be dying, we might even already be dead and finished, and worms are eating us, without smelling the stench that is coming out of us." Little did Toufic know it at the time, but his comment spoke to a rather peculiar experience I was continuously having: during the war, I went through an area that was militarily overrun by the militia, and I experienced that stench of death that Toufic was talking about—how it sticks to one's clothes and body for some time after. It left such an impact on me that I always associated the militia with it. This continued well after the war, and on many occasions when doing fieldwork with the militiamen, I became convinced that I actually smelled it, though I associated it not with decay and defeat in particular but, rather, with "war" in general. It was an encounter with a key informant that led me to start to seriously think the relation between bodily decay, and the experience of defeat and social decline. But as I will relate in this chapter, while I began by seeing defeat as an accelerator of a sense of decay, I soon realized that the relation was anything but that.

Tony: Rot and Atrophy

Tony was seventeen in 1976, when he began fighting in the Lebanese civil war with the Phalangists.[2] I interviewed him for my PhD thesis in 1986 and have known him ever since. When I met him, he had been fighting for ten years, and he looked it. He had a reputation for being a fierce fighter. He was also considered unpredictable and "mad." As such, he was feared, not so much by the enemy but by the militiamen in his unit. In 1989, he became suddenly ill and lost weight. He recovered. But by the time he did so, the civil war had ended. In 1991, he began experiencing paralysis of his right hand and arm up to his shoulder. By 1992 this had evolved into a full paralysis of his right arm. Medical tests could not reveal a cause for the symptom, nor did they show any links with his previous illness two years before. He was then referred to a psychiatrist, and later a psychoanalyst. He ended up being diagnosed as suffering from an unspecified psychological war injury. "They told me that this is what the war has done to me," he said. When I saw him in 1995, his right arm and hand had atrophied considerably. When he saw me, he said, "Look, my hand is rotting" (*'am tehteri*), and he kept repeating a variation indicating that the flesh of his hand was disappearing. I wasn't taking notes—I was seeing him just to inquire about his health at that time—but he repeated this so often that it stayed in my mind. In 1996, I was told that he had started recovering some movement in his hand. In 1997, I saw him when I was in Beirut, and he had almost fully recovered the capacity to use his fingers, but his arm had irreparably atrophied and still looked like just skin and bone.

It was in 1999 that a dramatic moment occurred. I was visiting all the ex-fighters at the same apartment mentioned above. I took Tony and a few others for dinner at a local restaurant. Late in the night, Tony took me aside and said: "There's something I've been wanting to tell you, and I know that you will want to hear it." He paused and said:

> I know what happened to my arm. These doctors, when they talk about psychological war injury, they know, and they don't know, what they are talking about. But it's partly my fault since I couldn't share this with them.... Something really crazy happened.... Bashir [his son, named after Bashir Gemayel, the assassinated founding leader of the Lebanese Forces]... when he started to have facial hair... something very strange happened. Every time I saw him, I started seeing this boy that I killed in the camps [Palestinian camps], he had exactly the same facial hair. I entered his house and he and a woman, probably his mother, were hiding behind a sofa. When I saw them, the woman ran to me with a knife and I shot her. Then he ran to me screaming, his eyes looked totally wild, and he bit me like a feral dog. I put the gun on his head, and I shot him. I've shot many people in this war, some at close range. But his was different. Don't ask me why, but his facial hair stood out. I still remember this straight after I killed him. His facial hair stayed with me. And that's why, later, when Bashir developed some facial hair, the boy's facial hair came back to my mind and I couldn't shake it. It got so bad I started having nightmares. But worst of all, I just could no longer touch Bashir. I come to him to give him a cuddle and all I could concentrate on was his hair. That's when my hand started to become paralyzed. I not only had to deal with this, but I had to deal with Bashir, who started noticing that I was no longer being affectionate toward him. Everything around me was going to pieces.... I don't know. Perhaps if we had won this war, I would have felt different. But we didn't.

It was with this text, which I wrote from memory the day after Tony talked to me,[3] that I started thinking seriously about the way a sense of bodily disintegration and decay, a sense of social decay (that "everything around me was going to pieces"), and the discourse of defeat that was prevalent in the late twentieth and early twenty-first century in the milieus of the ex-Christian militiamen were all articulated together. Even those who identified politically as "Christians" but had not been militiamen spoke of themselves as being defeated. There is significant journalistic literature in Arabic, French, and English that documents and validates this experience of decline and defeat (AsiaNews.it 2018; *L'Orient–Le Jour* 2018; MTV 2015). And, as noted above, no doubt there were many "objective" indicators to make the external observer accept that this sentiment of defeat had a real basis in the way Lebanese society was transforming. It was not a mere "subjective" feeling. This was the case even though there was no clear sentiment on the Muslim/leftist side of the war of any political force that saw itself as a winner. Except for minor, explicitly pro-Syrian forces, both sides experienced the Syrian presence as a kind of defeat.

One ethnographic issue that kept coming up as my research evolved was the fact that the sense of decline in general, and the discourse of defeat in particular, were far more pronounced among militiamen from working-class/underclass backgrounds than they were among the more middle-class militiamen. The latter had taken most leading political and military positions in the militia from the start of the war. What's more, I could clearly note that while the discourse of defeat was decreasing in the general population and being replaced by a less partisan discourse on the dehumanizing nature of war, it continued to be pervasive among the militiamen (see Hermez 2019). I thought this was simply because they were fighters and were experiencing the result of the war more intensely. Consequently, for a time I continued to take "defeat" and "the sentiment of defeat" as causal forces in themselves, working with the socioeconomic decline to explain at least a dimension of the sentiment of decay—that is, of physical, political, and moral degeneration and depression—that prevailed in some of the Christian socioeconomic milieus from which the fighters came. I even began reading works on Germany after World War II, wondering if I could find similar traces of cultural disintegration and a depressive sense of decline. Accounts of high rates of suicide and personal decline in some of this literature reinforced my belief in the idea that defeat works to accelerate both cultural and bodily decay. However, another dramatic interview with a different militiaman changed the course of my thinking. This encounter made me see the relation between the culture of defeat and the sense of decay in a radically different light.

Paul: Decomposition

Paul was another fighter I interviewed for my PhD research, and I became particularly close to him. I had already known him superficially as a kid: he was the son of the concierge where my mother's maternal aunt lived. It was an apartment I often visited in my youth. For the same reason, I also knew Paul's wife, Rose, from when we were children. Her mother cleaned and cooked at my aunt's house in the 1960s and early 1970s, and I saw her on many occasions there when she accompanied her mother. For some time in the 1970s, Rose, in her early teens, helped her mother. It was when I came back to Beirut, after leaving for Australia, and was visiting my aunt in 1978 that I saw her again. And to my surprise, she was now married to Paul. He was already a militiaman of some standing, simply based on his involvement in many crucial battles in the early stages of the war. People in the building referred to him as Rayyess Paul (meaning "Chief Paul"). He described it to me in an interview once: "When the fighting is intense it is always 'Rayyess Paul, we need bread,' 'Rayyess Paul, we need water.'"

Paul's father, the concierge, died, along with occupants of the first-floor apartment when the building was bombed in the first year of the war. Paul got the Phalangist Party to help him financially so he could fix the first-floor apartment, and he moved into it. The ground floor where he grew up was left, and is still, in ruins. He didn't pay any rent, but he continued to service and "protect" the building. I saw Paul and Rose on many other visits since, and Paul was the first militiaman I interviewed for my thesis in 1984. I've stayed many times in their first-floor apartment when in Lebanon for research for weeks on end from the mid-1980s to the mid-1990s (my aunt had died by then).

This brief history above is to highlight that I had a certain degree of intimacy with both Paul and Rose. It was this intimacy that allowed me to note a slow but marked deterioration in Paul's physical and mental health over the years and until Paul died in 2006. Already in 1998, Paul had to go to hospital because of heart problems. He was nonetheless still chain-smoking when I saw him that year. He gave me a very disaffected interview in which he pointedly noted that "people in the building have stopped calling me Rayyess.... I am back to being Paul, the son of the concierge," he said bitterly. What he did not say, but I knew, was that he was not just the son of the concierge, but effectively the concierge now. Given that he was still occupying the first floor of the apartment without paying rent, the owner of the building had agreed to let him do so in exchange for working as the concierge. After telling me he was back to being the son of the concierge, he perceptively added, "Isn't that what this war was about? Rich people got people like me to put their life on the line protecting them, and once they've finished with us, they kept their wealth and dumped us in the garbage bin?" During that interview, Paul was already totally obsessed with the Syrian army in Lebanon: "We are occupied by a Muslim country. And they control everything.... Will I be able to go and pray in Saint Elie [a Beyrouth cathedral] next Christmas? I am not sure." He then said, without a hint of irony, "We in Lebanon are famous for our freedom; even when we were fighting, we freely and openly abused each other. Now, look at everyone whispering. Since when do people do politics in Lebanon by whispering? That's what has happened to us."

There was no doubt that I could identify with some of what Paul was saying. Even at the American University of Beirut, I had noted that, for the first time in my experience of public politico-intellectual chit chat in Lebanon, people were more "careful" and worried about who could hear what they were saying. It was beyond doubt that the Syrian Army brought with them a political authoritarianism that was largely foreign to Lebanon's political and intellectual culture and that this authoritarianism weighed oppressively on those involved, however marginally, in politics. But there was no doubt that Paul was also linking this situation to changes that he was himself experiencing, and the situation was making his experience of these changes particularly intense. He was finding it hard to get any paid job, and Rose had reverted to cooking for households as her mother did thirty years ago. In 1999, I witnessed a full-blown argument between Paul and Rose because he was drinking and smoking too much. And Rose looked at me and said, in front of him, "He hit me. He's never hit me before. Why don't you tell Ghassan how you hit me, war hero [*yaa batal*], go on." It was an awful moment, and he told her, "Shut up. Shut up. Go away and leave us alone." She said, "I'll go. But not because I am afraid of you. I just hope Ghassan can talk some sense into your head." Paul was clearly very ashamed of himself, and when she left, he said, "I know I shouldn't have done that. I know that's not something you approve of. But I've had it. I've had it. It's not her fault. But I've had it." And he started sobbing.

Over the next two years, Paul's health deteriorated, and he had a continuous smoker's cough. Though he managed to get the owner of the building to pay him a small sum for his work as a concierge (it was, in fact, Rose who was doing most of the work), his economic position was even more precarious than it had been. Rose's brother, who lived in Australia, became unemployed and was no longer able to help them financially. His obsession with the Syrians, however, grew and he talked endlessly and carelessly about resistance. Even other ex-militiamen were pointing out to me that he was not careful and that they would not be surprised if the Syrians arrested him and put him in jail at any moment. One of them, though, said, "Hopefully the Syrians will notice that he is just *katteer hakeh* [a big talker] and he doesn't have it in him to do any of the things he says he will do. The only thing he can do is cough on the Syrians until they run away."

In 2003, I took up a visiting professorship at the American University of Beirut. I lived in an apartment near the university, which is in what, in war parlance, was designated as West Beirut (the area of the city that was under Muslim/leftist control during the war). I called Paul to tell him that I was going to be in Beirut for a while now, and said to him that he and Rose should come and visit me and meet my wife and daughters, who were with me this time. He said he couldn't wait to see me and meet my family and that he had something important to tell me but that he "cannot go to *manta'etun* ["their area," i.e., the Muslims' area]." It was indicative of the way people like him continued to think themselves in a state of war at the time, despite the war having ended, officially, thirteen years earlier.[4] Two weeks later, Paul rang me and said: "How come you haven't visited me yet?" His eagerness was a bit surprising, and I explained that I was settling in and teaching, which takes time. He said: "Come soon and bring your tape recorder. I have something important to tell you."

When I finally saw Paul and Rose a month later, Paul seemed pleased to see me, but he also came across as overanxious and hyped-up. He also looked like he had aged a lot in a very short time, and there was a noticeable nervous twitch in his right eye. Rose took me aside and said: "He has not been very good." She told me, "Ma'o mitl hastiria" (He has something like hysteria). She started to tell me that the doctor had given him tablets, and was about to say more, but Paul was very eager to talk to me. He kept calling me and asking me to come to the living room. He then asked me to sit down and activate my tape recorder. I did, and he immediately asked:

PAUL: Did Rose tell you? Did she tell you?

ME: Tell me what?

PAUL: How I got arrested

ME: No. What happened? Why did you get arrested?

PAUL: Some *darak* [gendarmes] came here from the police station asking for me. I wasn't here. They told Rose that I should go and see them. So I did. And before I know it, they arrested me and put me in a cell. I kept saying, "What have I done? What have I done?" but they said, "We don't know." Finally, one of them I've known for many years came to me and said: "It's not us. It's the Syrians." I said to him: "You should be ashamed of yourself. You are Lebanese police and you're doing what the Syrians ask you to do." He just couldn't say anything.

DECAY AS DECLINE IN SOCIAL VIABILITY | 117

> But then the next day, these guys came. They handcuffed me and put a bag over my head and suddenly I was being driven for a long time, I am not sure where to. When we arrived, they left me blindfolded and handcuffed and put me in a cell. Then they walked me somewhere, made me sit down, and took the bag off, and here I was looking at these three guys. I immediately knew who they were. Syrian *mukhaabaraat* [intelligence officers]. And the guy looked at me and he said with a Syrian accent: "So, Rayyess Paul, we hear you want to re-create the Lebanese Forces and fight us, do you? Don't you know that it is illegal for the Lebanese Forces to exist?"
>
> I looked him straight into his eyes, and I said: "It's not up to the Syrians to decide what is illegal and what is not illegal in Lebanon." I swear to you he was furious, and he started sweating. He got up, and he whacked me across the face to the right and the left. There wasn't much I could do. I kept thinking how shameful it is that the Lebanese *darak* have helped deliver me to the Syrians. *'Ayb. 'Ayb.* [Shameful! Shameful!]

Paul was looking very angry, distraught, and nervy now. He was breathing heavily and perspiring, and I was a bit scared that he was going to have a heart attack. But he continued talking.

> PAUL: I've spent days and nights not far from here [*he pointed to the street outside*] under heavy Syrian bombardments. I got hit by a bullet in my leg here and Sheikh Bashir was walking around and he saw me and he said, "You need to go to hospital," and I said to him, "I am not moving from here until the Syrians go." They thought they will cow us into submission, and they did not succeed. That's where the real battle ended. And then the politicians started playing their dirty games. We were defeated by politicians, not on the battlefield. And look at us now. You go to a Lebanese police station and you end up being interrogated by a Syrian. *Kess ekht hal haaleh. Shee ma byenhamal.* [Fuck this situation. It is unbearable.]

As he screamed the last sentence, Paul got up, put his two hands underneath the coffee table in front of us where the tape recorder and the coffee cups were, and threw everything flying up in the air. Needless to say, I was looking at Paul, stunned and worried that he might harm himself, as he looked completely out of control. But he quickly calmed himself down. He looked embarrassed but still angry. "Maa twehkhizneh" (Forgive me), he said, "bass shee hakikatan ma byenhamal" (but it is really something unbearable).

From the corner of my eye, however, I see Rose coming toward us with tears in her eyes. She was looking angry rather than worried, and said, "See what I mean?—he's lost it completely. It's become like this every day. He just looks for some reason to be violent. Did he tell you that he got arrested? Did he tell you why? Or did he make up yet another one of his heroic resistance stories?"

"What?" I said. Paul looked at her and started screaming at the top of his lungs: "Shut up! Shut up. You bitch." But Rose was clearly unstoppable. She looked at me and said:

> He got arrested because he was telling someone that he would be happy to make some money selling drugs if someone can provide him with the merchandise. The guy turned out to be a policeman. If it weren't for Mr. Firas [a local politician and businessman, and an ex-Lebanese Forces local leader who was Paul's superior during the war], he would still be in jail. Ever since that date, he starts telling himself, or whoever is around, these made-up stories, and they always end up with him having a violent fit. I am sick of it. He hit me again last month.

As she talked, Paul continued to say: "Shut up. Just shut up. You bitch. They did hit me." He said, "They did hit me," four times in a row. Then he went and picked up the table and put it back where it was, picked up the tape recorder too, and just sat down on the sofa looking dazed.

While it took me a bit of time to fully understand what had just unfolded before me, it was clear that it was not safe to leave Rose with Paul, and it was not safe to leave Paul by himself. I stayed with Rose, and we arranged with Mr. Firas's help for Paul to be taken to a psychiatric clinic. He stayed there for a few days and was put on stronger medication. I have seen Paul and Rose a couple of times since that day. The pills he received succeeded at pacifying him, but he looked like a shell of his previous self. Rose had her unmarried sister move from North Lebanon and come and live with them in Beirut.

From the Stench of Defeat to the Stench of the Fantasy of Defeat

For what are more or less obvious reasons, Paul's fabulation transformed the way I looked at the discourse of defeat. It made me suspect that in the form it continued to exist after the war, the importance of the discourse for the militiamen I was researching was anything but simply its status as an expression and representation of actual experience. Paul—the son of the concierge who rose during the war to become "Chief Paul" but by the end of the war saw himself return to being the son of the concierge—is paradigmatic of a class of militiamen who neither managed to steal enough money to become one of the postwar nouveau riche, nor had enough social, cultural, or educational capital to reintegrate in a relatively successful way in postwar society. There is no doubt that the defeat they experienced had an objective basis in reality. It contributed to accentuating their feelings of belonging to a declining social group, and to experience that sense of decline personally. But there was a lot more to them hanging on to this experience well after it happened than the explanatory function they have given it. In what follows, I will argue that while defeat can be seen as an original accelerator of their sense of decline and decay, clinging to its memory worked in the opposite direction. Paradoxically, it became an antidecay "maintenance" mechanism, a desperate attempt at forging for themselves what I will call "a fantasy of viability" that made life bearable and livable. To understand this, we need to understand the importance of social fantasy in the composition and decomposition of the human social subject.

The Durkheimian distinction between social and psychological facts is foundational to the social sciences. While it mainly aims to distinguish between collective and individual phenomena, one of its other corollaries is the idea that the individual social subject is more than a biological subject. Importantly, though, this does not mean that the social subject is not *also* a biological subject. It is because of this that the decay of the human body associated with aging is intricately entangled with social processes. Clearly aging itself is never a "purely" biological process, since it is affected by the history of the social practices (both working and leisure-time practices) that a body has engaged in, as well as all kinds of nutritional, environmental, and psychosocial factors that affect health.

At the end of the war, the militiamen I was working with were all reaching their forties, showing not only signs of their age but also what looked to me like signs of premature aging. They all invariably led and continued to lead an unhealthy life of heavy smoking and drinking, with a marked absence of any form of exercise. Most of them were very visibly overweight. And they clearly carried the weight and the scars of the war they fought for about fifteen years. Because I was the same age as they were, I could very clearly see, even if at a simple observational level, that they were aging in a more pronounced way, and far more rapidly, than I was: their hair was grayer, their wrinkles were more pronounced, they tired more quickly when we went for a walk, and they invariably had many more health issues than I did. Their conversation was becoming already increasingly marked by the sharing of medical problems and more general aches and pains. This process of rapid aging continued to intensify over the next twenty years.

Already, it can be seen from the above that the "natural" process of bodily decay associated with aging is not purely biological. At the same time, it is also clear that just as one's biological being declines, one's social being can also decline: one's status, one's social power, one's capacity to earn money. But all aspects of one's social being do not need to decline together. Parts of one's social existence may thrive—one's status or one's business, for instance—while one's body is decaying. In such circumstances, the social can have an effect of slowing the overall, and even the strictly bodily, decaying process of the social subject. Unfortunately, this was not the case for the militiamen. "The social world gives what is rarest, recognition, consideration, in other words, quite simply, reasons for being," Bourdieu famously wrote. Accordingly, "one of the most unequal of all distributions, and probably, in any case, the most cruel, is the distribution of symbolic capital, that is, of social importance and of reasons for living," and "there is no worse dispossession, no worse privation, perhaps, than that of the losers in the symbolic struggle for recognition, for access to a socially recognized social being, in a word, to humanity" (Bourdieu 2000, 241). The militiamen were undoubtedly an example of social subjects located at the wrong end of this distributional process. While war society had offered them the opportunity to exist in a meaningful manner, postwar society left them with no means of self-realization. They had no fulfilling jobs, they had no prospect of a better social future, and they were getting poorer.

For Paul, as for many other former militiamen, this was compounded by a loss of recognition and respect. This was not just about people not calling him "chief," though that was crucial. Paul, once a genuinely feared fighter, was now laughed at by his companions, the very people who used to fear him—such as the person I quoted earlier saying about him that he "talked too much" but the only way he could hurt the Syrians would be by coughing at them. Even Rose mocked his warrior status by sarcastically calling him "Mr. War Hero."

It is in looking at the above that the importance of "fantasies of the self" come to the fore. The concept of fantasy here is not used in the sense of something that is opposed to reality. It has a psychoanalytic genealogy. It signifies a mode of imagining and staging oneself in a way such that what we are becomes entangled with what we aspire to be. If we see the social subject as a strictly sociobiological entity that seeks to satisfy bodily needs, social status, and financially fulfilling socioeconomic positions in society, we will come to a very bleak conclusion regarding the militiamen. Having lost their health, their warrior status, and their income as fighters, the loss of social recognition and respect, and their inability to get a decent job, there was very little left to stop them from accelerating toward oblivion and disintegration. However, if we add to these social and biological dimensions of being the psychosocial dimension of fantasy, we note that there was, in fact, something left: they had their fantasy of themselves as defeated warriors. This is how the discourse of defeat ends up having a positive antidecaying function.

The militiamen slowly realized that being "a defeated warrior" was infinitely better than being an unemployed and unemployable person with no social worth living on the margins of the spaces where economic and moral viability was constructed. Unlike such a sorry figure, a defeated warrior is still a warrior. On a good fantasy day, it is someone who can plan or at least dream of "resistance." But even warriors who are not planning a future "resistance" are people whose past could still help define them as viable beings in the present, if by nothing other than the respect they can still summon. It is in this sense that it is important to recognize the function of social fantasies as "maintenance mechanisms" that work at slowing the decaying of the social subject. But just like any other dimension of social being, social fantasies can themselves decay. This is what we witnessed in the case of Paul.

Social fantasies are more particular, less structural, and less all-encompassing variants of myths. In that sense, they share myths' crucial social function as a mode of staging the viability of the subjects that are created through them, protecting such subjects from symbolic disintegration, and as a counterentropic technology aimed at slowing down the inevitable material decay of the social, and even the subject's biological decay. But at the same time, social fantasies—again, like myths—need a minimal empirical anchor for them to thrive and perform their function. If not, rather than preventing a society or a social group from decaying, the fantasies become groundless and turn into mere hallucinations. They themselves begin to decay and disintegrate. Here we come to an important difference between societal myths and the social fantasy of a particular group. In the case of myths, the whole of society conspires in struggling to maintain the material conditions for the flourishing of the myths that in turn sustain it. In the case of a group's social fantasy, this reproduction is dependent on its compatibility with the dominant fantasies of society as a whole. This compatibility does not always exist.

The Lebanese state, a neoliberal state *avant la lettre*, has never been into the production and distribution of social goods: just as it is not into the distribution of social welfare, it is not into the distribution of collective psychological help. As such, the militiamen of the Lebanese civil war were left to find their own private means of maintaining their viability in postwar society. The fantasy of the defeated militiaman was a private means of sustaining the self. It helped to marginally protect these men from facing the process of socioeconomic and bodily decay that they were experiencing. But it was not actively supported by the state, nor did the state feel responsible for reproducing the material anchors on which the fantasy was dependent. In the early postwar stages, the material anchors were more readily available. Social groups still spoke the language of conflict, which was transported into the political as opposed to the military arena. Just as importantly, even the urban environment of decaying infrastructure and crumbled war-torn buildings helped to anchor a sense of continuation of the state of war (see Kanafani 2017).

But the fantasy became harder and harder to sustain as Lebanon moved away from the civil war, not only because of postwar urban and financial reconstruction but also because the ruling classes that participated in the civil war decided to hide their responsibility for it by blaming the figure of the militiaman. "The combatant" (*al muhaareb*) increasingly became, in the early twenty-first century, construed as a vilified figure. "The combatant" was portrayed not as the means through which war was conducted, but as the very causal force that led the war to happen. The state had never actively helped inflate the social status of the militiamen, and now it was actively working to deflate it. The state was also actively working at removing the memory of the war and demarcation lines. While the militiamen still wanted to cling to the language of "East Beirut and West Beirut," they were increasingly alone in doing so.

It is in the above sense, then, that the fantasy—the militiamen's last resort in the face of their accelerating biological and social decline and decay—was itself decaying, becoming increasingly irrelevant and nonreproducible, as we saw dramatically in Paul's case. Perhaps that stench of death I kept smelling when in touch with the militiamen was not so much the smell of defeat as much as the smell emanating from the disintegrating fantasy of defeat. The latter, again as we saw graphically in the case of Paul, compounded its decay with the rot of the social and biological body of the warrior, which it could no longer stop from decaying.

A Concluding Note: Toward an Olfactory Ethnography

In a search for *decay*'s synonyms, one might come across words such as *ruins, disintegration, decline, degeneration*, and *deterioration*. Yet such terms offer us a partial understanding of *decay*. They leave out both the visual sense of dread and, most importantly, the unbearable smell that the experience of decay implies. These are better communicated with another class of synonyms such as *decompose, rot, putrefy, go bad, go off, spoil*, and *fester*. "Jazz is not dead," Frank Zappa once quipped, "it just smells funny." While spoken in jest, it is a reminder of the complex sensory world that decay entails. Indeed, it is hard to read someone describing an experience of decay without reference to its stench. The overwhelming and undescribable stench of death mentioned above looms as a limit experience on the horizon. As in Baudelaire's poem, also mentioned in the introduction:

> The sky regarded as the carcass proud
> Oped flower-like to the day;
> So strong the odour, on the grass you vow'd
> You thought to faint away. (Baudelaire 1869, 11)

And according to the Nirvana Sutra, even the gods stink when they decay. The sutra notes five signs of decay affecting heavenly beings when their lives are about to end: (1) their clothes become soiled, (2) the flowers on their heads wither, (3) their bodies become dirty and smell bad, (4) they sweat under the armpits, and (5) they do not feel happy, wherever they may be.[5]

It is interesting that Ann Laura Stoler, in her essay "Imperial Debris," where she concentrates on the trail of ruins and ruination that colonialism leaves behind, encounters the stench of decay in many places, but her gaze at them from a ruins perspective reduces them to precisely that: ruins without the sensory and affective dimension that is attached to them. This is so despite choosing as an epigraph for her essay (Stoler 2008, 191) these lines from a Derek Walcott poem:

> The world's green age then was a rotting lime
> Whose stench became the charnel galleon's text.
> The rot remains with us, the men are gone.[6]

This collapsing of decay into "ruins," crucial for the rich concept of imperial ruins that she develops, continues as she treats Fanon's reference to the "tinge of decay" that marked the aftermath of direct French colonial rule in Algeria:

> As Frantz Fanon wrote in his study of the extensive mental disorders that followed French rule in Algeria, it is the "tinge of decay"—the indelible smack of degraded personhoods, occupied spaces, and limited possibilities—that were (and remain) hardest to erase. They are also the hardest to critically locate. Fanon worked between two poles of decay: at one pole was an evocative figurative sense that situated the breakdown of persons, their pathologies, and mental disabilities as imperial effects. As he argues, it was more than the future of such patients that was already "mortgaged" by the "malignancy" of their psychological states. "A whole generation of Algerians" who were subject to "generalized homicide" would be "the human legacy of France in Algeria."
>
> But the ruinous "tinge of decay" for Fanon was never figurative alone. At the other pole lay the material, tangible, and physical destruction of Algerian landscapes, drained swamps, burnt-out homes, and corroded infrastructures of over a century of French rule and nearly a decade of colonial war. To work between these two poles is to acknowledge both the potential and the problems in sustaining a balance between the analytic power that to ruin carries as an evocative metaphor and the critical purchase that it offers for grounding processes of decomposition and recomposition, degradation, and decay. These latter processes are of our time as they reactivate the traces of another. (Stoler 2008, 195)

This is not to take anything away from Stoler's essay, which is both imaginative and analytically and politically powerful. It is to argue, however, that despite making all the gains she does, Stoler also misses a whole important dimension of what she wants to analyze by thinking her "ruins" in such a nonsensory way. Nor is this, it should be added, about imposing on her questions she does not want to contemplate, for this is entirely in line with her own questioning. As she notes at the beginning of a section where she ends up noting that the resonance between Walcott's "rot that remains" and Fanon's "tinge of decay" is striking: "Perhaps the most critical task is to address, if not answer, a question prompted again by Derek Walcott, which provides the epigraph for this article. What constitutes, what he so searingly captures in 'Ruins of a Great House,' 'the rot that remains' when the men are gone? What are the forms that rot can take? What does it corrode, from what interior spaces does it take hold, and where is it that it remains?" (Stoler 2008, 200). My point is not to reduce all decay to organic decay. But at the same time, I do want to argue that this olfactory dimension is more metonymic

DECAY AS DECLINE IN SOCIAL VIABILITY | 125

than metaphoric: it connects us to an unavoidable sensory-affective dimension of decay that needs to be captured ethnographically if we are to fully answer questions such as "What form does rot take?" This is the sensory-affective dimension where Fanon was particularly at home and which made his experience of a "tinge of decay" a nonmetaphoric one. Nietzsche is also at home in this domain:

> May I still venture to sketch one final trait of my nature that causes me no little difficulties in my contacts with other men? My instinct for cleanliness is characterized by a perfectly uncanny sensitivity so that the proximity or—what am I saying?—the inmost parts, the "entrails" of every soul are physiologically perceived by me—smelled.
>
> This sensitivity furnishes me with psychological antennae with which I feel and get a hold of every secret: the abundant hidden dirt at the bottom of many a character—perhaps the result of bad blood, but glossed over by education—enters my consciousness almost at the first contact. If my observation has not deceived me, such characters who offend my sense of cleanliness also sense from their side the reserve of my disgust—and this does not make them smell any better. (Nietzsche 1967, 233)

In this sense, an ethnography of decay, unlike an ethnography of ruins, would have to capture decay, bodily and sensually. In the case of the militiamen I discussed above, articulating their social and symbolic decay to their organic decay did not mean simply that the organic was always social; it also meant that the social and symbolic was also organic and, as such, an organic stench was continuously entangled with social and symbolic decay. This is why I felt it necessary not only to analyze and intellectualize the social injustice that lies within this decay but also to try and help the reader experience its stench and feel the disgust of being present in its proximity. I have only timidly gestured toward it, but it seems to me that an ethnography of decay that can fully convey its subject matter can only be a disgusted ethnography.

Notes

I would like to thank Michael Jackson and Sami Hermez for reading and commenting on an early draft of this chapter.

   1. The Lebanese Forces was formed through unifying the Christian militias during the Lebanese civil war. In the aftermath of the war, in 1990, they were transformed into a political party. The Syrian army, which for all practical purposes occupied and controlled Lebanon after the war, banned the party in 1994. It remained banned until

2005, when the Syrian occupation was ended following what became known as the Cedar Revolution.

2. The Phalangists were the main Lebanese Christian militia at the beginning of the civil war.

3. I showed it to him. He agreed to its accuracy and said, "Use it after I die." (He died in 2011, but I also asked his son's permission to publish it.) To be clear, I am not saying here that what Tony believes has triggered his paralysis is necessarily correct. I am neither inclined, nor qualified, to make a judgment regarding this. But nor do I want to rush into explaining his symptoms as "war trauma" even if this seems obvious. Again, I am not qualified to make a judgment regarding this. But I am interested in the connections he has made between defeat and his symptoms, not in terms of their veracity, but as a dramatic individual manifestation of the more culturally and collectively pervasive mode of thinking about defeat and decline that I am analyzing.

4. Some of my militia informants still think this way today, more than thirty years after the war has ended.

5. Nirvana Sutra, s.v. "five signs of decay," Soka Gakkai Nichiren Buddhism Library, accessed December 15, 2020, https://www.nichirenlibrary.org/en/dic/Content/F/87.

6. Thanks to Bart Klem for directing me to this reference at the early stages of this project.

10

RELATIONAL DECAY

White Helpers in Australia's Indigenous Communities

Cameo Dalley

It started with a cough. Well, maybe the sore came first. The stench being emitted from the sore was remarkable given the sore's size, something akin to an olive. A couple days previously, I had noticed a small red mark just above my elbow, an insect bite probably, but at the time I'd not thought much of it. On the second or third day, my arm felt hot, tight, and swollen, and it seemed like it was time to act. Wincing at the pain, I gently and then more forcibly squeezed the sore into a tissue. A thick green pus with a consistency like toothpaste oozed out until what remained was a deep, red, angry hole. Pleasure and relief washed over me. "It should be right now," I told myself as I peered down at my arm. I bathed the sore in a diluted antiseptic solution and put a small bandage over the top to stop it from weeping on my bedsheets.

The next morning, I gingerly peeled back the bandage to check the wound. Overnight, the sore had refilled and was now fuller and angrier than the previous day. This triggered a renewed attention to my skin: I now looked more intently at what had been small irritations on other parts of my body, one on my chin and another on my leg. Both now exhibited the telltale green pus. I went outside to smoke and contemplate a course of action. I rolled a cigarette and inhaled deeply before coughing and spluttering, launching a gelatinous wad of mustard-colored phlegm across the yard and into the dirt. How had it come to this? Since I'd started fieldwork in the remote Aboriginal community of Mornington Island in northern Australia, my body had been in a slow state of decay that I'd been reluctant to observe or acknowledge.

It was only some days later, when I started to feel generally unwell, that I dragged my putrid body to the local health service. The waiting room was air-conditioned and had the clinical, austere functionality of a room able to be hosed out and disinfected with ease. I slipped my dirty sandals off my tanned feet and lay down on the bench with my cheek pressed on the cold metal. Most Aboriginal people wanting to see a doctor chose to wait outside in the heat, where they could watch the passing traffic, smoke, and eat. Outside, children could play without worrying that they were disturbing sick patients or, more to the point, provoking the ire of medical staff. Aboriginal people, many of whom referred to me using a kin term, wandered in and out, some clutching plastic bags with freshly dispensed prescription medicines. Some paused to ask, "You right?," to which I would nod and close my eyes again.

Eventually the nurse called my name and ushered me into a small room to take my blood pressure and the details of my ailment before a doctor would see me. At the time, there were only about one hundred *marndagi* (Whitefellas, in local parlance) living in the community, and most of us were somewhat acquainted. We exchanged brief pleasantries before she moved on to the reason for my visit.

"What can we help you with today?"

"I've got a sore," I told her, lifting my elbow up toward her. "I think it might be infected."

"That's staph," she said, looking unimpressed. "Anything else?" she asked.

"I've also got a bit of a cough," I replied. She listened to my chest, telling me to breathe in and out as she pressed the cool face of a stethoscope onto my skin. "You've probably got pleurisy," she said nonchalantly before launching into a lecture. "You really must take better care of yourself," she said. "People see you walking around town. That's really mad, you know!" I laughed. Like most Aboriginal people living in the community, at the time I didn't have a car. Aside from the odd lift that I could sponge, walking (also referred to as the "Foot Falcon" after the iconic Australian car, the Ford Falcon) was my only mode of transport. My laughter incensed her. "It's serious, you know!" What the nurse seemed to be getting at was that my bodily decay was not at all separate from a view, held by some Whitefellas living in the community, that I was becoming too socially close to Aboriginal people.

At that point I'd spent about six months living full-time in the Aboriginal community on Mornington Island. Being far from my friends and family, I had embraced the Aboriginal polity around me, doing what I could to "fit in," trying hard to become recognized as kin. After all, this was the expectation of my chosen field of anthropology and part of my transition from an outsider to the highly feted insider status. I was so focused on this endeavor that I had allowed my basic health care to lapse. I'd given up on eating anything nutritious: the community store provided few appealing options that didn't come in brightly colored packets and filled with preservatives to keep them alive across the long journey from the Australian mainland. Wilted vegetables and bruised fruit far past their best sat gloomily in boxes at the store, condensation running down their flesh, their sad tears ignored by most shoppers. Instead I drank soft drink (soda), ate potato chips and chocolate, and made my way through packets of low-quality, high-fat frozen meat whose volumes were intended to feed extended Aboriginal families. I'd half-heartedly taken up smoking, the roll-your-own cigarettes a welcome preoccupation to fill the long awkward silences and waiting around associated with "island time." I couldn't remember the last time that I'd purposefully exercised. It was bloody hot, after all, and not having a car meant that I was doing a lot of incidental exercise, wasn't I?

White Helpers in Remote Australia

My experience of somatic decay and the nurse's comments have given me pause to reflect on the role that decay plays in structuring relationships between Indigenous people and the non-Indigenous people who go to work in remote Australia. Here I refer to these people as "white helpers." At the heart of these relationships is an essentially unresolvable tension. On the one hand, community development discourses encourage helpers to want "in" with Indigenous people, to come to know them in socially intimate, culturally informed ways so that the projects they're sent to deliver land sensitively and successfully among their intended audience. Yet generating this "in" can be fraught with the difficulties of navigating unfamiliar social and cultural terrain and becoming proximate to Indigenous people. This proximity can result in the kinds of bodily ill-health I've described. On the other hand, not enough "in" ends in accusations of being an exploitative careerist, maintaining a safe colonial distance while profiting off the exotic misery of Indigenous people. Many of these professionals take up remote positions to "do their time" before returning to the city, their résumés considerably improved.

Like most other health workers at the Mornington Island hospital, the nurse who tended to me was on a short-term contract. These often-lucrative contracts enable health workers, some of them on international work visas, to come to Australia and gain employment. Working in a remote community also enables newly qualified but inexperienced helpers the opportunity to treat conditions rarely encountered in the broader population. Syphilis, congenital heart conditions, trachoma, and rheumatic fever are just some of the ailments prevalent in the local Aboriginal population. Another common ailment is *Staphylococcus aureus*, also known as golden staph, a strain of skin flora that a portion of the population hosts in their nasal cavities. Under a weakened immune system and the right climatic conditions, the flora proliferate and colonize the body, sometimes resulting in the eruption of pus-filled sores like mine. These sores look so toxic that when the anthropologist Elizabeth Povinelli (2006, 31) presented hers at a North American medical service, she was (mistakenly) diagnosed with the deadly bacteria anthrax.

In the figuring of helpers, some are so desirous of an "in" that they succumb to decay, while another portion claims to cure it, and both are frowned on. The holy grail in remote Indigenous communities, then, is the white helper with chameleonic bodily qualities and a compartmentalized mind: a person able to blend into a foreign biotope without decaying but also firmly grounded in their own society. This person remains a mythical figure, however, and not only because of the impossibility of holding two contrasting modes of being in the world in a seamless embrace. Inevitably, at various points in one's life, most are called on by those with whom they share intimate social space to stake a claim to the places and people with whom they most belong. When it comes to remote Indigenous communities, at risk are the lauded figure of the white helper and the very idea that helping can help. In their place is the disingenuous and uninformed, ultimately another production of coloniality and an exercise in expanding and reaffirming its withering but controlling tendrils. In this chapter I explore the social and bodily contours of experience for white helpers, discuss their historical resonances, and contemplate what "relational decay" means in these settings.

In Australia, as in other development contexts, what brings white helpers to remote communities is based on particular racialized notions of Indigenous decay—bodily, societal, and cultural—and what can and should be done to ameliorate the symptoms of these states. Rafts of government initiatives fund helpers to live in these parts of Australia so that they can deliver various programs based on the well-worn trope of "closing the gap" of statistical inequity between Indigenous and non-Indigenous people. Nevertheless, much of what defines non-Indigenous people's experiences in these settings is related to their own autonomy relative to Indigenous people. This includes changes that they observe in their bodies, which are vulnerable to unfamiliar kinds of health decay and their social proximity to Indigenous people. It is the interplay between the social and pathological that defines decay, as Ghassan Hage has highlighted in the introduction to this volume. It is the intention of being "the helper" rather than being a person in need of help that erodes any expectation of becoming sick. The longer they remain in communities, the more their prospects of being a helper decay, replaced with more ambivalent engagements with Indigenous people. In this sense, their relationality to Indigenous people decays.

Ambivalence has been recounted in memoirs by helpers themselves (e.g., M.-E. Jordan 2005; Shaw 2009) and also by a small cohort of anthropologists who have made them their primary focus of study (e.g., Kowal 2015; Lea 2008). Of health workers in the Northern Territory, Tess Lea (2008, 211) observes: "They are well able to identify the discordance between the fractious complexity of Aboriginal existences they glimpse and the alternately uplifting or melancholy dot-pointed abstractions that they conscientiously reproduce as explanations for Aboriginal pathology. Their representations of their work are imbued with contradiction." But Lea's sympathetic animation of the figure of the remote bureaucrat and their experiences in and of decay is not an approach shared by all writing in this space. The anthropologist Gillian Cowlishaw (2010, 52), who has generally urged for studies of white helpers, also disparages such workers who "cannot know what they do" when it comes to the transformation of Indigenous people's lives.

A widely discussed account by writer Kim Mahood similarly typifies Cowlishaw's critique. Mahood (2012) detailed the bodily and mental decay of a fictive non-Indigenous worker who arrives in an Aboriginal community in Central Australia. Working in an understaffed, under-resourced Aboriginal art center, the worker whom Mahood calls "New Kartiya" begins her job enthusiastically, full of the hopes and expectations of being able to put her skills to good use. Over time, New Kartiya becomes overwhelmed by the demands of Aboriginal people, and she allows her physical and mental health to decay until it becomes necessary for her to leave the community to recover. "Kartiya are like Toyotas," Mahood quotes an Aboriginal woman as saying; the punch line to this phrase is "When they break down, we get another one." Presumably, New Kartiya is a real person, perhaps even someone who Mahood knew well, or a bricolage of people, and it's this familiarity that makes the rendering so evocative. Anthropologist Danny Fisher (2016, 187) has even suggested that Mahood herself is New Kartiya. Among colleagues who study white health workers, many have reveled in her characterization of what she describes elsewhere as "the white slaves, abject and ingratiating, whose desire to serve Aboriginal people undermines basic mutual respect" (Mahood 2015, 50). Some even describe Mahood's New Kartiya essay as "mandatory reading for anyone going into remote Australia."

Yet Mahood's satirical rendering of New Kartiya and others who wander into the frame reads as a thinly veiled attempt at casting aspersions on those who now work in the community she used to know—a rhetorical "What do you think you're doing in *my* community?" It's curious that Mahood's account of fictive New Kartiya eschews reflection on her own status, particular given its centrality to much of her other published work. In her memoir-inflected books *Craft for a Dry Lake* (2000) and *Position Doubtful* (2016), Mahood writes passionately about the intertwined nature of her family's settler history in Central Australia and the close association with Aboriginal people that it has entailed. Mahood seems to urge proximity, while she herself lives in the outskirts of Canberra among a different set of kin. As Mahood rightly points out, it's other Whitefellas who are the most critical of one another's motivations, each presuming that they know Indigenous people more intimately.

I recall my own feelings of indignation when confronted with a similar experience on Mornington Island. In 2016, during one of my return visits, the number of *marndagi* living on the island had grown to over one hundred. Men in particular were on the island working on an upgrade to the airstrip and the boat jetty. I'd never seen so many tanned, muscular *marndagi* lining up at the shop, their shopping baskets overflowing with frozen food, the black plastic handles straining as they shuffled toward the registers. During the same visit the Aboriginal family that I regularly stay with had loaned me their car so I could drive around the community and visit other Aboriginal families. When I arrived at one of these houses, a white woman pulled up in a car next to me; expecting to see an Aboriginal person in the driver's seat, she looked shocked. Taken aback, she reversed and drove off. Later, when we were introduced by Aboriginal friends, the woman told me that her first thought on seeing me had been, "Who the fuck are you?" I laughed, wondering who the fuck she was. She then asked me probing questions about how long I'd lived in the community and why I'd eventually left. Her questions felt accusatory, and I sensed in her the same types of feelings I had experienced when I first started doing fieldwork in the community.

Relations in Decay or Relations of Decay?

On Mornington Island, the trappings of moral and societal decay and their health manifestations seem omnipresent. Anthropologists writing before me have pathologized the community and the so-called destruction of Aboriginal culture and society, leaving remnants described by John Cawte (1972) as "cruel, poor and brutal nations" and David McKnight (2002) as a community "bereft of an identity." Cawte, McKnight, and a number of other scholars have written extensively of the damage done to Mornington Islanders' sociality since settler occupation of the region began in the late 1880s. A particular trigger for this damage has been high rates of alcohol consumption, patterns of intake that began to escalate among Mornington Islanders during the 1960s. Even the term "Mornington Islanders," which is now in common parlance, represents the forced coming together by missionaries of what were once distinct Aboriginal groups (Dalley, 2021; Dalley and Memmott 2010). Before the Presbyterian mission was established in 1914, Lardil, Yangkaal, and Kaiadilt Aboriginal people lived dispersed across the Wellesley Island archipelago. For many anthropologists working in Australia, including the renowned W. E. H. Stanner, it was the desire to witness and record the "degradation and decay of the essentially noble Aboriginal culture" in proximity to non-Indigenous people that drove their interest in ethnography (Cowlishaw 2017, 330).

What was seen as the inevitable end of days of and for Aboriginal people has been a feature of anthropological discourse in other parts of the world as well, particularly those with violent settler histories (Bessire 2012). More than just a reflection on societal or cultural decay, apocalyptic visions are a product of colonized Indigenous peoples' experiences of systemic ill-health and premature death. On Mornington Island the unexpected deaths of young people from suicide, accidents, and chronic health conditions are the source of considerable trauma, or what anthropologists have described for other remote Indigenous communities as a kind of "stress" or "existential stress" (Burbank 2011; Eickelkamp 2017, 240). It has been the fetishization of these forms of decay, and what Lea (2012, 112) describes as the resulting "emotional thrill of surfing crises," that justifies many of the policy interventions that take place in Indigenous people's lives. However, policy interventions are only one of the ways in which the state, and the policy makers and service providers that constitute it in remote Australia, grapple with decay.

The "make live or let die" politics of Indigenous lives, as Tanya Murray Li (2010) refers to it, is a contemporary manifestation of a particular biopolitics, where policies of paternalism (make live) and abandonment (letting die) sit alongside one another in the state's role as a care provider for Indigenous people (after Fassin 2009). Though the state in its many manifestations moves away from Indigenous people, such as through the withdrawal of basic services in some locations, in other places a different change is stealthily occurring. This change is reflected in an analysis of census statistics between 2006 and 2011 by demographers Nick Biddle and Francis Markham (2013). When examining the inward and outward migration of Indigenous and non-Indigenous people across seven location types, they found that the highest net migration of any sector (5.3 percent) was non-Indigenous migration to "remote dispersed settlements"—that is, "communities" (Biddle and Markham 2013). By and large these "migrants" are non-Indigenous people who move to communities to take up jobs, broadly tasked with ameliorating Indigenous disadvantage. On Mornington Island, the proportion of the non-Indigenous population has been growing over time and now constitutes about 12 percent of the total population (Dalley 2021, 87). This growth is evident across a number of employment sectors, including health and education.

The proximity with Aboriginal people that white helpers usually experience as part of their work contrasts with the distance that is maintained in residential patterns within the community of Gununa, where they live on Mornington Island. The settlement itself consists of about two hundred houses spread across a dozen or so residential streets, mostly Aboriginal housing provided by a local council. Hospital staff are accommodated in what is referred to as a "compound," a residential block that includes the health service, surrounded by six-foot fencing topped with razor wire and a locked gate. This spatial zoning and the materiality that accompanies it are potent symbols to Aboriginal people that they are not welcome. Among the health workers themselves, there were a range of opinions about why they were accommodated in this way. Some said that it reflected concerns about the need to protect non-Indigenous autonomy against the invasiveness of Aboriginal sociality. For instance, one white helper described to me how the compound enabled a separation, a buffer that allowed non-Indigenous people to evade what she called "all kinds of unreasonable requests," such as being visited by Aboriginal people at nighttime and asked for lifts or for money.

These socially and spatially created divisions mimic those of an earlier history: a remnant of the layout of the settlement as a Presbyterian church mission station. In the early settler history of the region, it was partly evidence of sexually transmitted infections among Aboriginal people that enabled the Presbyterian church to successfully lobby the Queensland government to establish a mission station on Mornington Island. At the time, traders were sailing through the region, often forcibly taking Aboriginal people to work as slave labor. Under the guise of protectionism, Aboriginal people were moved from around the Wellesley Islands to Mornington Island and settled in a camp at the mission station (Dalley and Memmott 2010, 115–16). This proximity was the first sustained contact that most Aboriginal people had had with *marndagi*; nevertheless, a strong sociospatial division was maintained in the local geography. While some Aboriginal people recall fondly their relationships to specific missionaries or to the arrival of Christianity, they do so while living through the disastrous impacts on language and cultural transmission. The most profound technique was the removal of Aboriginal children into dormitories, allowing only minimal contact with their adult family. Though most people alive during the dormitory times have now died, the trauma has had ongoing intergenerational impacts.

Relationality and Decay

Relationality is sometimes used to conceptualize sociality at the interface between people or more specifically groups of people (Brigg 2019; Moreton-Robinson 2017). Anthropologists emphasize the intimate ways in which these bonds are developed and performed over time, often in ways that transgress expected structural hierarchies (Carsten 2011). These relations are expressed and experienced in a multitude of ways, including the process by which Aboriginal people categorize and name non-Indigenous others. For example, the terms *balanda* in Arnhem Land, *marndagi* in the Gulf of Carpentaria, and *kartiya* (also *gardiya*) in parts of Central Australia and the Kimberley region are all used to refer to non-Indigenous people. As Stephen Muecke (2014, 262) pointed out in his own explanation of "turning into a *gardiya*," these terms do not necessarily apply to all people of the "non-Indigenous" category. Rather, they are used in zones of remote Australia to refer to those "who have been given a place in Indigenous Australia that they are more or less aware of, more or less accepting of." In Muecke's analysis, the situatedness of this ascription means that "if you turn into *gardiya* you can turn back again, as soon as you head south." As I and others have pointed out (Dalley and Martin 2015, 2; Merlan 2009, 304–5), *gardiya* and other categories that refer to non-Indigenous people do not exist as total social facts but exist in relation to Indigenous categories of being and are embedded in specific geopolitical contexts.

Non-Indigenous people working in remote Australia have sometimes been incorporated into Indigenous kinship systems through the granting of kin terms or what Redmond (2005, 234) describes as "extending the kinship web indefinitely outwards." Redmond continues, "The local kinship modality means that many different categories of relatives can be expected to contribute in different ways to the maintenance of not just a person's physical body but to their overall emotional well-being" (239). Though often referred to as "fictive," the application of kinship structures to include non-Indigenous people has been a means to stress social coherence rather than disjuncture in the interpretation of relations. Nevertheless, the seamlessness with which such terms are applied or adapted is sometimes the cause of disputes among Indigenous people. In 2017 Warren H. Williams, an Arrernte country music singer from Central Australia, stirred controversy by saying that non-Indigenous people should not be given "skin names" (quoted in Terzon and Simpson 2017). For Aboriginal people, "skins" are part of a broader kinship system that prescribes relationships and therefore behaviors between people living in a society. For example, people belonging to particular skin groups should not marry, while others within one's own skin group may be expected to support kin during ritualized initiation ceremonies. Williams's objection to the practice stemmed from his experiences at community meetings in Alice Springs, where, as he described it, non-Indigenous people too readily claimed to belong. It was Williams's view that rather than an attempt at symbolically recognizing socially intimate connections, these acts of figurative incorporation were intended by Indigenous people to act as formalized opportunities for material exploitation. In other words, it was expected that non-Indigenous people who received such gestures at social proximity would perform the kin relation by giving Indigenous people money or resources when they sought it.

What Williams's critique also hinted at was the misconception among non-Indigenous people that situatedness in the kinship milieu acts as a fixed ordering principle for the experience of social life. In reality, to keep this relation from decaying, one must continually cultivate and perform it. In 2007, during a yearlong stay on the island, I became incorporated into the kinship system, being categorized as the daughter (*kambin*) of a senior Lardil Aboriginal man then in his sixties. Over time this relationship became the indicator by which Aboriginal people reckoned their relationship to me: *yaku* (sister), *jembe* (cousin), and so on. Far from being a naturalized or inherent connection, my relationships with Mornington Islanders have been nurtured by return visits to the island in 2006, 2007, 2008, 2009, 2010, 2012, 2014, 2016, and 2018. The iterative nature of these returns over time has ensured some level of continued potency for kin relations.

Not everyone in the community sees me as kin or as in a kinship relationship that they choose to acknowledge. On Mornington Island in 2007, an Aboriginal woman whom I knew asked me for money, referring to me as her "daughter-in-law." As I had no small amounts of money at the time, I shrugged off her requests, telling her that I was "cleaned out." Because the woman's repeated attempts to get money from me and to perform my kinship relationship to her were unsuccessful, she finally shouted angrily, "Ah, you got no fucking family! You nothing!" I was also sometimes referred to (mostly humorously) as *wuurldijin*, a term from the local Lardil Aboriginal language meaning a person who has no one or no proximate family. This was mostly on account of being a childless woman without a long-term partner, something of a rarity among Mornington Islanders. The elapse of time is another indicator by which social proximity and relatedness decays. I often grasp for the names of children who have grown into adults and now have their own children: my familiarity with their physical appearance has faded over time. Similarly, many who used to know me well now don't recognize me or perhaps refuse to recognize me when I visit. Whereas I was once commonly known as an "auntie" or "sister," children often refer to me now as "Miss," the generic term used for white women in the community, reflecting that most are schoolteachers. In part this rejection of a relation highlights the significance of correctly performing a relationship, renewing it as a means of ensuring its vitality.

Decaying Relations

In 2016, while working in the remote East Kimberley region of Western Australia, I noticed a sore on my leg and the next day visited the local health service. I explained to them that the sore was exhibiting what I now know to be the green pus that I associate with a *Staphylococcus* infection. In the interim I have contracted staph several times, including an episode in 2014 that resulted in an extended hospital stay. Over time I've become intimately familiar with staph and its presentation; I know how my body will react when placed under a particular set of conditions. The more I understand about staph—that it lives within me or, more precisely, in my nose—the more I can put its symptoms down to the creative potential of my body itself. It seems quite extraordinary to me that although it will eventually precipitate decay, it first rapidly grows and disperses bacteria, like a flowering field bursting into life and spreading out a hypercolorful blanket all over my body. Under UV lighting, I imagine I'd glow like a Christmas tree covered in tiny neon bacteria baubles. The bodily decay experienced by those living in remote Aboriginal communities, though, does not always provide such productive visual schema to draw on or such relatively manageable symptoms.

Continued attention to the decay of others obscures our own view of ourselves, and the specter of relational decay is always avoided. It's easy to be dismissive of the desires of white helpers to be drawn into relational frames with Indigenous people, particularly when those expectations rarely come to fruition. White helpers are part of broader state-mandated processes imbued with fundamentally ameliorative stances about remote Indigenous people. Their presence is part of a colonial fantasy of the white savior that remains seductive. At the same time, unless non-Indigenous experiences of decay are narrated, what remains is a continuing fiction that it is only or predominantly Indigenous people that decay under trying conditions, not those who have been sent to help them.

During a visit to Mornington Island in 2018, I again met the woman whom I had encountered in 2016 while driving through the community. By then she had become the mother of a small baby fathered by a local Aboriginal man and had moved in to live with the man's extended Aboriginal family. After taking time away from work to have her child, she had (re)applied for a teaching job at the local school where she had worked but had been turned down. It seemed that her former colleagues now harbored suspicions about her, since her relationship within the local community had changed with the arrival of her son. When I saw her, she was in her last few days of living on the island: she had decided to return to her family, a few thousand kilometers to the southeast on the mainland. Just as her relational proximity to Aboriginal people had seemed assured, it slipped away again.

Note

Thanks to Akhil Gupta, Bart Klem, and Debra McDougall for their incisive comments on earlier drafts. Writing was supported by the McArthur Postdoctoral Fellowship in Anthropology at the University of Melbourne and the ARC Discovery Indigenous project IN180100055, "Beyond Recognition: Strengthening Relationality across Difference in Postcolonial Contexts," at the Alfred Deakin Institute for Citizenship and Globalisation at Deakin University.

11

DECAY, ROT, MOLD, AND RESISTANCE IN THE US PRISON SYSTEM

Tamara Kohn

To study decay is to observe and analyze ambiguous and multidimensional processes of transformation. Alongside decay that is understood to be degenerative, painful, dangerous, and potentially lethal, one often finds processes of generation, growth, resistance, and hope. While decay can appear as an expression of neglect—of entropy or the cost of nature taking control—it can also be understood as a structural condition that demands an active political response but is too often allowed to fester. I explore these and other ambiguities around *decay* (and the associated terms *rot* and *mold*) via a brief thought tour on the state of maximum-security prisons in the United States. Such prisons are where human bodies are often resolutely put "to rot" (SBS News 2018; News.com.au 2019). And while many do indeed perish there—"snapping down" (committing suicide), "snapping out" (going crazy), or being killed—some "snap up": they rise to the challenge of defying the decay and expectation of decay that is visible, audible, and otherwise sensed all around them.[1] In this chapter I explore the meanings of decay in this context and ask readers to challenge their expectations regarding the "total" embodied experiences of caged individuals and to recognize their unwitting participation in the ongoing reproduction of an ever-decaying carceral society.

Let us begin deep beneath the ground in a visiting booth in a maximum-security prison outside Philadelphia, where I was talking for six straight hours with Cush, an inmate who had, at that time, already served twenty-eight years in solitary confinement on death row.[2] I strained to hear and to remember his words as he spoke urgently into his phone receiver. We were deep into a conversation about his family, his martial arts practice experience "before," the studying, writing, and painting he had done in prison, and the legal casework he had managed successfully for fellow inmates. A guard opened the door to Cush's small holding cell and ordered him to move to the other one. Cush raised his voice in protest: "Why should we move?! The window's broken and we won't be able to see each other—I've been complaining about this for years, and it's never fixed! And look up there!" (He raised his voice and pointed energetically at the ceiling.) "Black mold. And the cells have it too." We moved to the other booth, and we both leaned in closer to the dirty, crazed pane of glass. He told me about guys in other cells who had asthma and one who had died from respiratory issues, and he said the mold was to blame: "You don't treat lions like this and dogs like this. But evil can only continue as long as it can hide."

I have thought a lot about Cush's words from that first visit in 2015 and the spirit he projects in person and in the hundreds of times we have corresponded. Arrested in his early twenties for a crime he claims he did not commit, he spent just under three decades in solitary confinement (and for the first nine years he had not even been sentenced). Please stop and try to imagine thirty years in a windowless moldy space six by eight feet with no view of the sky and the desperate sounds and smells of other people's suffering. In 2017, Cush's death sentence was vacated, and he was released into the general prison population, although he is still periodically placed in "the hole." He speaks in his letters about his exoneration and dreams for his future in freedom. He "snaps up" whenever he can—by naming and shaming; even when it results in his further isolation and punishment, he works to bring "evil" out of hiding as his guards and the state work to keep "evil" off the streets. The recognition of and abhorrence of decay is an important part of his quest for individual growth and creative productivity in a remote and isolating space that defies all expectations of such a possibility. As he says, it "feeds him."

I am starting with the palpable mold that I could see in the prison visiting booth and Cush's words about it, but in a sense such visible decay only gestures at a series of relationships that are built around the *ideas* of mold and decay. Indeed, many newer prison spaces are free of physical mold, but the ideas presented in this chapter around an expectation of decay associated with lack of care and the dismissal of human value are as relevant to those sites as they are to prisons that are physically molding and crumbling. Exploring these ideas of mold and decay involves considering relationships between prisoners and their (often) moldy, decay-filled environment, relationships between inmates and prison staff who are also exposed to and affected by structural and human decay, and relationships between individual voices of protest and the structures of power that react to silence them behind bars or in the bowels of solitary confinement.

Let us put this set of relationships in scalar context. I may draw in this discussion from one extraordinary individual I know well,[3] but there are 2.3 million people incarcerated at any given time (a figure that explodes to 10.6 million admissions annually when considering the huge traffic through smaller jails) (Sawyer and Wagner 2019), and when you add in people on parole and probation, there are at any one time 7 million people under correctional control by the justice system in the United States, the so-called land of the free.[4] There are more people of color in prison or on parole in the United States now than there were enslaved at the beginning of the Civil War (Alexander 2012). Prisoners are America's disappeared. Many factors have contributed over centuries to the disappearing act of mass incarceration—cultural legacies of slavery; poverty; gang and family violence; mental illness; conspicuous racial profiling, policing, and prosecuting; Nixon's war on crime; Reagan's war on drugs;[5] recidivism; "tough on crime" policies like "stop and frisk";[6] Clinton's "three strikes" rule;[7] the zero tolerance policy.[8] But all those policies and social conditions rest on a series of presumptions around human value—who has it and who does not, as well as how it is seen to live and grow (or not) in the body of the accused.

Not only are millions of individual inmates disappeared, in the sense that they are removed from everyday "free" life and from their families and social networks; they are also removed from some public's consciousness—some, not all, as there are some urban neighborhoods where thinking about selves or loved others in prison is a fearful reality. Ta-Nehisi Coates's extremely moving and important memoir *Between the World and Me* (2015) explores why.[9] But for those of us who do not carry that fear of being shot or arrested in our neighborhoods or who do not have loved ones behind bars, this is not the case. The more prison numbers increase in the United States, the larger the "public secret" becomes regarding how prisons are populated and what goes on inside them (Daniel 2006, 1). Any consciousness most of us do have comes not from our personal relationships with imprisoned individuals but from our contact with a range of fetishizing media representations of the people they might be, or that we imagine or desire them to be. And I believe that these representations fail us and fail our society by misleading us all, causing us to turn a blind eye.

Social theorists have examined the prison complex from a range of perspectives. Some describe the broad structural conditions that have supported the production and maintenance of the carceral institution, including the penalization of poverty, worlds of crime, and histories of prison architectures. Michel Foucault's *Discipline and Punish* (1977), for example, demonstrated that prisons were designed to be instruments of transformation (like hospitals) but failed bitterly from the start, only producing more violence. Abolitionists like Angela Davis (2003, 2012) have critically explored the prison complex's history and future in relation to modern capitalism, to slavery, racism, and segregation. Other researchers have homed in on how the system operates inside the prison walls, affecting the bodies and minds of inmates. Erving Goffman (1961), for example, described the ritual function of the "total institution" that produces a "mortification of self" in prisons and asylums through meaningless tasks—a "disculturalization" process that strips selfhood and perpetuates powerlessness. And there is a rich body of published, mostly biographical literature written by prisoners, ranging from stories of redemption to protest writing about the pain of incarceration and the racial injustices prisoners experience (e.g., Stanley "Tookie" Williams's redemption stories written for black youths; Ernie Lopez, writing on the arbitrary torture of black bodies; George Jackson, who penned on rage, on war).

These and many more are all critical works addressing big issues, revealing major injustices, and demanding reform. I would suggest, however, that they tend to divert our attention away from developing and "knowing" long-incarcerated individuals who refuse to be represented as generalizable victims and/or perpetrators of violence. They also refuse to allow Hollywood's fetishized representations of life inside substitute for the real thing. These are people who see themselves as political prisoners—freedom fighters for a larger cause that not only permits survival but allows them to make meaning in their lives. Evil in its many guises can only continue as long as it can hide.

You might think that I am exaggerating the "evil" meaning of mold. Surely, you think, mold in an old prison cell is just what you should expect—an expression of human neglect and "natural" decline, perhaps, but not a form of discipline? But mold in the free world and mold in prison are two different beasts. We attend to them differently.

Decaying Dwellings and Their Mold

The "natural world" always whittles away at seemingly solid structures, and occasionally it crashes into them violently—they crack, they weaken, they cave in. Pipes rust and structures get flooded. The decomposition of houses produces an industry of management and employs many skilled workers. When the decay is deemed unmanageable, there are structural systems in place to help safely dispose of it. When decay is manageable, the experts are expected to step in to fix, clean, rebuild, and even improve the extant structure. It is easy to imagine that most home-dwellers will engage with structural decay at some point. Some decay requires immediate attention; some can wait a bit.

There is an expected sense of urgency around building decay when it exposes people to risk—for example, collapsing ceilings, asbestos exposure, and black mold.[10] A prison inmate at Eastham unit in Texas who was once a contractor in the home-building industry attests to this urgency with reference to his previous work experience and raises a question at the end that I want to pursue:

> Anytime black mold is found present in an establishment, all people are relocated while the black mold is eliminated! Workers using paper face masks will go to such measures: if residential, all sheet rock and insulation are torn out and replaced along with any carpeting even suspected to have had moisture damage. Air ventilation ducts are sanitized or replaced. Industrial strength oil based Kilz primer paint is used throughout the home or establishment. That is before the new material and fresh finish paint. If industrial, with concrete walls (e.g., schools, rec centers), the paint is removed by using bens-o-matic torches and tools to scrape the burning paint. A stone soap and scrub brush are used on the porous concrete and then the abovementioned precautions are followed. Should these measures not be followed and black mold is again found in future inspections, the place is condemned! Why not here? Because we are convicted criminals? (Coffin and Washington 2017)

I would suggest that the answer to his final question is yes. Decay is a problem when it touches valued members of society. It is ignored when it touches the untouchables, even if they make its presence loudly known. This would appear to connect ideas about material "decay" (of spaces and things) with a public expectation (rampant in public discourse) that you do not just put people away for life or condemn them to death in prison: you put them there to rot.

Putting someone away "to rot" in a building that is also rotting deep in its most hidden cells of solitary confinement is a brutal act of violence not only on the bodies affected by their (moldy) environments but also on the body politic that allowed the institution to grow while at the same time turning a blind eye to its reality. This is not to say that publics don't think about prisons but, rather, to say that they are seduced by media and other popular representations of prisons to imagine them in a particular light. For some, an idea of prison for retribution embraces conditions of cruelty, and the punishment could never be too harsh—being in prison removes all qualities of personhood. For others, the idea of the prison as a place (out of public view) for people to "do time" produces an expectation of that time being unproductive, of no value, and thus meaningless. In all cases, the state of the prison, the mechanisms of control and punishment that are produced within it, and the sometimes aggressive and sometimes passive ways we react to its inevitability are all cultural productions that are felt to be natural and hence slip into our "nothing can be done about it" box of realities.

Prison policy-makers and managers in the United States alongside the private companies that prisons employ often produce and maintain decay.[11] This is part of what Davis has wisely noted: how the prison "produces the conditions of its own expansion, creating a syndrome of self-perpetuation" (2012, 67). The irony is important to notice here—that against the enforced and expected decay of spaces and persons, there is also a deliberate program of maintenance taking place.[12] But what if it were possible to halt this and produce something different? What if we could all override our expectations of spiritual and physical and environmental decline in prison with the recognition of human positive growth, of potential societal contribution, of something of value produced out of truly attending to and rejecting that which we have dismissed as a "natural" order (of separation from society and decay)? Mold is a particularly telling focal point. Simply as a mental exercise here, to help our decay-centered theorization, let us consider the *cultural production* of blue cheese—an orientation that manipulates a potentially degenerating and even toxic process to produce something regarded as valuable.

Claude Lévi-Strauss considered the way human "cultural" transformations of things in nature are both structured in relation to one another and given value. In pondering what he called *le triangle culinaire* (the culinary triangle), he described how, unlike (most) animals, which just eat foods found in their environments, humans often modify products to make them palatable (to humans)—they invest in the transformation of the foods that they ingest (using cultural tools such as fire and pots), and they accord the resultant foods different levels of prestige. To skip straight to the cheese: Lévi-Strauss would suggest that a fine blue-veined cheese is made by skillfully controlling with tools of culture the rotting process, which he described as natural (see Lévi-Strauss 1969; Leach 1970). Generally, a milk product that is totally left to its own devices over a long time (like a body left to rot in jail) is far from palatable (indeed, it may be extremely dangerous to ingest and would be best disposed of in a receptacle that will prevent it from contaminating anything else). A cultural process of guided fermentation, however, reveals delicious potential. The controlled growth of the dark mold in the cheese may become both "safe" and highly valued, not just to cheesemakers and connoisseurs, but potentially to whole nations of consumers. Roquefort is one of the moldiest of French cheeses, with its blue-green veins and dots of *Penicillium roqueforti* throughout; requiring great control and skill to produce, it is sometimes called "the King of Cheese." As such, this cheese features in state banquets and contributes value to the French tourist industry. The message I take away here is that it is not the mold itself that is the potential problem—what is important is what you do or do not do with it. This is not all trivial wordplay. Let us go back to the prison to see why.

The Bodies and Minds That Can Resist Rot

I send Cush books through Amazon. Sometimes we read them "together" (meaning we read them separately at around the same time and then write letters to each other about our thoughts). Recently I sent him Viktor Frankl's great memoir on surviving life in a Nazi death camp, *Man's Search for Meaning* ([1959] 2006). When he received it, he wrote this in his next letter:

> The book *Man's Search for Meaning* is one of the books I'd been looking to get my hands on again. I've read and studied it twice before.... This book is so significant to me. It is a book that tells the experience that I felt when put into this criminal Justice System and prison/death-camp. I was not prepared for an existence among a group of captives that had accepted the dehumanization and were active participants in the perpetuation of the torture of their fellow prisoners. Everything he describes is real and without sugar-coating.
>
> Have you seen the News about the internment calls that the USA is putting to the families who are asylum seekers? It is sickening to see history repeating itself in such a horrendous way. Fortunately, many are actively protesting and willing to go to jail to bring attention to

this inhumane treatment of people. They have literally taken infants (9 months old) from their mother's arms and put the babies and children into cages. This is madness!

. . . I feel as though another big step towards my freedom is about to be made. I'm preparing myself for the transition. I can't follow my dreams as if I will face no opposition. My goals will be challenged and in many circumstances vigorously opposed. I must continue to be well disciplined and focused on the process and planning of my projects. Like U.

The heat and sunshine has given me a burnished bronze healthy skin. It feels so good to have relieved myself of the death row pallor. I feel the health changes from my innermost being to my expanded Aura. My psychological health is improving rapidly too.

. . . loving the books that you sent to me. I've been sharing them with others who appreciate wisdom.

Here is a person who embodies Frankl's notion of "tragic optimism." He brings evil out of hiding—he studies the law to give voice to his "comrades" from the inside, he shouts *no* to mold that grows dangerously on damp prison cell walls, and he says *yes* to living and growing his mind and body productively. Being positive is believing in his own power. For Cush, waiting within the chaos and ritualized order of the institution is not living in a state of suspension (see Kohn 2009); instead, it is a place that can be reframed as an active source of connection—to changing ideas about oneself and one's relations with others. Cush sees that in his case, profound transformations need to come from his own labor inside, and rather than further removing him from society and family, the work he does with his mind and his body allows him to see himself as connected and valuable to others and able to plan how to move forward in a richly imagined future even while the state imagines his warehousing, rotting, and disposal.[13] He defies the expectation of decay through his persistence, his development of skills, his devotion to practice, his care for himself and for others, and it is this activity that produces a gem out of a vat of rot and decay. Just imagine what would be possible if we all could recognize and free this potential—if we could all give it the value it deserves.

A Decaying Prison System

The degree of civilization in a society can be judged by entering its prisons.
—Fyodor Dostoevsky, *The House of the Dead*

Something is rotten in the state of Denmark.
—William Shakespeare, *Hamlet*

"The prison system": this label is used all the time and produces an illusion of a well-oiled structure, but the "system" is broken.[14] Not only is it not doing what it set out to do (reducing crime); it is also fraught with tensions between what is actually experienced (but kept out of sight), what is imagined, and what is supported through the associations that most people make around notions of decay. Everyone within "the system" is affected by the conditions that it produces, forming an "ecology of cruelty" (Haney 2008). This extends beyond inmates to the guards and many other employees who work within prison walls. Mold spreads *dis-ease*—it literally often permeates the bread that is served (see Perkins 2017), and ominously, it contributes to the dark and dangerous growth of violence, of trauma. People who physically and emotionally (mis)handle rot and mold become rotten and moldy. In his ethnographic study of waste workers in Detroit, Joshua Reno positions waste as social relationship—"waste" describes "unwanted people" as much as unwanted things (2016, 14–15). In his case, waste workers "become paradoxically stigmatized (as filthy) as well as privileged (as white and male)" (15). In the prison case, this paradox could be seen to apply to prison staff who live in a harsh and sometimes moldy environment that is filled with inmates who are collectively perceived as dangerous waste that deserves to rot (despite our knowledge that the penal system is broken—that it is racist, targets the poor, and frequently makes many incarceration and execution mistakes). The prison workers are socially tarnished by their proximity to the collective prison rot, much as waste workers are tarnished by their proximity to waste, and death workers are stigmatized by their proximity to death.[15] Yet, as Reno observes, such proximity paradoxically produces a sense of relative privilege and authority. One can see from this discussion that prison workers and the managers who employ them would be seriously threatened if out of their maintained environment of decay there was a public reveal of incarcerated persons with moral and productive value—this would undoubtedly destabilize their senses of relative privilege and deserved authority. This may help explain why my friend Cush (and others like him) are pushed for decades into the deepest bowels of the prison system, into a state of isolation, where their productive growth and practiced humanity cannot be witnessed and cannot rock the boat.

While prison institutional structures are imagined to be preventing societal decay (locking up or executing dangerous "criminals," shielding publics from violent crime), they also accelerate it through sustaining racially biased mass incarceration practices that strive to permanently remove many thousands of productive individuals from public social life. Productivity and physical, mental, and spiritual growth can be a biproduct of resistance to the maintenance of institutional rot and decay that unsuccessfully poses as governance.[16] It is because the residues of decay have this clear potential for animation, for resistance, for life, that I feel it is imperative to shine a light on them. And then, looking forward, we can all take some responsibility to employ our greater powers of creativity and care to imagine a decarceration scenario in which we learn to attend fully to all of our fellow human beings.

Some Additional Thoughts in the Time of COVID-19

In the year leading up to the publication of this book, 2020, we have all come to the shocking realization that a global pandemic can significantly alter our ways of life and ways of thinking about ourselves and the connections to others in our social worlds—ways of thinking about responsibility, touch, distance, breath. From the comfort of my isolation at home in Australia, I can only imagine the fear felt by those incarcerated in or near coronavirus hotspots in the United States. Trapped in close quarters with others in often "sick buildings" that already attack their respiratory systems, people "inside" are sitting ducks. When I first read in the US press about how some prisons in the United States are reducing their prison populations to push back against a fear of virus epicenters—"flattening the (virus) curve" by releasing prisoners who had nearly served their time or were old, ill, or in other ways particularly vulnerable—I thought with hope about the response to the virus as a wake-up call. Sadly, a closer reading only affirms the essentializing public values and expectations explained in the chapter above. Basically, the call for action has little to do with public and state concern for people in prison and everything to do with concern for the protection of the public outside the prison walls. If mold spores attack the respiratory systems of prisoners, or if poor medical care leads to the demise of an already "rotting" body in the public imaginary, then action is not urgently called for.[17] Those bodies breathe in the consequences of what is seen to be the "natural," gradually growing and deadly decay around them. Their inhalation of potential illness is understood to be part and parcel of their punishment "inside"—an inevitable consequence of their own criminal pasts. However, coronavirus particles, wherever they proliferate, pay no attention to the prison walls as they get carried out by prison staff and others into the community.[18] The fear of the exhalation of deadly coronavirus out into the "innocent community" at large is what has made a modicum of decarceration acceptable for many and has stimulated attention to the prison's overcrowded and decaying spaces as a public health liability. To me, however, this is not enough. We should not accept this as an "exceptional" rationale for "exceptional" times. Here, instead, is an opportunity to think differently—to confront our *own* values and expectations around prison decay and to help develop, communicate, and embrace a broad humanistic response for a healthier and freer future.

Notes

I wish to thank Ghassan Hage for persevering in bringing together this collaborative book project on decay, and to all the other contributors for their useful ideas and critiques. Special thanks to Michael Herzfeld, Violeta Schubert, Hannah Gould, Ben Russell, and Jessica Kohn McGuire—I am grateful for all of your wise reflections on the text. Last but not least I am infinitely grateful to Robert L. Cook, who is also known as Dr. Cush, and whose spirit and brilliance features in this thought piece.

1. Cush shared these descriptions when I visited him in a state correctional institution in Pennsylvania in 2015—they gesture to how he manages, against all odds, to "snap up"—to name and resist decay and to grow.

2. For this first visit, I was accompanied by friend and colleague Dr. Ellen Kaplan (professor of acting and directing at Smith College), who subsequently produced a play, *Someone Is Sure to Come* (2018), that brings together voices of men and women on death row.

3. Cush is one of five individuals I have exchanged letters with over many years, who all have spent decades inside US maximum-security prisons. These epistolary exchanges are not extractive but produce thoughtful conversations—where intersubjective reflections on actions, ideas, and desire have voice.

4. The idea of the United States as the land of the free is publicly associated with the oft-heard lyrics of the national anthem, written by Francis Scott Key in 1814: "O say does that star-spangled banner yet wave . . . O'er the land of the free and the home of the brave?"

5. In 1971 US president Richard Nixon declared drugs "public enemy number one" and established drug control and treatment agencies with federal funding. With the presidency of Ronald Reagan in the early 1980s, the "war on drugs" shifted to increasing drug-related punishment over treatment, which led to huge increases in incarceration rates for nonviolent offenses. The Comprehensive Crime Control Act of 1984,

followed by the Anti-Drug Abuse Act of 1986, poured federal funding into expanding penalties and established minimum sentences.

6. "Stop and frisk," or the "Terry stop" (outside New York), refers to policy in the United States since the 1960s permitting police officers to detain anyone for questioning and perform an on-the-spot body search on persons they believe could be armed or may be involved in a crime. Black and Latino people are targeted through this policy, which persists despite evidence that it does not reduce crime.

7. In 1994, President Bill Clinton took the war on drugs to yet another level with the establishment of the "three strikes" bill (inspired by baseball, where the batter "strikes out" after three misses). This law required life sentences for anyone convicted of a felony who had two or more prior convictions, which could include drug crime or even, in many cases, misdemeanors. The "three strikes" rule has contributed to mass incarceration and the imposition of disproportionate penalties.

8. A "zero tolerance" policy is one that calls for punishment for any breaking of rules. It was written into many school regulations starting in the 1990s to reduce crime and misbehavior. These policies have been criticized for focusing on punishment and suspensions rather than restorative practices, putting many students at risk, criminalizing poverty, and contributing to what has been called the "school-to-prison pipeline."

9. This nonfiction story draws from the author's experiences growing up in Baltimore and is written as a letter to his teenage son about the racist violence endemic in the streets and policing of black youths in America.

10. Toxic black mold (*Stachybotrys chartarum*) reproduces through spreading highly allergenic and toxic spores called mycotoxins, which contaminate food or invade the body through the skin or through inhalation.

11. Even government-run prisons outsource to private contractors to manage food services and maintenance.

12. This deliberate maintenance of the decay of people and buildings is not unrelated to the process discussed in Michael Herzfeld's discussion (this volume) of Roman conservators' insistence that all historic preservation should permanently reflect the reality of decay and mortality.

13. See Johnson 2019 on how life on death row is understood as warehousing for death.

14. Note here that this critique focuses on some of the orientations that accompany mass incarceration in the United States, and they may not apply as readily to parts of the world where imprisonment is more clearly aligned with discourses and practices of rehabilitation rather than rot and decay.

15. Sensorial connections among rot, decay, and death are frequently evoked in prisoner testimonials. Buildings can be "sick," with cell air vents that smell of death—see Tsolkas 2019.

16. "Resistance to decay" is referred to as "maintenance" in Akhil Gupta's chapter on infrastructure (this volume). Here, from the prisoner's position, resistance to decay is a political stance and impetus for activity that desires to do more—to lift the spirit and disrupt the infrastructure.

17. The sense that it is appropriate for prison bodies to work in a rotting environment since they are rotting themselves is evident around the care of the dead on Hart Island in the northeastern Bronx region of New York City. For decades, inmates from Rikers Island Prison have been transported to the island to dig the graves of the homeless and poor, and now, during this time of coronavirus, unmarked mass graves are prepared by the inmates, then bulldozers move caskets into the trenches. See Kilgannon 2020.

18. Sociologist Ashley Rubin (2020) raises this point in a recent *Conversation* article about the permeability of coronavirus through the walls of the prison and also usefully reminds us of the irony that the first large US prisons were built in the colonial era as a reaction to overcrowding, violence, and the fear of spreading disease in local jails.

REFERENCES

Aldern, Natalie. 2018. "Get Up Close and Personal with the Most Beautiful Buildings in Rome." *TimeOut*, April 30. https://www.timeout.com/rome/things-to-do/most-beautiful-buildings-in-rome.
Alexander, Michelle. 2012. *The New Jim Crow: Mass Incarceration in the Age of Colorblindness*. New York: New Press.
Altman, Jon. 2007. "The Howard Government's Northern Territory Intervention: Are Neo-paternalism and Indigenous Development Compatible?" Working Paper 58. Canberra: Center for Aboriginal Economic Policy Research.
Altman, Jon. 2010. "What Future for Remote Indigenous Australia? Economic Hybridity and the Neo-liberal Turn." In *Culture Crisis: Anthropology and Politics in Aboriginal Australia*, edited by Jon Altman and Melinda Hinkson, 259–80. Sydney: University of New South Wales Press.
Altman, Jon. 2014. "Indigenous Policy: Canberra Consensus on a Neoliberal Project of Improvement." In *Australian Public Policy: Progressive Ideas in the Neo-liberal Ascendancy*, edited by Chris Miller and Lionel Orchard, 117–34. Bristol: Policy Press.
Altman, Jon. 2015. "Basic Income a No-Brainer for Remote Indigenous Australia." *New Matilda*, September 17. https://newmatilda.com/2015/09/17/basic-income-no-brainer-remote-indigenous-australia/.
Altman, Jon. 2018. "Raphael Lemkin in Remote Australia: The Logic of Cultural Genocide and Homelands." *Oceania* 88, no. 3: 336–59.
Altman, J. C., M. C. Gray, and W. G. Sanders. 2000. "Indigenous Australians Working for Welfare: What Difference Does It Make?" *Australian Economic Review* 33, no. 4: 355–62.
Altman, Jon, and Elise Klein. 2017. "Lessons from a Basic Income Programme for Indigenous Australians." *Oxford Development Studies* 46, no. 1: 132–46.
Amirthalingam, Kopalapillai, and Rajith Lakshman. 2009. "Displaced Livelihoods in Sri Lanka: An Economic Analysis." *Journal of Refugee Studies* 22, no. 4: 502–24.
Anda-Harapa, Panga-Kulu. 2018. "O'Neill Government Not Interested in Finding Out the Cause of Devastating Earthquake." *Papua New Guinea Mine Watch* (blog), April 9. https://ramumine.wordpress.com/2018/04/09/oneil-government-not-interested-in-finding-out-the-cause-of-devastating-earthquake/.
Argyrou, Vassos. 1993. "Under a Spell: The Strategic Use of Magic in Greek Cypriot Society." *American Ethnologist* 20, no. 2: 256–71.

Asianews.it. 2018. "Card Raï: Citizenship and Belonging to Counter Christian 'Desertification' in the Middle East." Asianews.it, October 22. http://www.asianews.it/news-en/Card-Ra%C3%AF:-citizenship-and-belonging-to-counter-Christian-'desertification'-in-the-Middle-East-45266.html.

Australian Human Rights Commission. 2016. *Social Justice and Native Title Report 2016*. Sydney: Australian Human Rights Commission.

Bailey, Kenneth D. 1990. *Social Entropy Theory*. Albany: State University of New York Press.

Ballard, Chris. 1994. "The Centre Cannot Hold: Trade Networks and Sacred Geography in the Papua New Guinea Highlands." *Archaeology in Oceania* 29, no. 3: 130–48.

Ballard, Chris. 2000. "The Fire Next Time: The Conversion of the Huli Apocalypse." *Ethnohistory* 47, no. 1: 205–25.

Barnes, Jessica. 2017. "States of Maintenance: Power, Politics, and Egypt's Irrigation Infrastructure." *Environment and Planning D: Society and Space* 35, no. 1: 146–64.

Bateson, Gregory. 1972. *Steps to an Ecology of Mind: Collected Essays in Anthropology, Psychiatry, Evolution, and Epistemology*. San Francisco: Chandler.

Baudelaire, Charles. 1869. "A Carcass." In *Translations from Charles Baudelaire*, edited by Richard Herne Shepherd. London: John Camden Hotten, 1869. https://fleursdumal.org/poem/126.

Baxendale, Rachel. 2018. "More Money No Solution to Dysfunction in Indigenous Communities: Dan Tehan." *Weekend Australian*, July 4. https://www.theaustralian.com.au/nation/politics/more-money-no-solution-to-dysfunction-in-indigenous-communities-dan-tehan/news-story/b4fac51753dab7c69cdbf762eef67134.

Belford, Audrey, Saska Cvetkovska, Biljana Sekulovska, and Stevan Dojčinović. 2017. "Leaked Documents Show Russian, Serbian Attempts to Meddle in Macedonia." OCCRP, June 4. https://www.occrp.org/en/spooksandspin/leaked-documents-show-russian-serbian-attempts-to-meddle-in-macedonia/.

Berlant, Lauren. 2007. "Slow Death (Sovereignty, Obesity, Lateral Agency)." *Critical Inquiry* 33, no. 4: 754–80.

Bessire, Lucas. 2012. "The Politics of Isolation: Refused Relation as an Emerging Regime of Indigenous Biolegitimacy." *Comparative Studies in Society and History* 54, no. 3: 467–98.

Biddle, Nicholas, and Francis Markham. 2013. "Mobility." In *Indigenous Population Project: 2011 Census Papers*. Canberra: Centre for Aboriginal Economic Policy Research.

Bielenin-Lenczkowska, Karolina. 2010. "Different Models of Labour Migration in Contemporary Macedonia—or What Does Pecalba Mean Today?" In *Migration in, from, and to Southeastern Europe*, part 2: Ways and Strategies of Migrating. *Ethnologica Balkanica 14*, edited by Klaus Roth and Jutta Lauth Bacas, 11–26. Munich: Ludwig Maximillian University.

Bjerregaard, Peter, Anders Emil Rasmussen, and Tim Flohr Sørensen, eds. 2016. *Materialities of Passing: Explorations in Transformation, Transition and Transcience*. London: Routledge.

Blong, Russell J. 1982. *The Time of Darkness: Local Legends and Volcanic Reality in Papua New Guinea*. Canberra: Australia National University Press.

Bonfiglioli, Chiara. 2014. "Gender, Labour and Precarity in the South East European Periphery: The Case of Textile Workers in Štip." *Contemporary Southeastern Europe* 1, no. 2: 7–23.

Bourdieu, Pierre. 2000. *Pascalian Meditations*. Translated by Richard Nice. Cambridge: Polity.

Bradnick, David. 2009. "Entropy, the Fall, and Tillich: A Multidisciplinary Approach to Original Sin." *Theology and Science* 7, no. 1: 67–83.

Brand, Stewart. 1994. *How Buildings Learn: What Happens after They're Built*. New York: Viking.

Brandi, Cesare, 1977. *Teoria del restauro*. Torino: Giulio Einaudi.

Brigg, Morgan. 2019. "Registers for Knowing Indigenous-Settler Politics." In *Questioning Indigenous-Settler Relations: Interdisciplinary Perspectives*, edited by Sarah Maddison and Sana Nakata, 15–31. New York: Springer.

Broad, William J. 2005. "Deadly and Yet Necessary, Quakes Renew the Planet." *New York Times*, January 11. https://www.nytimes.com/2005/01/11/science/deadly-and-yet-necessary-quakes-renew-the-planet.html.

Brontë, Charlotte. 1993. *Shirley*. Ware, UK: Wordsworth Classics.

Brown, Keith. 1998. "Contests of Heritage and the Politics of Preservation in the Former Yugoslav Republic of Macedonia." In *Archaeology under Fire: Nationalism, Politics and Heritage in the Eastern Mediterranean and Middle East*, edited by Lynn Meskell, 68–86. London: Routledge.

Brown, Keith. 2003. *The Past in Question: Modern Macedonia and the Uncertainties of Nation*. Princeton, NJ: Princeton University Press.

Brown, Keith. 2013. *Loyalty unto Death: Trust and Terror in Revolutionary Macedonia*. Bloomington: Indiana University Press.

Buch, Elana D. 2015. "Anthropology of Aging and Care." *Annual Review of Anthropology* 44, no. 1: 277–93.

Burbank, Victoria. 2011. *An Ethnography of Stress: The Social Determinants of Health in Aboriginal Australia*. New York: Palgrave Macmillan.

Carbonara, Giovanni. 2009. "Alcune riflessioni, da parte italiana, sul restauro architettonico." In *Conserving the Authentic: Essays in Honour of Jukka Jokilehto*, edited by Nicholas Stanley-Price and Joseph King, 27–36. Rome: ICCROM.

Carsten, Janet. 2011. "Substance and Relationality: Blood in Contexts." *Annual Review of Anthropology* 40: 19–35.

Castiglione, Baldassare. [1528] 1910. *Il Cortegiano*. Edited by Vittorio Cian. Florence: G. C. Sansoni.

Cawte, John. 1972. *Cruel, Poor and Brutal Nations*. Honolulu: University of Hawai'i Press.

Christakos, George. 2010. *Integrative Problem-Solving in a Time of Decadence*. Dordrecht: Springer.

Clapp, Alexander. 2016. "Skopje, City on the Make." *Baffler*, no. 32: 8–13. https://thebaffler.com/salvos/skopje-city-make-clapp.

Coates, Ta-Nehisi. 2015. *Between the World and Me*. New York: Spiegel and Grau.

Coffin, Noah "Comrade Cado," and Keith "Comrade Malik" Washington. 2017. "Black

Mold and Toxic Prisons: An Update on Dangerous and Unsanitary Conditions at the Eastham Unit in Texas." Incarcerated Workers Organizing Committee, September 3. https://incarceratedworkers.org/news/black-mold-and-toxic-prisons.

Comaroff, Jean, and John L. Comaroff, eds. 2001. *Millennial Capitalism and the Culture of Neoliberalism*. Durham, NC: Duke University Press.

Commonwealth of Australia. 2015. *Our North, Our Future: White Paper on Developing Northern Australia*. Canberra: Government of Australia.

Commonwealth of Australia. 2019. *Closing the Gap: Report 2019*. Canberra: Government of Australia.

Commonwealth of Australia. 2020. *Closing the Gap: Report 2020*. Canberra: Government of Australia.

Constable, Liz, Matthew Potolsky, and Dennis Denisoff. 1999. Introduction to *Perennial Decay: On the Aesthetics and Politics of Decadence*, edited by Liz Constable, Dennis Denisoff, and Matthew Potolsky, 1–34. Philadelphia: University of Pennsylvania Press.

Coombs, H. C. 1989. "The Ideology of Development." In *Land of Promises: Aborigines and Development in the East Kimberley*, edited by H. C. Coombs, H. McCann, H. Ross, and N. M. Williams, 1–20. Canberra: ANU and Aboriginal Studies Press.

Coulthard, Glen. 2014. *Red Skin, White Masks: Rejecting the Colonial Politics of Recognition*. Minneapolis: University of Minnesota Press.

Cowan, Jane K., ed. 2000. *Macedonia: The Politics of Identity and Difference*. London: Pluto.

Cowan, Jane K., and K. S. Brown. 2000. "Introduction: Macedonian Inflections." In Cowan 2000: 1–27.

Cowlishaw, Gillian. 2010. "Helping Anthropologists, Still." In *Culture Crisis: Anthropology and Politics in Aboriginal Australia*, edited by Jon Altman and Melinda Hinkson, 45–60. Sydney: University of New South Wales Press.

Cowlishaw, Gillian. 2017. "Tunnel Vision Part One: Resisting Post-colonialism in Australian Anthropology." *Australian Journal of Anthropology* 28, no. 1: 324–41.

Cronin, Darryl. 2007. "Welfare Dependency and Mutual Obligation: Negating Indigenous Sovereignty." In *Sovereign Subjects: Indigenous Sovereignty Matters*, edited by Aileen Moreton-Robinson, 179–200. London: Routledge.

Dalley, Cameo. 2021.*What Now: Everyday Endurance and Social Intensity in an Australian Aboriginal Community*. New York: Berghahn.

Dalley, Cameo, and Richard Martin. 2015. "Dichotomous Identities? Indigenous and Non-Indigenous People and the Intercultural in Australia." *Australian Journal of Anthropology* 26, no. 1: 1–23.

Dalley, Cameo, and Paul Memmott. 2010. "Domains and the Intercultural: Understanding Aboriginal and Missionary Engagement at the Mornington Island Mission, Gulf of Carpentaria, Australia from 1914–1942." *International Journal of Historical Archaeology* 14, no. 1: 112–35.

Danforth, Loring. 1995. *The Macedonian Conflict: Ethnic Nationalism in a Transnational World*. Princeton, NJ: Princeton University Press.

Daniel, Sharon. 2006 "The Public Secret: Information and Social Knowledge."

Intelligent Agent 6, no. 2. http://www.intelligentagent.com/archive/vo16_no2_community_domain_daniel.htm.

Daskalovski, Zhidas. 2017. "Clashing Historical Narratives and the Macedonian Name Dispute—Solving the Unsolvable." *Trames* 21, no. 4: 327–43.

Davis, Angela Y. 2003. *Are Prisons Obsolete?* New York: Seven Stories Press.

Davis, Angela Y. 2012. *The Meaning of Freedom and Other Difficult Dialogues.* San Francisco: City Lights Books.

Davis, Philip J. 2011. "Entropy and Society: Can the Physical/Mathematical Notions of Entropy Be Usefully Imported into the Social Sphere?" *Journal of Humanistic Mathematics* 1, no. 1: 119–36.

Dawdy, Shannon Lee. 2016. *Patina: A Profane Archaeology.* Chicago: University of Chicago Press.

Dawisha, Karen. 2014. *Putin's Kleptocracy: Who Owns Russia?* New York: Simon and Schuster.

Dawson, Andrew. 2002. "The Mining Community and the Aging Body." In *Realizing Community: Concepts, Social Relationships and Sentiments*, edited by Vered Amit, 21–37. London: Routledge.

Demetriou, Olga. 2006. "Streets Not Named: Discursive Dead Ends and the Politics of Orientation in Intercommunal Spatial Relations in Northern Greece." *Cultural Anthropology* 21, no. 2: 295–321.

D'Emilio, Frances. 2016. "Rome's Colosseum Sparkles after Magnate-Funded Restoration." *Star Tribune* (Newark, NJ), July 1. https://www.startribune.com/rome-s-colosseum-cleaner-after-magnate-funded-restoration/385182041/.

Deng, Grazia (Ting). 2018. "Chinese Espresso: Immigrant Entrepreneurship and Ethnic Encounters in Bologna, Italy." PhD diss., Chinese University of Hong Kong.

Dimova, Rozita. 2013. *Ethno-Baroque: Materiality, Aesthetics and Conflict in Modern-Day Macedonia.* New York: Berghahn.

Douglas, Mary. 1966. *Purity and Danger: An Analysis of Concepts of Pollution and Taboo.* London: Routledge and Kegan Paul.

Dwyer, Peter D., and Monica Minnegal. 2000. "El Niño, Y2K and the Short Fat Lady: Drought and Agency in a Lowland Papua New Guinean Community." *Journal of the Polynesian Society* 109, no. 3: 251–72.

Dwyer, Peter D., and Monica Minnegal. 2018. "Refugees on Their Own Land: Edolo People, Land and Earthquakes." *Envirosociety* (blog), June 9. http://www.envirosociety.org/2018/06/Refugees-On-Their-Own-Land-Edolo-People-Land-And-Earthquakes/.

Eberstein, Amanda, and Rebecca Holland. 2017. "A Design Lover's Guide to Rome." *Architectural Digest*, March 29. https://www.architecturaldigest.com/story/rome-italy-design-guide.

Eickelkamp, Ute. 2017. "Finding Spirit: Ontological Monism in an Australian Aboriginal Desert World Today." *Hau: Journal of Ethnographic Theory* 7, no. 1: 235–64.

Elinoff, Eli. 2017. "Despotic Urbanism in Thailand." *New Mandala*, May 4. https://www.newmandala.org/despotic-urbanism-thailand/.

Empowered Communities. 2019. "East Kimberley." Accessed November 17, 2020. https://empoweredcommunities.org.au/our-regions/east-kimberley-3/.

Errington, Frederick K., Deborah B. Gewertz, and Tatsuro Fujikura. 2013. *The Noodle Narratives: The Global Rise of an Industrial Food into the Twenty-First Century*. Berkeley: University of California Press.

Fassin, Didier. 2009. "Another Politics of Life Is Possible." *Theory, Culture and Society* 26, no. 5: 44–60.

Fay, Elizabeth A. 1994. *Eminent Rhetoric: Language, Gender, and Cultural Tropes*. London: Bergin and Garvey.

Fazioli, K. Patrick. 2017. *The Mirror of the Medieval: An Anthropology of the Western Historical Imagination*. Oxford: Berghahn.

Fisher, Daniel. 2016. *The Voice and Its Doubles: Media and Music in Northern Australia*. Durham, NC: Duke University Press.

Fisher, Tom. 2013. "A World of Colour and Bright Shining Surfaces: Experiences of Plastics after the Second World War." *Journal of Design History* 26, no. 3: 285–303.

Flanagan, Paul, and Luke Fletcher. 2018. *Double or Nothing: The Broken Economic Promises of PNG LNG*. Sydney: Jubilee Australia.

Fonseka, Bhavani, and Mirak Raheem. 2009. *Trincomalee High Security Zone and Special Economic Zone*. Colombo: CPA.

Forrest, Andrew. 2014. *The Forrest Review: Creating Parity*. Canberra: Department of Prime Minister and Cabinet.

Foucault, Michel. 1977. *Discipline and Punish: The Birth of the Prison*. Translated by Alan Sheridan. New York: Pantheon.

Fowkes, Lisa. 2016. "Impact on Social Security Penalties of Increased Remote Work for the Dole Requirements." Working Paper 112. Canberra: Center for Aboriginal Economic Policy Research.

François, Charles, ed. 2001. *International Encyclopedia of Systems and Cybernetics*. Munich: K. G. Saur.

Frankl, Viktor E. (1959) 2006. *Man's Search for Meaning*. Boston: Beacon.

Frederiksen, Martin Demant. 2016. "Material Dys-Appearance: Decaying Futures and Contested Temporal Passage." In *Materialities of Passing: Explorations in Transformation, Transition and Transcience*, edited by Peter Bjerregaard, Anders Emil Rasmussen, and Tim Flohr Sørensen, 49–65. London: Routledge.

Friedman, Victor A. 2010. "Challenging Crossroads: Macedonia in Global Perspective." *Slavic Review* 69, no. 4: 811–15.

Gabrys, Jennifer. 2013. "Plastic and the Work of the Biodegradable." In *Accumulation: The Material Politics of Plastic*, edited by Jennifer Gabrys, Gay Hawkins, and Mike Michael, 208–27. London: Routledge.

Gabrys, Jennifer, Gay Hawkins, and Mike Michael. 2013. "Introduction: From Materiality to Plasticity." In *Accumulation: The Material Politics of Plastic*, edited by Jennifer Gabrys, Gay Hawkins, and Mike Michael, 1–14. London: Routledge.

Gal, Susan, and Judith T. Irvine. 1995. "The Boundaries of Languages and Disciplines: How Ideologies Construct Difference." *Social Research* 62, no. 4: 967–1001.

Garond, Lise. 2014. "The Meaningful Difference of 'Aboriginal Dysfunction' and the

Neoliberal 'Mainstream.'" e*Tropic: Electronic Journal of Studies in the Tropics* 13, no. 2: 7–13.

Geertz, Clifford. 1963. *Agricultural Involution: The Process of Ecological Change in Indonesia*. Berkeley: University of California Press.

Geertz, Clifford. 2000. "'The World in Pieces: Culture and Politics at the End of the Century." In *Available Light: Anthropological Reflections on Philosophical Topics*, 218–64. Princeton, NJ: Princeton University Press.

Gewertz, Deborah B., and Frederick K. Errington. 2010. *Cheap Meat: Flap Food Nations in the Pacific Islands*. Berkeley: University of California Press.

Gibson, Paddy. 2012. "Return to the Ration Days: The Northern Territory Intervention—Grassroots Experience and Resistance." *Ngiya: Talk the Law* 3: 58–107.

Glanz, James, Gaia Pianigiani, Jeremy White, and Karthik Patanjali. 2018. "Hanging by a Thread: Behind a Bridge Collapse." *New York Times*, September 7.

Goffman, Erving. 1961. *Asylums: Essays on the Social Situation of Mental Patients and Other Inmates*. Garden City, NJ: Doubleday Anchor.

Gökarıksel, Saygun. 2017. "The Ends of Revolution: Capitalist De-democratization and Nationalist Populism in the East of Europe." *Dialectical Anthropology* 41, no. 3: 207–24.

Goodhand, Jonathan. 2010. "Stabilising a Victor's Peace? Humanitarian Action and Reconstruction in Eastern Sri Lanka." *Disasters* 34, s3: S342–67.

Goodhand, Jonathan, Bart Klem, and Benedikt Korf. 2009. "Religion, Conflict and Boundary Politics in Sri Lanka." *European Journal for Development Research* 21, no. 5: 679–98.

Graan, Andrew. 2013. "Counterfeiting the Nation? Skopje 2014 and the Politics of Nation Branding in Macedonia." *Cultural Anthropology* 28, no. 1: 161–79.

Graham, Stephen, and Nigel Thrift. 2007. "Out of Order: Understanding Repair and Maintenance." *Theory, Culture and Society* 24, no. 3: 1–25.

Grenier, Amanda, Chris Phillipson, and Richard A. Settersten Jr., eds. 2020. *Precarity and Ageing: Understanding Insecurity and Risk in Later Life*. Bristol, UK: Policy Press.

Grudnoff, Matt, and Rod Campbell. 2017. "Dam the Expense: The Ord River Irrigation Scheme and the Development of Northern Australia." *Australia Institute Discussion Paper*, 1–24. Canberra: Australia Institute.

Gupta, Akhil. 2018. "The Future in Ruins: Thoughts on the Temporality of Infrastructure." In *The Promise of Infrastructure*, edited by Nikhil Anand, Akhil Gupta, and Hannah Appel, 62–79. Durham, NC: Duke University Press.

Gwynne, Paul, and Flavia Marcello. 2015. "Speaking from the Walls: Militarism, Education, and *Romanità* in Rome's Città Universitaria (1932–35)." *Journal of the Society of Architectural Historians* 74, no. 3: 323–43.

Hage, Ghassan. 2017. *Is Racism an Environmental Threat?* Cambridge: Polity.

Haley, Nicole. 2007. "Cosmology, Morality and Resource Development: SHP Election Outcomes and Moves to Establish a Separate Hela Province." In *Conflict and Resource Development in the Southern Highlands of Papua New Guinea*, edited by Nicole Haley and Ronald J. May, 57–68. Canberra: Australian National University Press.

Halpern, Joel M. 1965. "Peasant Culture and Urbanization in Yugoslavia." *Human Organization* 24, no. 2: 162–74.

Halpern, Joel M., and Barbara K. Halpern. 1975. "The Pecalba Tradition in Macedonia, a Case Study." *Anthropology Department Faculty Publication Series* 58, University of Massachusetts, Amherst. https://scholarworks.umass.edu/anthro_faculty_pubs/58/.

Haney, Craig. 2008. "A Culture of Harm: Taming the Dynamics of Cruelty in Supermax Prisons." *Criminal Justice and Behavior* 35, no. 8: 956–84.

Hawkins, Gay. 2013. "Made to Be Wasted: PET and Topologies of Disposability." In *Accumulation: The Material Politics of Plastic*, edited by Jennifer Gabrys, Gay Hawkins, and Mike Michael, 49–67. Oxford: Routledge.

Hawkins, Gay. 2018. "Plastic and Presentism: The Time of Disposability." *Journal of Contemporary Archaeology* 5, no. 1: 91–102.

Hegel, G. W. F. 1977. *The Phenomenology of Spirit*. Translated by A. V. Miller. New York: Oxford University Press.

Hell, Julia, and Andreas Schönle, eds. 2010. *Ruins of Modernity*. Durham, NC: Duke University Press.

Hermez, Sami. 2019. "Dehumanization in War and Peace: Encounters with Lebanon's Ex-Militia Fighters." *American Anthropologist* 121, no. 3: 583–94.

Herzfeld, Michael. 1982. "The Etymology of Excuses: Aspects of Rhetorical Performance in Greece." *American Ethnologist* 9, no. 4: 644–63.

Herzfeld, Michael. 1987. *Anthropology through the Looking-Glass: Critical Ethnography in the Margins of Europe*. Cambridge: Cambridge University Press.

Herzfeld, Michael. 2009. *Evicted from Eternity: The Restructuring of Modern Rome*. Chicago: University of Chicago Press.

Herzfeld, Michael. 2015. "Practical Piety: Intimate Devotions in Urban Space." *Journal of Religious and Political Practice* 1, no. 1: 22–38.

Herzfeld, Michael. 2016. *Cultural Intimacy: Social Poetics and the Real Life of States, Societies, and Institutions*. 3rd ed. New York: Routledge.

Herzfeld, Michael. 2017. "The Blight of Beautification: Bangkok and the Pursuit of Class-Based Urban Purity." *Journal of Urban Design* 22, no. 3: 291–307.

Herzfeld, Michael. 2020. "Seeing like a Village: Contesting Hegemonic Modernity in Greece" *Journal of Modern Greek Studies* 38, no. 1: 43–58.

Higgs, Paul, and Gilleard, Chris. 2016. *Personhood, Identity and Care in Advanced Old Age*. Bristol, UK: Policy Press.

Hislope, Robert. 2008. "Corrupt Exchange in Divided Societies: The Invisible Politics of Stability in Macedonia." In *Transnational Actors in Central and East European Transitions*, edited by Mitchell Orenstein, Stephen Bloom, and Nicole Lindstrom, 142–61. Pittsburgh: University of Pittsburgh Press.

Hunt, Janet. 2017. "The Cashless Debit Card Trial Evaluation: A Short Review." CAEPR Topical Issue 1. Canberra: Center for Aboriginal Economic Policy Research.

Hutchens, Gareth. 2017. "Turnbull Says Cashless Welfare Card about 'Practical Love' while Announcing New Site." *Guardian*, September 1. https://www.theguardian.com/australia-news/2017/sep/01/coalition-hails-success-of-cashless-welfare-card-and-says-kalgoorlie-will-be-next-site.

Infomax. 2018. "Selo Gori, Baba Se Češla: 'Državata Ni Gori, Ti Za Dve Sliki Plačeš'—Komentar Na Profilot Na Lila Hit Na Internet" [Village is burning, grandma is combing (her hair): "Our country is burning, you are crying for two pictures"—comment on Lila hit's profile]. April 13. https://infomax.mk/wp/село-гори-баба-се-чешла-државата-ни-г/.

Jackson, Steven J. 2014. "Rethinking Repair." In *Media Technologies: Essays on Communication, Materiality, and Society*, edited by Tarleton Gillespie, Pablo J. Boczkowski, and Kirsten A. Foot, 221–39. Cambridge, MA: MIT Press.

Jaisaard, Rapeepun, Garry Christensen, Gary Smith, David Gue, and Aleksandar Nacev. 2002. FYR *Macedonia: Agriculture Sector Review*. World Bank, Environmentally and Socially Sustainable Development Europe and Central Asia Region 25829, October 30. Washington, DC: World Bank.

Janev, Goran. 2017. "Burdensome Past: Challenging the Socialist Heritage in Macedonia." *Studia Ethnologia Croatia* 29, no. 1: 149–70.

Johnson, Robert. 2019. *Condemned to Die: Life under Sentence of Death*. 2nd ed. New York: Routledge.

Jokilehto, Jukka. 1986. "A History of Architectural Conservation: The Contribution of English, French, German and Italian Thought towards an International Approach to the Conservation of Cultural Property." PhD thesis, University of York, England. https://www.iccrom.org/publication/history-architectural-conservation.

Jordan, Kirrily, ed. 2016. *Better Than Welfare? Work and Livelihood for Indigenous Australians after CDEP*. Canberra: Australian National University Press.

Jordan, Mary-Ellen. 2005. *Balanda, My Year in Arnhem Land*. Crow's Nest, NSW: Allen and Unwin.

Kanafani, Samar. 2017. "Made to Fall Apart: An Ethnography of Old House and Urban Renewal in Beirut." PhD diss., University of Manchester.

Karakasidou, Anastasia. 1997. *Fields of Wheat, Hills of Blood: Passages to Nationhood in Greek Macedonia, 1870–1990*. Chicago: University of Chicago Press.

Kastens, Kim. 2010. "The Second Law of Thermodynamics as a Unifying Theme of Geosciences." *Earth and Mind* (blog), May 21. https://serc.carleton.edu/earthandmind/posts/secondlaw.html.

Kelly, Raymond C. 1976. "Witchcraft and Sexual Relations: An Exploration in the Social and Semantic Implications of the Structure of Belief." In *Man and Woman in the New Guinea Highlands*, edited by Paula Brown and Georgeda Buchbinder, 36–53. Washington, DC: American Anthropological Association.

Khatchadourian, Raffi. 2020. "End-Times." *New Yorker*, June 1: 13–14.

Kilgannon, Corey. 2020. "As Morgues Fill, N.Y.C. to Bury Some Virus Victims in Potter's Field." *New York Times*, April 10. https://www.nytimes.com/2020/04/10/nyregion/coronavirus-deaths-hart-island-burial.html.

Kimberley Development Commission. 2013. *Aboriginal Wellbeing: Assessing Aboriginal Wellbeing in the Kimberley*. Report prepared for the Kimberley Development Commission, Wunan, Kununurra.

Klein, Elise. 2014. "Academic Perspectives on the Forrest Review: Creating Parity." Topical Issue 2. Canberra: Center for Aboriginal Economic Policy Research.

Klein, Elise. 2020. "The Indigenous Development Assemblage and Contemporary Forms of Elimination in Settler Colonial Australia." *Postcolonial Studies*: 1–22. https://doi.org/10.1080/13688790.2020.1838811.

Klein, Elise, and Sarouche Razi. 2017. "The Cashless Debit Card Trial in the East Kimberley." Working Paper 121. Canberra: Center for Aboriginal Economic Policy Research.

Klem, Bart. 2014. "The Political Geography of War's End: Territorialisation, Circulation, and Moral Anxiety in Trincomalee, Sri Lanka." *Political Geography* 38, no. 1: 33–45.

Klem, Bart. 2018. "The Problem of Peace and the Meaning of 'Post-war.'" *Conflict, Security and Development* 18, no. 3: 233–55.

Klem, Bart, and Thiruni Kelegama. 2020. "Marginal Placeholders: Peasants, Paddy and Ethnic Space in Sri Lanka's Post-war Frontier." *Journal of Peasant Studies* 47, no. 2: 346–65.

Klem, Bart, and Sidharthan Maunaguru. 2017. "Insurgent Rule as Sovereign Mimicry and Mutation: Governance, Kingship and Violence in Civil Wars." *Comparative Studies in Society and History* 59, no. 3: 629–56.

Klem, Bart, and Sidharthan Maunaguru. 2018. "Public Authority under Sovereign Encroachment: Community Leadership in War-Time Sri Lanka." *Modern Asian Studies* 52, no. 3: 784–814.

Knauft, Bruce M. 1985. *Good Company and Violence: Sorcery and Social Action in a Lowland New Guinea Society*. Berkeley: University of California Press.

Kohn, Tamara. 2009. "Waiting on Death Row." In *Waiting*, edited by Ghassan Hage, 218–27. Melbourne: Melbourne University Press.

Korf, Benedikt. 2006. "Who Is the Rogue? Discourse, Power and Spatial Politics in Post-war Sri Lanka." *Political Geography* 25, no. 3: 279–97.

Korf, Benedikt, and Shahul Hasbullah. 2013. "Muslim Geographies, Violence and the Antinomies of Community in Sri Lanka." *Geographical Journal* 179, no. 1: 32–43.

Kowal, Emma. 2008. "The Politics of the Gap: Indigenous Australians, Liberal Multiculturalism, and the End of the Self-Determination Era." *American Anthropologist* 110, no. 3: 338–48.

Kowal, Emma. 2015. *Trapped in the Gap: Doing Good in Indigenous Australia*. New York: Berghahn.

Krause, Elizabeth K. 2018. *Tight Knit: Global Families and the Social Life of Fast Fashion*. Chicago: University of Chicago Press.

Law, Kara Lavender, and Richard C. Thompson. 2014. "Microplastics in the Seas." *Science* 345, no. 6193: 144–45.

Lea, Tess. 2008. *Bureaucrats and Bleeding Hearts: Indigenous Health in Northern Australia*. Sydney: University of New South Wales Press.

Lea, Tess. 2012. "When Looking for Anarchy, Look to the State: Fantasies of Regulation in Forcing Disorder within the Australian Indigenous Estate." *Critique of Anthropology* 32, no. 2: 109–24.

Lea, Tess. 2015. "What Has Water Got to Do with It? Indigenous Public Housing and Australian Settler-Colonial Relations." *Settler Colonial Studies* 5, no. 4: 375–86.

Lea, Tess, and Paul Pholeros. 2010. "This Is Not a Pipe: The Treacheries of Indigenous Housing." *Public Culture* 22, no. 1: 187–209.

Leach, Edmund. 1970. *Claude Lévi-Strauss*. London: Penguin.

Lévi-Strauss, Claude. 1962. *Totemism*. Translated by Rodney Needham. London: Merlin Press.

Lévi-Strauss, Claude. 1969. *Mythologiques*. Vol. 1, *The Raw and the Cooked*. Translated by John and Doreen Weightman. New York: Harper and Row.

Lévi-Strauss, Claude. 1976. *Structural Anthropology*. Vol. 2. Translated by Monique Layton. New York: Basic Books.

Lévi-Strauss, Claude. 2013. *Anthropology Confronts the Problems of the Modern World*. Translated by Jane Marie Todd. Cambridge, MA: Harvard University Press.

Li, Tania Murray. 2010. "To Make Live or Let Die? Rural Dispossession and the Protection of Surplus Populations." *Antipode* 41, s1: 66–93.

Livingston, Julie. 2019. *Self-Devouring Growth: A Planetary Parable as Told from Southern Africa*. Durham, NC: Duke University Press.

L'Orient-Le Jour. 2018. "Chrétiens d'Orient, de l'inquiétude à l'exil." July 8. https://www.lorientlejour.com/article/1124524/chretiens-dorient-de-linquietude-a-lexil.html.

Lovell, Melissa. 2012. "A Settler-Colonial Consensus on the Northern Intervention." *Arena Journal*, nos. 37–38: 199–219.

Macintyre, Martha. 1995. "Violent Bodies and Vicious Exchanges: Personification and Objectification in the Massim." *Social Analysis*, no. 37: 29–43.

Mahood, Kim. 2000. *Craft for a Dry Lake*. Sydney: Anchor.

Mahood, Kim. 2012. "*Kartiya* Are like Toyotas: White Workers on Australia's Cultural Frontier." *Griffith Review*, no. 36: 43–59.

Mahood, Kim. 2015. "White Stigma." *Monthly*, August: 50–51. https://www.themonthly.com.au/issue/2015/august/1438351200/kim-mahood/white-stigma#mtr.

Mahood, Kim. 2016. *Position Doubtful: Mapping Landscapes and Memories*. Brunswick, VIC: Scribe.

Main, Ian G., and Mark Naylor. 2010. "Entropy Production and Self-Organized (Sub) Criticality in Earthquake Dynamics." *Philosophical Transactions of the Royal Society A* 368, no. 1910: 131–44.

Main, Michael. 2017. "Papua New Guinea Gets a Dose of the Resource Curse as ExxonMobil's Natural Gas Project Foments Unrest." *Conversation*, March 8. https://theconversation.com/papua-new-guinea-gets-a-dose-of-the-resource-curse-as-exxonmobils-natural-gas-project-foments-unrest-70780.

Main, Michael. 2018. "How PNG LNG Is Shaking Up the Earthquake." *Envirosociety* (blog), March 28. http://www.envirosociety.org/2018/03/Michael-Main-How-Png-Lng-Is-Shaking-Up-The-Earthquake/.

Major Stackings. 2012. "Why Do the Walking Dead Zombies Stop Decomposing?" Science Fiction and Fantasy Message Board, June 11. https://scifi.stackexchange.com/Questions/18033/Why-Do-The-Walking-Dead-Zombies-Stop-Decomposing.

Malaby, Thomas M. 2003. *Gambling Life: Dealing in Contingency in a Greek City*. Urbana: University of Illinois Press.

Mannheim, Karl. 1972. "The Problem of Generations." In *Karl Mannheim: Essays*, edited by Paul Kesckemeti, 276–322. London: Routledge.

Marcuse, Herbert. 2007. *The Essential Marcuse: Selected Writings of Philosopher and Social Critic Herbert Marcuse*. Edited by Andrew Feenberg and William Leiss. Boston: Beacon.

Marinov, Tchavdar. 2010. "Historiographical Revisionism and Re-articulation of Memory in the Former Yugoslav Republic of Macedonia." *Sociétés Politiques Comparées*, no. 25: 1–19.

Markham, Francis, and Nicholas Biddle. 2018. "Income, Poverty and Inequality." CAEPR Census Paper 2. Canberra: Center for Aboriginal Economic Policy Research.

Marsh, Selina Tusitala. 2018. "Tokotoko Tales." Keynote presentation at the Biennial Meeting of the Australian Association for Pacific Studies, Adelaide, South Australia, April 4–7.

Marx, Karl. 1954. *Capital*. Vol. 1. Moscow: Progress.

Marx, Karl. 1969. "Theses on Feuerbach." In *Marx/Engels Selected Works*, vol. 1, 13–15. Moscow: Progress.

Mattioli, Fabio. 2014. "Unchanging Boundaries: The Reconstruction of Skopje and the Politics of Heritage." *International Journal of Heritage Studies* 20, no. 6: 599–615.

Mattioli, Fabio. 2020. *Dark Finance: Illiquidity and Authoritarianism at the Periphery of Europe*. Stanford, CA: Stanford University Press.

Mattioli, Fabio. 2021. "Innovation after Prespa." In *Macedonia and Identity Politics after the Prespa Agreement*, edited by Vasiliki P. Neofotistos, 206–26. London: Routledge.

McDougall, Debra. 2016. *Engaging with Strangers: Love and Violence in the Rural Solomon Islands*. New York: Berghahn.

McKnight, David. 2002. *From Hunting to Drinking: The Devastating Effects of Alcohol on an Australian Aboriginal Community*. London: Routledge.

Merlan, Francesca. 2009. "Indigeneity: Global and Local." *Current Anthropology* 50, no. 3: 303–33.

Michaels, Mike. 2013. "Process and Plasticity: Printing, Prototyping and the Prospects of Plastic." In *Accumulation: The Material Politics of Plastic*, edited by Jennifer Gabrys, Gay Hawkins, and Mike Michael, 30–46. Oxford: Routledge.

Miyazaki, Hirokazu. 2004. *The Method of Hope: Anthropology, Philosophy, and Fijian Knowledge*. Stanford, CA: Stanford University Press.

Moreton-Robinson, Aileen. 2009. "The Good Indigenous Citizen: Race, War and the Pathology of Patriarchal White Sovereignty." *Cultural Studies Review* 15, no. 2: 62–79.

Moreton-Robinson, Aileen. 2017. "Relationality: A Key Presupposition of an Indigenous Research Paradigm." In *Sources and Methods in Indigenous Studies*, edited by Chris Andersen and Jean M. O'Brien, 69–77. Oxford: Routledge.

Morin, Edgar. 2005. *Introduction à la pensée complexe*. Paris: Seuil.

Mosse, David. 2010. "A Relational Approach to Durable Poverty, Inequality and Power." *Journal of Development Studies* 46, no. 7: 1156–78.

MTV. 2015. "Hal yasbah al-massihiyyoon ithnay 'ashar bil mi'at min al-lubnahniyyen?" [Will Christians become 12 percent of the Lebanese?]. November 30. https://www.mtv.com.lb/news/local/536559/؟هل_يصبح_المسيحيون_12___من_اللبنانيّين.

Muecke, Stephen. 2014. "Turning Into *Gardiya*." In *Ngapartji Ngapartji, in Turn in Turn: Ego-Histoire, Europe and Indigenous Australia*, edited by Vanessa Castejon, Anna Cole, Oliver Haag, and Karen Hughes, 259–70. Canberra: Australian National University Press.

Munn, Nancy. 1986. *The Fame of Gawa: A Symbolic Study of Value Transformation in a Massim (Papua New Guinea) Society*. Durham, NC: Duke University Press.

Napolitano, Valentina. 2016. *Migrant Hearts and the Atlantic Return: Transnationalism and the Roman Catholic Church*. New York: Fordham University Press.

Natali, Andrea. 2008. "Some Considerations on Conservation and Restoration in Contemporary Art." *Conservation Science in Cultural Heritage* 8. https://conservation-science.unibo.it/article/view/1406.

Navarette, Susan J. 1998. *The Shape of Fear: Horror and the Fin de Siècle Culture of Decadence*. Lexington: University Press of Kentucky.

Neofotistos, Vasiliki. 2012. *The Risk of War, Everyday Sociality in the Republic of Macedonia*. Philadelphia: University of Pennsylvania Press.

Neofotistos, Vasiliki P. 2021. Introduction to *Macedonia and Identity Politics after the Prespa Agreement*, edited by Vasiliki Neofotistos, 1–27. London: Routledge.

News.com.au. 2019. "'I Want Him to Rot in Jail': Pell Victim's Father Speaks on Eve of Sentencing." March 13. https://www.news.com.au/national/crime/i-want-him-to-rot-in-jail-pell-victims-father-speaks-on-eve-of-sentencing/news-story/b10cb8689332c835c39d0d9576f61013.

Nietzsche, Friedrich. 1964. *Thus Spoke Zarathustra: A Book for All and None*. London: Penguin.

Nietzsche, Friedrich. 1967. *On the Genealogy of Morals and Ecce Homo*. New York: Random House.

Nietzsche, Friedrich. 1996. *Human, All Too Human: A Book for Free Spirits*. London: Penguin.

Orima Research. 2017. "Cashless Debit Card Trial Evaluation: Final Evaluation Report." Australia Department of Social Services. Canberra: Orima Research. https://www.dss.gov.au/sites/default/files/documents/10_2018/cashless-debit-card-trial-final-evaluation-report_2.pdf.

Pearson, Noel. 2000. *Our Right to Take Responsibility*. Cairns: Noel Pearson and Associates.

Perkins, Tom. 2017. "More Maggots and Mold Found in Michigan's Prison Food." *Metro Times* (Detroit), November 8. https://www.metrotimes.com/table-and-bar/archives/2017/11/08/more-maggots-and-mold-found-in-michigans-prison-food.

Pianigiani, Gaia. 2020. "Italy Leaders Hail Genoa's New Bridge as Sign of Resilience." *New York Times*, August 3. https://www.nytimes.com/2020/08/03/world/europe/genoa-italy-new-bridge.html.

Pianigiani, Gaia, Elisabetta Povoledo, and Richard Pérez-Peña. 2018. "Corrosion at 'Unthinkable Pace' before Italy Bridge's Deadly Fall." *New York Times*, August 15.

https://www.nytimes.com/2018/08/15/world/europe/italy-genoa-bridge-collapse
.html.

Pina-Cabral, João De. 1992. "The Primary Social Unit in Mediterranean and Atlantic Europe." *Journal of Mediterranean Studies* 2, no. 1: 25–41.

Pond, Elizabeth. 2006. "Rescuing Macedonia." In *Endgame in the Balkans: Regime Change, European Style*, 168–87. Washington, DC: Brookings Institution Press.

Post-Courier (Papua New Guinea). 2018a. "Theories Must Not Be Relied On." March 13.

Post-Courier (Papua New Guinea). 2018b. "Highlands Earthquake Aftermath." July 12. https://postcourier.com.pg/highlands-earthquake-aftermath/.

Post-Courier (Papua New Guinea). 2018c. "Revisiting the Earthquake Devastated Communities." May 29. https://postcourier.com.pg/revisiting-earthquake-devastated-communities/.

Povinelli, Elizabeth. 2006. *The Empire of Love: Toward a Theory of Intimacy, Genealogy, and Carnality*. Durham, NC: Duke University Press.

Povinelli, Elizabeth. 2011. *Economies of Abandonment: Social Belonging and Endurance in Late Liberalism*. Durham, NC: Duke University Press.

Puar, Jasbir. 2015. "The 'Right' to Maim: Disablement and Inhumanist Biopolitics in Palestine." *Borderlands* 14, no. 1: 1–27.

Puar, Jasbir. 2017. *The Right to Maim: Debility, Capacity, Disability*. Durham, NC: Duke University Press.

Redmond, Anthony. 2005. "Strange Relatives: Mutualities and Dependencies between Aborigines and Pastoralists in the Northern Kimberley." *Oceania* 75, no. 3: 234–46.

Regenauer-Lieb, Klaus, David A. Yuen, and Florian Fusseis. 2009. "Landslides, Ice Quakes, Earthquakes: A Thermodynamic Approach to Surface Instabilities." *Pure and Applied Geophysics* 166, nos. 10–11: 1885–1908.

Rendina, Claudio. 2003. "Quegli archi trionfali ai fori nel medievo il massimo degrado." *La Repubblica*, June 29, Rome section.

Reno, Joshua O. 2016. *Waste Away: Working and Living with a North American Landfill*. Berkeley: University of California Press.

Reuters. 2019. "Macedonian Parliament Agrees to Change Country's Name to End a 27-Year Dispute with Greece." *NBC News*, January 12. https://www.nbcnews.com/news/europe/macedonian-parliament-agrees-change-country-s-name-end-27-year-n957771?cid=sm_npd_nn_fb_nw.

Rogers, Susan Carol. 1987. "Good to Think: The 'Peasant' in Contemporary France." *Anthropological Quarterly* 60, no. 2: 56–63.

Royal Australian and New Zealand Society of Psychiatrists. 2017. Letter regarding Social Services Legislation Amendment (Cashless Debit Card) Bill 2017. September 17. https://www.ranzcp.org/files/resources/submissions/08560-president-to-committee-secretary-re-cashless.aspx.

Rubin, Ashley. 2020. "Prisons and Jails are Coronavirus Epicenters—But They Were Once Designed to Prevent Disease Outbreaks." *Conversation*, April 9. https://theconversation.com/prisons-and-jails-are-coronavirus-epicenters-but-they-were-once-designed-to-prevent-disease-outbreaks-136036.

Russell, Andrew, and Lee Vinsel. 2016. "Hail the Maintainers." *Aeon*, April 7. httpss:// aeon.co/essays/innovation-is-overvalued-maintenance-often-matters-more.

Russell, Robert J. 1984. "Entropy and Evil." *Zygon: Journal of Religion and Science* 19, no. 4: 449–68.

Salmang, Grace Auka. 2018. "Quake Described as a 'Curse' from God." *Post-Courier* (Papua New Guinea), March 8. https://postcourier.com.pg/quake-described-curse-god/.

Sawyer, Wendy, and Peter Wagner. 2019. "Mass Incarceration: The Whole Pie 2019." Northampton, MA: Prison Policy Initiative.

SBS News. 2018. "'Rot in Jail': Dutton to Prakash." July 20. https://www.sbs.com.au/news/rot-in-jail-dutton-to-prakash.

Schieffelin, Edward L. 1976. *The Sorrow of the Lonely and the Burning of the Dancers*. New York: St. Martin's.

Schotten, Heike. 2009. *Nietzsche's Revolution: Décadence, Politics, and Sexuality*. New York: Palgrave Macmillan.

Schubert, Violeta. 2005. "Dynamics of Macedonian Kinship in a Mediterranean Perspective: Contextualizing Ideologies and Pragmatics of Agnation." *Journal of Mediterranean Studies* 15, no. 1: 25–50.

Schubert, Violeta. 2020. *Modernity and the Unmaking of Men*. London: Berghahn.

Shapiro, Nicholas, and Eben Kirksey. 2017. "Chemo-Ethnography: An Introduction." *Cultural Anthropology* 32, no. 4: 481–93.

Shaw, Bruce. 1992. *When the Dust Come in Between: Aboriginal Viewpoints in the East Kimberley prior to 1982*. Canberra: Aboriginal Studies Press.

Shaw, Paula, 2009. *Seven Seasons in Aurukun: My Unforgettable Time at a Remote Aboriginal School*. Crow's Nest, NSW: Allen and Unwin.

Shevchenko, Olga. 2008. *Crisis and the Everyday in Postsocialist Moscow*. Bloomington: Indiana University Press.

Siegel, Gerald. 1996. "Balkan Culture as Revealed in Legends of Vampires and Spirits: Folklore of the Former Yugoslav Republic of Macedonia." *CEA Critic* 59, no. 1: 51–59.

Silverman, Sydel. 1975. *Three Bells of Civilization: The Life of an Italian Hill Town*. New York: Columbia University Press.

Simmel, Georg. 1958. "Two Essays." *Hudson Review* 11, no. 3: 371–85.

Simmel, Georg. 1965. "The Ruin." In *Essays on Sociology, Philosophy, and Aesthetics*, edited by Kurt H. Wolff, 259–66. New York: Harper and Row.

Skyring, F. 2012. "Low Wages, Low Rents, and Pension Cheques: The Introduction of Equal Wages in the Kimberley, 1968–1969." In *Indigenous Participation in Australian Economies II: Historical Engagements and Current Enterprises*, edited by Natasha Fijn, Ian Keen, Christopher Lloyd, and Michael Pickering, 153–70. Canberra: Australian National University Press.

Smith, Pamela A. 2000. "Station Camps: Legislation, Labour Relations and Rations on Pastoral Leases in the Kimberley Region, Western Australia." *Aboriginal History* 24: 75–97.

Spencer, Jonathan. 2003. "A Nation 'Living in Different Places': Notes on the Impossible Work of Purification in Postcolonial Sri Lanka." *Contributions to Indian Sociology* 37, nos. 1–2: 1–23.

Spencer, Jonathan, Jonathan Goodhand, Shahul Hasbullah, Bart Klem, Benedikt Korf, and K. Tudor Silva. 2015. *Checkpoint, Temple, Church and Mosque: A Collaborative Ethnography of War and Peace*. London: Pluto.

Spinoza, Benedictus de. 1988. *Ethics*. In *The Collected Works of Spinoza*. Vol. 1. Edited and translated by Edwin Curley. Princeton, NJ: Princeton University Press.

Standing Committee on Legal and Constitutional Affairs. 2006. *Unfinished Business: Indigenous Stolen Wages*. Senate Printing Unit, Department of the Senate, Parliament House, Canberra. https://www.aph.gov.au/Parliamentary_Business/Committees/Senate/Legal_and_Constitutional_Affairs/Completed_inquiries/2004-07/stolen_wages/report/index.

Star, Susan Leigh. 1999. "The Ethnography of Infrastructure." *American Behavioral Scientist* 43, no. 3: 377–91.

Stoler, Ann Laura. 2008. "Imperial Debris: Reflections on Ruins and Ruination." *Cultural Anthropology* 23, no. 2: 191–219.

Tambiah, Stanley. 1989. "Ethnic Conflict in the World Today." *American Ethnologist* 16, no. 2: 335–49.

Terzon, Emilia, and Mikaela Simpson. 2017. "Arrernte Country Singer Warren H Williams Questions Skin Names Given to Non-indigenous People." *ABC News*, January 12. https://www.abc.net.au/news/2017-01-12/arrernte-singer-questions-skin-names-for-non-indigenous-people/8172482.

Thiranagama, Sharika. 2011. *In My Mother's House: Civil War in Sri Lanka*. Philadelphia: University of Pennsylvania Press.

Thiranagama, Sharika, Tobias Kelly, and Carlos Forment. 2018. "Introduction: Whose Civility?" *Anthropological Theory* 18, nos. 2–3: 153–74.

Thompson, Richard, Shanna H. Swan, Charles J. Moore, and Frederick S. Vom Saal. 2009. "Our Plastic Age." *Philosophical Transactions of the Royal Society B: Biological Sciences* 364, no. 1526: 1973–76.

Todorov, Petar. 2013. "Skopje, od Pochetok na XIX Vek do Krajot na Osmanlinskoto Vladeenje" (Skopje, from the beginning of the XIX century until the end of Ottoman rule). PhD diss., Ss. Cyril and Methodius University in Skopje.

Todorova, Maria N. 2009. *Imagining the Balkans*. Updated ed. Oxford: Oxford University Press.

Torzillo, Paul J., Paul Pholeros, Stephan Rainow, Geoffrey Barker, Tim Sowerbutts, Tim Short, and Andrew Irvine. 2008. "The State of Health Hardware in Aboriginal Communities in Rural and Remote Australia." *Australian and New Zealand Journal of Public Health* 32, no. 1: 7–11.

Toynbee, Arnold J. 1934. *The Study of History*. Vol. 1, *Introduction: The Geneses of Civilizations*. Oxford: Oxford University Press.

Tsolkas, Panagioti. 2019. "'It Smelled Like Death': Reports of Mold Contamination in Prisons and Jails." *Prison Legal News*, April 2. https://www.prisonlegalnews.org/news/2019/apr/2/it-smelled-death-reports-mold-contamination-prisons-and-jails/.

US Department of State. 2018. "2018 Trafficking in Persons Report—Macedonia." June 28. https://www.refworld.org/docid/5b3e0ae7a.html.

Verdery, Katherine. 2003. *The Vanishing Hectare: Property and Value in Postsocialist Transylvania*. Ithaca, NY: Cornell University Press.

Voegtle, Simone. 2012. "Admiror, paries, te non cecidisse ruinis / qui tot scriptorum taedia sustineas: Graffiti und Karikaturen als Medien der Kommunikation im städtischen Raum." In *Kommunikationsräume im kaiserzeitlichen Rom*, edited by Felix Mundt, 105–21. Berlin: De Gruyter.

Wallace, Anthony F. C. 1949. "Revitalization Movements." *American Anthropologist*, n.s., 58, no. 2: 264–81.

Watson, Irene. 2009. "In the Northern Territory Intervention, What Is Saved or Rescued and at What Cost?" *Cultural Studies Review* 15, no. 2: 45–60.

Weiner, Myron. 1971. "The Macedonian Syndrome: An Historical Model of International Relations and Political Development." *World Politics* 23, no. 4: 665–83.

Wiener, Norbert. 1948. *Cybernetics: Or Control and Communication in the Animal and the Machine*. New York: Wiley.

Wiener, Norbert. 1950. *The Human Use of Human Beings: Cybernetics and Society*. Boston: Houghton Mifflin.

Wilg, Alan, and Jonathan Silver. 2019. "Turbulent Presents, Precarious Futures: Urbanization and the Deployment of Global Infrastructure." *Regional Studies* 53, no. 6: 912–23.

Williams, Caroline. 2016. "Unravelling the Subject with Spinoza: Towards a Morphological Analysis of the Scene of Subjectivity." *Contemporary Political Theory* 16, no. 3: 342–62.

Williams, Raymond. 1977. *Marxism and Literature*. Oxford: Oxford University Press.

Wolfe, Patrick. 2006. "Settler Colonialism and the Elimination of the Native." *Journal of Genocidal Research* 8, no. 4: 387–409.

Wolfe, Patrick. 2016. *Traces of History: Elementary Structures of Race*. London: Verso.

Yanagisako, Sylvia Junko. 2002. *Producing Culture and Capital: Family Firms in Italy*. Princeton, NJ: Princeton University Press.

Yu, Peter. 1994. "Aboriginal Peoples, Federalism and Self-Determination." *Social Alternatives* 13, no. 1: 19–21.

Zahirovic, Sabin, Gilles Brocard, John Connell, and Romain Beucher. 2018. "Aftershocks Hit Papua New Guinea as It Recovers from a Remote Major Earthquake." *Conversation*, April 9. https://theconversation.com/aftershocks-hit-papua-new-guinea-as-it-recovers-from-a-remote-major-earthquake-94176.

CONTRIBUTORS

CAMEO DALLEY is a sociocultural anthropologist and research fellow at Deakin University (Melbourne, Australia). Her research explores the relationships that emerge at the interface between Aboriginal and settler descendant (non-Aboriginal people) identities in northern Australia. This includes a focus on the politics of belonging, constructions of indigeneity, and contestations over land and development. She has long-term research relationships in two settings: a remote Aboriginal community where she conducted doctoral fieldwork and a racially diverse port town. Cameo's first book, *What Now: Everyday Endurance and Social Intensity in an Australian Aboriginal Community*, was published in 2021.

PETER D. DWYER is an honorary senior fellow in the School of Geography at the University of Melbourne. After many years of zoological research, a year in Papua New Guinea led to a reemphasis on anthropological questions. He has worked with commercial fishermen in Australia and with people of four language groups in Papua New Guinea. His research emphases concern the interplay of ecological and social processes, systems of nomenclature and classification, processes of change, and historical representations of social geography.

AKHIL GUPTA is president of the American Anthropological Association; professor of anthropology and director of the Center for India and South Asia at UCLA; and, formerly, professor of anthropology and development studies at the University of Melbourne. He is the author of *Postcolonial Developments* (Duke University Press, 1998), editor of *Culture, Power, Place* (Duke University Press, 1997) and *Anthropological Locations* (1997). His book *Red Tape* (Duke University Press, 2012) was awarded the Coomaraswamy Prize by the Association for Asian Studies. Recent publications include *The Promise of Infrastructure* (Duke University Press, 2018) and "Rethinking the Anthropology of Corruption" (2018). He is currently finishing a book manuscript on BPOs and call centers titled *Future Tense*.

GHASSAN HAGE is a professor of anthropology at the University of Melbourne. He has worked for many years on racism and White nationalism from a comparative perspective. His work *Is Racism an Environmental Threat?* (2017) deals with the common basis for the colonial practices of racialization and exploitation of people and the speciesist practices of exploitation of nature. His most recent work, *The Diasporic Condition: Ethnographic Explorations of the Lebanese in the World* (2021), is an ethnographic exploration of Lebanese diasporic culture. He has a long interest in critical anthropological theory and has written *Alter-Politics: Critical Anthropological Thought and the Radical Imaginary (2015)*. He is currently writing a book on Pierre Bourdieu, also for Duke University Press.

MICHAEL HERZFELD is Ernest E. Monrad Research Professor of the Social Sciences, Department of Anthropology, Harvard University; IIAS Visiting Professor at Leiden University; Chang Jiang Scholar and Visiting Professor at Shanghai International Studies University; and Honorary Professorial Fellow, University of Melbourne; he also holds honorary appointments at Thammasat University, Bangkok, and the University of Rome "Tor Vergata." His eleven published books include *Siege of the Spirits: Community and Polity in Bangkok* (2016) and *Cultural Intimacy: Social Poetics and the Real Life of States, Institutions, and Societies* (2016); his next book, *Subversive Archaism*, will be published by Duke University Press in 2021.

ELISE KLEIN is a senior lecturer at the Crawford School of Public Policy, Australian National University. She has a DPhil in international development from the University of Oxford and held a postdoctoral fellowship at the Centre for Aboriginal Economic Policy Research at the Australian National University. Her research interests include the rise of therapeutic cultures in development interventions, settler colonialism in social policy, and decoloniality. She has coedited collections titled *Postdevelopment in Practice: Alternatives, Economies, Ontologies* and *Implementing a Basic Income in Australia: Pathways Forward*.

BART KLEM is a senior lecturer in peace and development studies at the University of Gothenburg, Sweden. His research is focused on political order amid and after civil war. He is interested in state institutions, de facto sovereignty of rebel movements, and public authority. He is finishing a research project on the role of the Sri Lanka's provincial councils in conflict and peace. In connection to that, he is completing a book manuscript provisionally titled "Sovereignty, Nationalism and Make-Believe: Tamil Insurgency and Post-war Transition in Sri Lanka."

TAMARA KOHN is a professor of anthropology in the School of Social and Political Sciences at the University of Melbourne. She has conducted fieldwork in Scotland, Nepal, the United States, and Japan. Research interests include humanistic anthropology, communities of practice, the body and senses, prison lives, death studies, and research methods and ethics. She is part of the ARC-funded interdisciplinary DeathTech research team, studing death, commemoration, and new technologies of disposal and interment. Her latest books include *Sounding Out Japan: A Sensory Ethnographic Tour* (2020), with Richard Chenhall and Carolyn S. Stevens; and she is a coeditor of *Residues of Death: Disposal Refigured* (2019).

MICHAEL MAIN has a PhD in anthropology from the Australian National University. His PhD research focused on Huli people in the Papua New Guinea highlands and the impact on their lives of ExxonMobil's Papua New Guinea liquefied natural gas project. Michael has a professional background in geology and environmental science, which underpins his interest and work in the anthropology of development and resource extraction.

FABIO MATTIOLI is a lecturer in anthropology at the School of Social and Political Sciences at the University of Melbourne. Fabio is interested in innovation, speculation, and technology. His book *Dark Finance* (2020) describes the connection between financial expansion and illiberal politics at the periphery of Europe. Previously he was a postdoctoral fellow at NYU Center for European and Mediterranean Studies. He obtained a master's degree from the École des hautes études en sciences sociales and a PhD in anthropology from the Graduate Center of the City University of New York.

DEBRA MCDOUGALL is a senior lecturer in anthropology at the University of Melbourne, author of *Engaging with Strangers: Love and Violence in the Rural Solomon Islands* (2016), and coeditor of *Christian Politics in Oceania* (2013) and *Unequal Lives: Gender, Race and Class in the Western Pacific* (2021). Her current research focuses on a remarkable vernacular language movement, the Kulu Language Institute of Ranongga, and other grassroots challenges to socioeconomic, political, and epistemological inequality in Oceania.

MONICA MINNEGAL is an associate professor in anthropology at the University of Melbourne. She has spent many years conducting research among Kubo and Bedamuni people in Papua New Guinea, studying the impacts of modernity on their understandings and practices. She is increasingly interested in how some people emerge from local communities to broker relationships with church, state, and corporations, and how these people manage the ambivalence with which those who seek to bridge worlds are often treated.

VIOLETA SCHUBERT is an anthropologist and lecturer in development studies in the School of Social and Political Sciences at the University of Melbourne. A native Macedonian, Violeta's ongoing research of postsocialist Macedonia commenced with doctoral research in the mid-1990s conducting fieldwork across a band of villages surrounding the towns of Bitola and Ohrid. Her research advances understandings of kinship, gender, and marriage and sheds light on the plight of individuals and communities navigating existence in the face of precarity and rapid social transformation. Violeta is the author of *Modernity and the Unmaking of Men* (2020).

INDEX

abolition (of death penalty), 143
accumulation, 44; by dispossession, 101, 107–8
aesthetics, 40, 41, 45, 58, 59, 60, 62, 64, 71, 72n6
agency, 8, 12, 13, 14, 18, 20, 21, 23, 25, 55–56, 88, 94, 97; of microorganisms, 6
aging: human, 4, 8, 16n2, 54, 120, 121; of the urban fabric, 60
Altman, Jon, 99–100, 109
Anthropocene, 12, 37
Apocalypse, 55
Argyrou, Vassos, 23–24
assimilation (sociocultural), 14, 68, 83, 101, 105, 107
atrophy, 1, 112
Australia, viii, 13, 14, 15, 27n2, 48, 50, 52, 54, 99–101, 103–4, 106, 107, 109n2, 115, 116, 129–30, 131, 134; remote, 130–31, 133, 136–37, 149
authoritarianism, 70, 77, 90, 92–94, 116
Autostrade per l'Italia, 42

bakia, 32, 33
Balkans, Balkan people (*Balkanci*), 10, 19, 21, 92, 94; wars, 88
baroque, 63
Baudelaire, Charles, 6, 124
beauty. *See* aesthetics
Bedamuni [people], 51, 53, 54
behavioral change and management, 103–4, 107
Berlant, Lauren, 106
Bible, 51, 55
Bitola, 22, 24, 27n2
black mold. *See* mold

Bloch, Ernst, 9
bodies, 2, 4, 14, 15, 29, 30, 32, 33, 35, 45, 49, 56, 86, 103, 106, 111–14, 121, 123, 124, 126, 129–32, 139, 140, 143, 145, 149–50, 152n17; adornment of, 34; black, 143; fluids from, 53, 54; waste from, 34. *See also* embodiment
Book of Revelation, 55
Bosavi, 50, 51
Bourdieu, Pierre, 121
Brandi, Cesare, 59
breakdown, 39, 42, 44, 45; of garbage collection, 60; moral, 96; psychological, 125; social, 60
Brontë, Charlotte, 2
Brown, Keith, 23
builders, 90
buildings: as infrastructure, 40; decay of, 2, 7, 29, 45, 49, 63, 88–89, 90, 91, 144, 145, 151n12; design of, 40; high-rise, 41; sick, 149, 151n15; toxic, 35

capitalism, 4, 5, 27n9, 35, 37, 38, 39, 44, 98n5, 102–3, 111, 143
carceral society, 140
care, 8, 12, 37, 41, 49, 88, 90, 93, 103, 130, 135, 141, 147, 149; of the dead, 152
caste, 78, 79, 80, 81, 82, 83, 84
Catholicism, 58, 61, 66, 67, 72n10, 76. *See also* Christianity; Vatican
chaos, 21, 22, 47, 49, 56, 66, 70, 95, 147
cheese, 32, 62, 72n7, 145, 146
Christianity, 2, 3, 8, 12, 14, 50, 51, 53, 55, 56, 76, 81, 83, 110, 111, 113, 114, 126n1, 127n2, 136. *See also* Catholicism; evangelism; missionaries

circulation of information and people, 76, 77, 78–79; of images, 40; of objects, 34, 74; (with mixture and exposure) as source of decay, 81–82, 83. *See also* exposure; mixture

civility, 62, 65; decline of, 70; lack of, 66, 71; varieties of, 70

civilization, 19, 27n9, 37, 38–39, 64, 148; as project, 78

civiltà, 64, 68, 70

civil war: in Lebanon, 110–17, 119, 120, 121, 123, 126n1, 127n2; in Sri Lanka, 73–77, 78, 80, 81, 83; in the United States, 142

Clinton, Bill, 142, 151n7

Closing the Gap (Australian policy), 99, 100, 101, 105, 106, 131

Cold War, 92

collective: consciousness, 96; decay 17, 88, 96; experience, 17; hopes, 87; imaginary, 95, 97; identity, 96; norms 103, 105, 106–7, 108; topos, 18; ways of being, 14

colonialism, 8, 13, 14, 35, 37, 78, 124–25, 131, 139, 152n18; Australian colonial government, 15, 50; frontier of, 23; settler, 13, 14, 15, 99, 100, 101, 107, 108

commoditization of histor(icit)y, 60, 65

communism, 18, 20, 24

community development, 105, 130

conatus, 9–11

conservation, 59, 62, 69, 70, 72n6. *See also* restoration

conspiracy theories, 94–96

construction, 12, 37, 38, 39, 40, 41, 43, 44, 45, 60, 88, 89–90

consumption, 34–35; of alcohol, 76, 100, 134

coronavirus. *See* COVID-19; pandemic; virus

corrosion, 41, 42, 43, 68

corruption: bodily, 58; cultural, 92; moral and political, 10, 18, 20, 22, 24, 51, 58, 63, 65, 71n2, 79, 93; physical, 58

COVID-19, 149–50. *See also* pandemic; virus

Cowlishaw, Gillian, 132, 134

creativity, 12, 13, 15, 25, 44, 45, 60, 138, 141, 149

crime, 22, 141, 143, 144, 148, 149, 150, 151n6, 151n7, 151n8; petty, 61; war on (Nixon), 142

crisis, 5, 94; ecological, 10; refugee, 102

Cronin, Darryl, 100–101

Dalley, Cameo, 15, 35, 45, 61, 128–39

Davis, Angela, 143, 145

death, 2, 3, 4, 23, 25, 26, 27n9, 34, 35, 49, 51, 53, 54, 86, 111, 112, 123, 124, 134, 151n15; camps (Nazi), 146; in custody, 107; sentences (and death row), 15, 32, 141, 144, 147, 150n2, 151n13; slow, 106; workers, 148

debility, 106; social, 106–7

decadence/*décadence*, 3, 20, 21, 22, 26; visual, 62

decarceration, 149, 150

decay, vii, viii, 2; arrested, 4, 21, 60, 62, 69; as regeneration, 6; biological, 122, 125; bodily, 4, 8, 13, 15, 32, 35, 56, 106, 112, 113, 114, 120, 121, 123, 126, 129, 130, 131, 132, 138, 139; capitalist, 5; change as, 82; cultural, 74–75, 77–79, 81, 84, 85, 114, 123, 131, 134; deliberate, 4, 8, 13, 60, 71, 145, 148, 149, 151n12; ecological, 53; economic, 123; of history, 20–21; and identity, 20; infrastructural, 11, 37–46, 105–6, 123; institutional, 4; material, 9, 11, 15, 29, 50, 62, 86, 90, 98n5, 106, 122, 144; mental, 15, 87, 132; moral, 1, 7, 10, 12, 54, 57n1, 58, 70, 96, 134; national, 1; natural, 1, 6, 7–8, 13, 39, 54, 55; normal, 2–3; organizational, 7; pathological, 3, 4, 35; politics of, 10, 12–13, 14, 19, 20, 84, 96; premature, 41; relational, 15, 128–39; rhetoric of, 20; rural, 18–19; social, 1, 7, 9, 10, 12, 14–15, 22, 50, 54, 56n1, 58, 62, 70, 74, 77, 99–100, 101, 103, 107, 108, 113, 122, 123, 126, 131, 134, 140, 149; of spectacles, 21; structural, 4, 7; suspended, 35; symbolic, 126; tooth, 1, 31, 32; urban, 57, 58–72, 88, 97n3. *See also* decline; disintegration; purification

decline, 1, 17, 26n1, 49, 50, 54, 61, 113, 114, 143, 145; Christian, 110–11; of civility, 70; economic, 90, 110, 111, 114; infrastructural, 10; military, 111; personal, 114, 120–21 social, 15, 62, 99, 111, 114. *See also* decay; disintegration

defeat, 14, 15, 95, 97, 110, 111–14, 118, 119–23, 124, 127n3; of LTTE, 73, 76, 79, 83

degrado, 39, 62–66, 68, 69, 70–71, 72n9

deindustrialization, 90

destruction, 39, 44, 60, 69, 125; bodily, 106; cultural, 134; environmental, 38, 44; infrastructural, 38; of monuments, 24; sociopolitical, 87

disadvantage, 99–12, 105–8, 135

176 | INDEX

discourse, 2, 10, 14, 15, 19, 21, 64, 88, 97, 113, 114, 119, 122, 134, 144, 151n14; development, 38, 130; social decay, 99–109
discipline, 50, 63, 64, 75, 104, 108, 143; self-, 147
discrimination, 67, 100, 109n2. *See also* racism
disintegration, vii, 1, 3, 4, 6, 9, 18, 49, 122, 123, 124; bodily, 8, 113; cultural, 77, 79, 114; political, 18; social, 13
disorder. *See* order
Douglas, Mary, 3, 64, 78
durability, 11, 12, 28, 32–35, 59, 64
dvoličnost (two-facedness), 23
Dwyer, Peter, 3, 12, 47–57, 61

earthquakes, 3, 12, 31, 43, 47–49, 51–54, 55, 56, 90
East Kimberley, 101–5, 107, 108, 138
ecology/ecological and environmental issues, viii, 1, 2, 6, 10, 28, 29, 30, 33, 38, 47, 120; ecology of cruelty, 148; infrastructural, 44, 123, 142
Edolo (people), 47, 51, 53, 54
elegiac, 39
elimination: of decay, 39; of First Nations, 106, 107, 108; of mold, 144
El Niño, 54
embargo, 88, 92, 93
embodiment, 72n13
endo-decay, 6, 9, 11, 12, 13, 14. *See also* decay
Enlightenment, 39
entropy, 7, 11, 15, 47, 49, 55, 57n1, 122, 140
eschatology, 48
eternity and eternal life, 11, 565, 58; Eternal City (Rome), 62, 64
ethnography, 4, 6, 7, 8, 10, 33, 44, 46n7, 55, 71n2, 73, 81, 114, 125, 126, 134, 148; olfactory, 124–26
European Union, 92, 93, 94, 96, 98n6
evangelism, 76, 79, 81, 84. *See also* Christianity
excision, 96
exo-decay, 6, 11, 12, 14. *See also* decay; endo-decay
exploitation (of people), 67, 101, 102, 109
exposure, 13, 74, 75, 77, 79, 82, 84, 85; to asbestos, 144. *See also* circulation of information and people; mixture
expropriation, 101
evil, 12, 15, 54, 55, 57, 141, 143, 147

falling apart, 17, 18, 19, 21, 22–26, 47, 63, 77
familija (family), 24. *See also* kinship
fantasies of the self, 121
fascism, 1, 24, 64, 67, 71
fate/fatalism, 21, 22–23, 49, 55; fated subjectivity, 21–22
Fay, Elizabeth, 20
feminized labor, 41
First Nations, 14, 35, 99, 100, 101–2, 103–8
Former Yugoslav Republic of Macedonia (FYROM), 17–27
Foucault, Michel, 143
Frankl, Viktor, 146, 147
fresh contact, 13, 74, 81–84. *See also* Mannheim, Karl
function, functioning, 11, 37, 41, 42, 4, 44, 45, 122; functionality, 129; dysfunction and malfunction, 4, 10, 99, 100, 103, 107; explanatory, 120; ritual, 143; state, 93
future, 4, 5, 8, 9, 13, 23, 24, 29, 32, 45, 53, 66, 70, 76, 84, 87, 88, 91, 92, 93, 95, 96, 97, 107, 109, 121, 122, 125, 141, 143, 147, 150; dystopian, 92

garbage, 22, 28, 58, 60, 63, 64, 115. *See also* litter
Geertz, Clifford, 25–26
gender, 76, 82
generation, 35, 40, 68, 82–83, 84. *See also* Stolen Generations
Genoa, 41–42
gentrification, 60, 61
Germany, 67, 114
giving up, 87, 88, 95, 96, 97
Global North, 41
God's curse, 51
Golden Gate Bridge (San Francisco), 39, 40, 43
governance, viii, 18, 20, 62, 149, 151n11; Australian, 14, 50, 52, 54, 99–100, 101, 103–5, 107, 131; governmentality, 15, 22; Greek, 93; Italian, 42, 43, 63; Macedonian, 90, 92, 93, 94; Northern Territory (Australia), 109n2; Papua New Guinea, 50, 52, 53; Queensland, 135; Sri Lanka, 77, 80, 81; ungovernability, 10
graffiti, 58, 63, 64, 65, 68, 69
Graham, Stephen, 42
Gramsci, Antonio, 8
Great Papuan Plateau, 50, 53

INDEX | 177

Greece, 20, 22, 27nn2–3, 72n13, 92, 93, 94, 96
growth, 1, 35, 37, 38, 39, 86, 140, 141, 140, 141, 145; of mold, 146; spiritual, 149; of youth, 54
Gruevski, Nikola, 94

health, 23, 30, 49, 50, 53, 101, 106, 110, 111, 112, 116, 120, 122, 132, 134, 135, 147, 150; Aboriginal, 15, 120–32, 134–35; care, 88, 93, 129–30, 131, 132–33, 135, 138; as condition of decay, 3, 11; mental, 104, 115, 147; oral, 31; public, 14, 150
Hela province, 52
heroism, 21, 39, 40, 45, 119
Herzfeld, Michael, 7, 12, 22–23, 28, 39, 45, 46n7, 57, 58–72, 81, 151n12
historicity, 60
hope, 5, 9, 13, 15, 20, 26, 53, 87–88, 95–96, 97, 132, 140, 149; oblivion of, 88
Huli (people), 3, 48–52, 55, 56, 61
humanism, 9, 150; antihumanism, 45

imaginary, 1, 4, 97, 111, 149; capitalist, 5; national, 18, 95; social, 13
immigration, 63, 64, 68, 70
incarceration, 142, 143, 148, 149, 150n5, 151n14; mass, 142, 149, 151n7. *See also* maximum-security prison
income management, 103, 104, 108
Indigenous communities and peoples, 14, 81, 82, 100–101, 103, 107, 130, 131–32, 133, 134, 135–37, 136, 137, 139; non-, 130, 131, 132, 134, 135, 136, 137, 139
Industrial Revolution, 11, 37, 38
inequality, 43, 44, 45, 101
Infomax, 17
infrastructure, 11–12, 35, 37–46, 76, 86, 89, 105, 123, 126, 151n16
innovation, 25, 26, 40, 41, 42, 44, 45
Instagram, 17
internment, 146. *See also* incarceration
Italy, 13, 41–42, 69, 70

Jackson, Steven J., 45
Jesus, 56. *See also* Christianity
Jewish community (Rome), 67
junk food, 31, 32

kinship, 27n7, 80, 82, 136, 137, 138
Klem, Bart, 7, 11, 12, 56n1, 73–85
Kohn, Tamara, 6, 15, 35, 62, 72n7, 140–52
kudi, 80. *See also* kinship
kula, 33, 34
Kununurra, 101, 102, 103

Lea, Tess, 105, 132
Leach, Edmund R., 146
Lebanese Forces (militia), 110. 118, 119. 126n1
Lebanon, 110, 115–16, 118, 119, 123, 126n1
Lévi-Strauss, Claude, 2, 7, 16n1, 25, 62, 145–46
Liberation Tigers of Tamil Eelam (LTTE), 73, 80
life cycle, 39; rituals, 34. *See also* generation
litter, 31. *See also* garbage
Livingston, Julie, 1
Lovell, Melissa, 100, 108

Macedonia, Republic of North, 2, 10, 13, 17–27, 56n1, 63, 86–98
Marinov, Tchavdar, 24
Mahood, Kim, 132–33
Main, Michael, 3, 12, 47–57, 61
maintenance, vii, 11–15, 28, 37, 39–45, 46n7, 59, 67, 88, 95, 106, 120, 122, 137, 143, 145, 149, 151n11, 151n12, 151n16
Mannheim, Karl, 12, 74, 82–84
Marsh, Selina Tusitala, 33
Marx, Karl, 27n9
Marxism, 5, 82
masculinity, 11, 37, 41, 61
Mattioli, Fabio, 10, 13, 26, 35, 56n1, 86–98
maximum-security prison, 140–41. *See also* incarceration
McDougall, Debra, 3, 10–11, 28–36, 38, 45
McKnight, David, 134
media, 17, 27n3, 142, 145
medical treatment, 150n5; of dental problems, 31. *See also* health
migration. *See* immigration
Minnegal, Monica, 3, 12, 47–57, 61
missionaries, 50, 134, 136. *See also* Christianity
mixing, 13, 74, 81, 82. *See also* circulation of information and people; pollution; purity
Miyazaki, Hirokazu, 26
modernity, 3, 8, 18, 40, 41, 59, 68, 97n2

178 | INDEX

mold, 25, 29, 49, 105, 110–11, 140–52; black, 141, 144, 151n10
moral anxiety, 75
moral failure, 49, 54, 56n1, 78
Moreton-Robinson, Aileen, 106, 136
Mornington Island, 129, 130, 133–39
Monti, 61, 72n5, 72n10, 72n11
mortality, 59–60, 61–63, 66, 151n12. *See also* death

nationalism, 20, 83, 92, 93, 94
nation-state, 41, 64, 78, 92
natural gas, 35, 56; liquefied (as project) 48, 51, 52
nature, 6, 7–8, 11, 13, 26, 35, 38, 39, 54, 55, 62, 78, 121, 140, 143, 144, 145–46, 149; disasters in, 12, 53, 61
neoliberalism, vii, viii, 42, 122. *See also* capitalism
Nietzsche, Friedrich, 3, 96, 97n1, 98n8, 126
Nirvana Sutra, 124, 127n5
Nixon, Richard, 142, 150n5
nonhumans, 44
nostalgia, 28, 59, 61, 68, 82, 83, 84, 91; structural, 68–69
North Atlantic Treaty Organization (NATO), 93, 94, 98n6

order, 49, 70–71, 147; church, 63; colonial, 78; disorder, 49, 50, 55, 66; fascist, 64; social, 77; state, 63. *See also* fascism
origin stories, 53
original sin, 55, 56–57n1, 57n3, 58, 63, 68
Orochimaru, 2
Ottoman Empire, 18, 92

Pacific Islands, 10, 30
packaging, 10, 11, 29–31
pandemic, viii, 149. *See also* virus
Papua New Guinea, 12, 33, 48, 51–54, 61
patina, 59, 62, 71nn3–4
pečalba, 19
penalization of poverty, 143. *See also* poverty
personhood, 33, 125, 145
petroleum companies, 51–52
picturesqueness, 59, 66
piety, practical, 61

Piranesi, Giambattista, 59, 60, 64, 71, 72n6
plastic, 3, 10, 11, 28–35, 38, 45, 129, 133
plate tectonics, 48, 52
policy, 99–104, 106, 134, 142, 145, 151n6; abandonment, 101; assemblage, 102; punitive, 101, 102, 105. *See also* zero tolerance
political theory, 5
politics, 14, 25, 84, 111, 116, 134; biopolitics, 14, 134; of decay, 10; national, 10; necropolitics, 106; nihilist, 13, 14; of public health, 14
pollution, 29, 39; of the mind, 73. *See also* Mary Douglas; purity; Jonathan Spencer
Pompeii, 69
Ponte Morandi, 41, 44, 45, 46n6
postsocialism, 13, 88, 91, 98n9
poverty, 22, 63, 101–2, 105, 109nn1–2, 142, 143, 151n8. *See also* precarity
Povinelli, Elizabeth, 105, 131
power, 20, 21, 23, 24, 33, 43, 80, 92, 125, 147; economic, 111; lack of, 62, 94, 143; structures of, 142
precarity, 20, 21, 22, 66
Prespa agreement, 92, 93, 96
prison, 15, 35, 62, 140–52. *See also* carceral society; incarceration
productivity, 50, 141, 149
prophecy, 52
prostitution, 68, 72n11, 74, 75
proximity, 126, 130, 132–39, 148; to plastic production, 30; to seismic fault, 43
Puar, Jasbir, 106
public, 145, 149; discipline, 64; discourse, 144; secret, 142; space, 64, 74
purity, 12, 70, 78, 79, 84; cultural, 77. *See also* pollution

race and racism, 12, 14, 62, 64, 66–71, 72n11, 105, 143, 148, 151n9
Ranongga, 30–34
raspagja, raspagjanje, 17, 18–19, 21, 23, 26
rasipani, 18, 25; *kopilina*, 18, 24. *See also* rot
raspušteni, 18
rations, 104, 108
Reagan, Ronald, 142, 150n5
recidivism, 142
redemption, 61, 143
redistribution, 43, 44
referendum, 93, 94, 95

regulation, 42, 151n8
relatedness, subject to decay, 138
relationality, 15, 132, 136
replacement, 43; demographic, 65
representation: of experience, 119; media, 142–43; of prisons, 145
resistance, 15, 45, 106, 116, 122, 140, 149; "Christian" (Lebanon), 110; to decay, 151n16
responsibility, 12, 68, 84, 123, 149
restoration, 59, 64, 69. *See also* conservation
rice cultivation, 79, 81, 83
ritual, 34, 50, 137; prison, 143, 147
Rome, 12, 28, 39, 56–57n1, 58–72
rot, viii, 1, 4, 5, 6, 14, 15, 18, 20, 21, 23, 24, 25, 26, 31, 32, 34, 35, 60, 62, 82, 84, 86, 88, 90, 93, 96, 111, 112, 123, 124, 125–26, 140, 144, 145–47, 148–49, 151nn14–15, 152n17
routine, 40, 41, 42, 44, 45, 74, 95
ruin, 1, 4, 7, 8, 11, 12, 13, 19, 27n9, 34, 37–40, 58, 59, 62, 65, 69, 82, 124, 125, 126; socialist, 91, 92

Sampur, 79–81
science, 12, 42, 50, 53, 56; of plastics, 29
Scientology, Church of, 51, 57n2
Schubert, Violeta, 2, 10, 13, 17–27, 56–57n1, 63, 88
self-determination, 97, 99, 103, 107, 108
sentiment of defeat. *See* defeat
sexual morality, 18, 76
Shirley (novel), 2
Simmel, Georg, 7–8, 13, 27n9
simulacrum, 40
Skopje, 23, 24, 88, 90, 91, 95, 96, 97n3; in 2014, 20
slavery, 67, 102, 136, 142, 143; as metaphor for health workers, 133; "slave morality," 3
smell, 60, 63, 90, 91, 112, 123, 124, 126, 141, 151n15; of death, 111
Socialist Federal Republic of Jugoslavija (SFRJ). *See* Yugoslavia
sociospatial relations, 136
solitary confinement, 15, 141, 142, 145. *See also* incarceration
Solomon Islands, 30, 31
sorcery, 34, 54
Spencer, Jonathan, 12, 74, 78, 81
Spinoza, Baruch, 9, 10–11

Sri Lanka, 12, 56n1, 73–85; civil war in, 74, 76, 78; return to and reconstruction of, 79–80; and transition, 78
Staphylococcus, 131, 138
Star, Susan Leigh, 38, 39
state. *See* nation-state
stench, 61, 110, 111–12, 119, 123, 124, 126, 128. *See also* smell
Stoler, Ann Laura, 8, 13, 124–25
Stolen Generations, 102
sublime, 39, 40
surrender, 49, 97
Syrians (in Lebanon), 116–18, 121
system, 49, 66; belief, 66; caste, 82; eco-, 45; economic, 95; employment and labor, 109n2; immune, 131; infrastructural, 42; justice (US), 142, 146; kinship, 136, 137; prison (US), 140–52; respiratory, 149; of substrates, 38; subway, 11; theory, 7; of thought, 56; university, 4; writing, 65

Tambiah, Stanley J., 19
Tamils, 73, 75, 76, 77, 79–83
temporality, 3, 29, 33, 39, 40, 44, 49, 97n3, 130, 138; of darkness, 50
Thailand, 69
thermodynamics, second law of, 48, 55, 56
third space, 45
theodicy, 61, 68
Thrift, Nigel, 42
Todorova, Maria, 19
tokotoko, 33
tourism, 22, 40, 59, 60, 73, 75, 146
Toynbee, Arnold, 27n9
transformation, 64, 83, 92, 97, 132, 140, 143, 145, 147
trash, 28–36. *See also* garbage
Trastevere, 61
Trincomalee, 73, 74, 75, 79, 80, 82, 83, 84

"Une charogne" (Baudelaire), 6

valuables (traditional), 32–35
value, 29, 30, 32, 33, 34, 35, 40–41, 64, 70, 145, 146, 147, 148, 150; aesthetic, 45; cultural, 11, 75; human, 141, 142; moral, 65; public, 149; social, 65; of time, 145; Western, 19

Vatican, 63. *See also* Catholicism
Verdi, Giuseppe, 58, 70
violence, 8, 25, 33, 52, 63, 67, 70, 75, 87, 100, 108, 109, 119, 134, 142, 143, 145, 148, 149, 151n9, 152n18
virus, 149, 150, 152nn17–18
VMRO-DPMNE, 92
volcano, 50, 56, 57n2

Wallace, Anthony, 27
war, 12, 24, 33, 112, 143; Balkan, 88; colonial, 125; on crime, 142; on drugs, 142, 150n5, 151n7; injury (psychological), 112–13, 127n3; Israeli Palestinian, 106; veterans, 24; World, II, 29, 114. *See also* civil war; Cold War
warriors, 15, 121–22, 123
waste, 10, 34, 35, 63, 148; bodily, 34; food, 31; nuclear, 29; plastic, 29; workers, 148. *See also* garbage
waterfall, 53–55
welfare, 100, 101, 103, 104, 105, 106, 108, 123
white helpers, 35, 128–39
work-for-the-dole program, 105, 108

youth, 18, 23, 54, 63, 68, 75–77, 82, 83, 84, 143, 151n9
Yugoslavia (Socialist Federal Republic of Jugoslavija, SFRJ), 18, 20, 21, 27, 88, 89, 90, 92, 93, 97n2

Zaev, Zoran, 94
zero tolerance, 142, 151n8
zombie, 4–5, 95; capitalism, 5, 35; cells, 86; company, 89–90; parts, 89; workers, 90